PRELIMINARY EXCAVATION REPORTS:
BÂB EDH-DHRÂ^c, SARDIS, MEIRON,
TELL EL-HESI, CARTHAGE (PUNIC)

THE ANNUAL OF THE AMERICAN SCHOOLS OF
ORIENTAL RESEARCH
Volume 43

edited by
David Noel Freedman

PRELIMINARY EXCAVATION REPORTS:
BÂB EDH-DHRÂᶜ, SARDIS, MEIRON,
TELL EL-HESI, CARTHAGE (PUNIC)

PRELIMINARY EXCAVATION REPORTS: BÂB EDH-DHRÂᶜ, SARDIS, MEIRON, TELL EL-HESI, CARTHAGE (PUNIC)

Edited by
David Noel Freedman

Published by
AMERICAN SCHOOLS OF ORIENTAL RESEARCH

Distributed by

American Schools of Oriental Research
126 Inman Street
Cambridge, MA 02139

PRELIMINARY EXCAVATION REPORTS: BÂB EDH-DHRÂ᷎, SARDIS, MEIRON, TELL EL-HESI, CARTHAGE (PUNIC)

Edited by
David Noel Freedman

Library of Congress Cataloging in Publication Data
Main entry under title:

Preliminary Excavation Reports: Bâb edh-Dhrâ᷎,
Sardis, Meiron, Tell el Ḥesi, Carthage (Punic).

(Annual of ASOR ; no. 43)
Includes bibliographies.
1. Near East Antiquities—Addresses, essays,
lectures. 2. Excavations (Archaeology)—Near East—
Addresses, essays, lectures. 3. Carthage—Antiqui-
ties—Addresses, essays, lectures. 4. Excavations (Ar-
chaeology)—Tunisia—Carthage—Addresses,   es-
says, lectures. I. Freedman, David Noel, 1922- II.
Series: American Schools of Oriental Research.
Annual ; no. 43.
DS101.A45 no. 43 [DS56] 939   77–13341
ISBN 0-89757-043-X (previously 0-89130-193-3)

Printed in the United States of America
1 2 3 4 5

Table of Contents

A Preliminary Report of Excavations at Bâb edh-Dhrâᶜ, 1975

Walter E. Rast
Valparaiso University, Valparaiso, IN 46383
R. Thomas Schaub
Indiana University of Pennsylvania, Indiana, PA 15701

After a lapse of eight years following the late Paul W. Lapp's excavations at Bâb edh-Dhrâᶜ. work was resumed at this Early Bronze Age site between May 25 and July 2, 1975 with a number of institutions participating under the auspices of the American Center of Oriental Research in Amman. These new excavations differ from the earlier ones in that they are the beginning of a regional investigation of Early Bronze Age life in the southeast plain of the Dead Sea. The plan of the new expedition is to obtain data from several recently discovered Early Bronze Age sites and their environs in the Ghôr southeast and south of the Dead Sea (Rast and Schaub: 1974). As this plan unfolds, Bâb edh-Dhrâᶜ will be lifted from its isolation and set into the framework of what was apparently a system of interrelated Early Bronze Age towns along the southeast Dead Sea flatland with its well-defined natural boundaries.

In consonance with this long-range plan, and in order to begin a new approach to clarifying the large site of Bâb edh-Dhrâᶜ, the objectives of the present season were: (1) to concentrate most of the field work on the town components (fig. 1: Fields VIII, XI, XII, XIII), examined by Lapp in a limited way in 1965; (2) to determine the stratigraphic relation of the town to occupational remains on the exterior, spread out for nearly a half km. to the south and northeast sides of the town site (Fields XI, X); (3) to collect a stratified pottery sequence, especially for the transition from EB III to EB IV, this sequence to serve as a basis not only for clarifying Bâb edh-Dhrâᶜ, but also for examining other sites in the Ghôr; (4) to obtain data on the geologic and hydrologic features of Bâb edh-Dhrâᶜ and its environs, including the lower plateau on which the town site is situated, to the beginning of the Lisân proper, as well as the Wâdi Kerak and the spring just north of the site, and to ascertain the usage of these natural elements in antiquity; (5) to recover seed remains and other flora data by means of fine sifting and flotation; (6) and to explore one or two tombs in the cemetery area to obtain bone and skull groups, a preliminary effort intended to lead to a larger study of demographic continuity and change in the southern Ghôr (Tombs A 55, D 1).

The staff of the 1975 excavations was composed of the following: Walter E. Rast and R. Thomas Schaub (Co-Directors), Reuben Bullard (Geologist), Robert Johnston (Ceramic Technologist), Michael Finnegan (Physical Anthropologist), Christine Helms (Photographer), Jean Graham (Draftsman), Jeannine Schonta (Cartographer and Assistant to the Geologist), Alberic Culhane, Jack Graham, David McCreery (Field Supervisors), Robert M. Brown, James Engle, Dane Surra, Mary Vachon, Robert Zacour, Richard Zweig (Square Supervisors). Representatives from the Department of Antiquities of Jordan were Sami Rabaddi of Kerak and Faisal Quddah from Jerash. Technical men were Yahya M. Darwish from Nablus on the West Bank and Muhammad A. Darwish from Amman. Approximately 50 workers from the settlements at Mazraᶜ and Hadîtha supplied the labor force for the expedition. A word of thanks is due Mr. Yacoub Oweis, Director-General of Antiquities of the Hashemite Kingdom of Jordan, and Mr. Yousef Alami of the Department of Antiquities in Amman for much assistance in planning and carrying out the work. The expedition was financed by private gifts to be acknowledged in the final report and by a gifts and matching grant arrangement with the National Endowment for the Humanities (H-22974). Special visitors during the excavations were The Honorable Thomas Pickering, United States Ambassador to Jordan, Dr. Moawwiyah Ibrahim and Mr. Yousef Alami of the Department of Antiquities in Amman, Mrs. Remie Fenske, Secretary of the Friends of Archaeology in Amman, Mr. Kenneth Fanske, Vice-President of Alia Airlines, and a visiting group of Trustees of the American Schools of Oriental Research from the United States. Drs. George Mendenhall and James Sauer, successive directors of the American Center of Oriental Research in Amman, stood by to offer invaluable help prior to and during the season, as did also Mr. Thomas D. Newman and Dr. Edward F. Campbell in the United States.

Occupational History

The results of the 1975 season reinforce earlier proposals for the phasing and chronology of Bâb edh-Dhrâᶜ (Lapp 1968b: 38; 1970: 123-24). These are that Bâb edh-Dhrâᶜ experienced three principal occupational periods with sub-phases: an initial pre-urban one during EB I, followed by a lengthy urban settlement during EB II and III, and finally a post-urban period in EB IV.

The earliest usage of the site consisted of what appears to have been a settlement prior to EB IB and designated by Lapp as EB IA, since it was both post-Ghassulian and slightly earlier than the typical EB IB culture with its characteristic line-group wares (Lapp 1968b: 37; 1970: 104-6). Until the present season this phase was known entirely from shaft tombs in the cemetery. During the 1975 season traces of settlement belonging to the same period were discovered just west of the western defense wall in a hitherto unexplored area (F 3). The dating of this EB IA phase to between 3150 and 3050 B.C., as proposed by Lapp, still seems desirable (Lapp 1970: 124). The succeeding phase, then, was assigned in the earlier excavations to EB IB, represented previously by tombs in the cemetery and during the present season by the upper level of a tomb discovered to the west of the western defense wall (F 2). Lapp's date of between ca. 3050 and 2950 B.C. for this phase may again be retained (Lapp 1970: 124). No remains of EB IC, dated by Lapp between 2950 and 2850 B.C. (Lapp 1970: 124), were discovered during the 1975 season and they have generally been

lacking at Bâb edh-Dhrâᶜ. It is noteworthy, however, that the EB IA and EB IB phases discovered in the new area just west of the city fit exactly those of the large cemetery south of the town.

During EB II and III settlement was concentrated within the large walled town, along with some scattered suburban occupation. Preliminary study of the pottery shows that the interior of the town site was used exclusively during EB II and III. Only minimal amounts of either EB I or EB IV pottery have been discovered in the areas of the town excavated, and whatever occasional sherds of EB IV type were found in the town came from the surface and probably represent nothing more than sporadic contacts with the site.

In the 1965 excavations against the east wall of the town site (Field II), a mud brick defensive wall (Wall B) was discovered below the stone wall that rings much of the site (Wall A). The extent of this earlier wall remains undetermined, since it is not yet clear whether it circumscribed the entire town in an earlier phase, as Lapp (1968a: 5) proposed, or whether it was confined to the eastern end. The results of 1975 show, however, that the town site was occupied through most of EB II and III and came to an abrupt end late in EB III. The date for this urban occupation thus would be from ca. 2850 to 2300 B.C. (Lapp 1970: 124). During this period the town inhabitants buried their dead in distinctive funerary structures, designated charnel houses by Lapp, of which a further example (A 55) was excavated during the 1975 season.

The final period of occupation at Bâb edh-Dhrâᶜ was during EB IV, and this is a period of special importance. During this phase the areas south and east of the town, and possibly also to the west, were heavily used for the construction of dwellings made of mud brick and stone. Whether the settlers who built these structures arrived as newcomers or whether they simply continued in some form the native stock is a problem which needs further study. The continuity in the pottery traditions would suggest the latter, but other evidence must be found to draw firm conclusions. Whether they were also responsible for the destruction of the town is similarly a problem not resolved with certainty at this point. This last intensive occupation of the site may be assigned a date from ca. 2300 to 2200/2150 B.C. (Lapp 1970: 124).

Following the Early Bronze Age, the site does not seem to have been used again for settlement. Roman, Byzantine, and Arabic remains were found

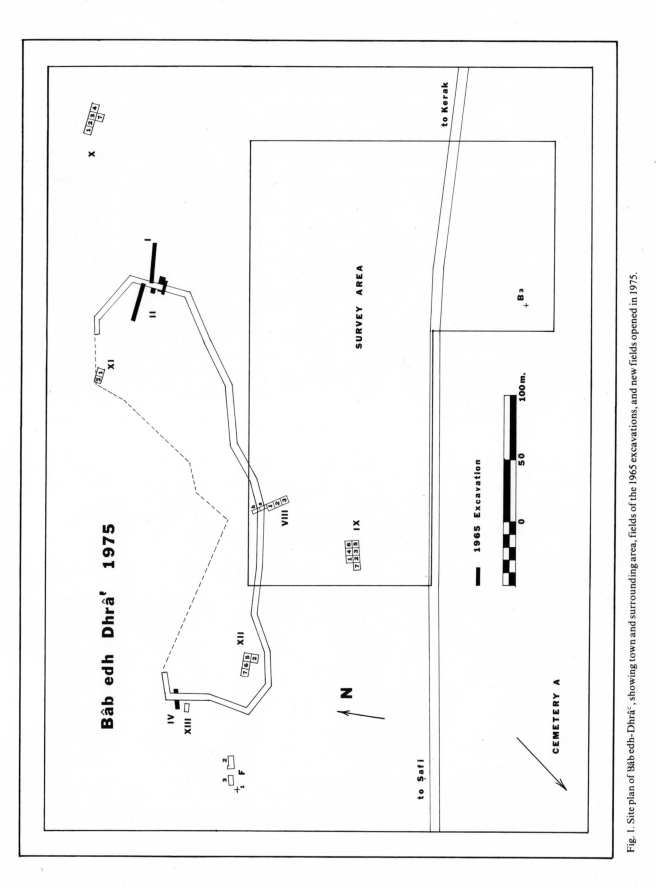

Fig. 1. Site plan of Bâb edh-Dhrâᶜ, showing town and surrounding area, fields of the 1965 excavations, and new fields opened in 1975.

Fig. 2. Tomb F 1 at Bâb edh-Dhrâᶜ, looking north with west half not yet excavated; robber trench is at bottom and remnants of doorway and shaft are on the north side.

Fig. 3. Tomb F 1 at Bâb edh-Dhrâᶜ, looking south at the elliptical end of the chamber; robber trench is in front of tomb and matting impression is visible under and to the left of pottery vessels.

in the vicinity, especially in the Wâdi Kerak and the Ghôr el-Mazra^c below Bâb edh-Dhrâ^c. An aqueduct in the Wâdi Kerak may be Byzantine or even Roman in date. Occasional later Roman, Byzantine and Arabic sherds were picked up around the site, and a new type of tomb in the eastern part of the cemetery (B 3) may belong to the Roman period, judging from its small number of sherds. But, in any case, these later remains are usually some distance from the site of Bâb edh-Dhrâ^c itself.

EB I Tombs and Settlement

An unexpected find of the 1975 campaign was the discovery of two EB I shaft tombs in a new area just west of the town wall. The same area provided evidence for what may be the earliest settlement at the site. Since the initial finds were of burials, the area as a whole was designated Field F, in line with the cemetery letter sequence begun by Lapp.

Field F is situated on the north slope of an eminence of Lisân sediment (figs. 1, 23). This hilly area is a continuation of the ridge on which the southern town wall was built, although it is lower in elevation. The opposite side of this part of the ridge had been cut recently for an access road to a hill farther west containing a gravel source. On the top of the knoll and on its north slope, local tomb robbers had scraped the area clean of the usual desert pavement, laying bare the Lisân marl immediately below. A number of trenches and pits had also been dug here by the tomb robbers, exposing several tomb chambers. Since the scattered sherds were similar to the EB IA and IB pottery of Cemetery A, it was decided to carry out a salvage operation. A series of trenches was laid out, with the first two, F 1 and F 2, coming down on burial chambers, while the third, F 3, yielded evidence for what appears to have been domestic occupation.

Tomb F 1

Tomb F 1 is a typical Bâb edh-Dhrâ^c EB I burial with shaft, narrow entryway, and rounded chamber (fig. 2). Due to slope erosion the shaft, 0.90 m. in diameter, was only partly preserved. Judging by the angle of the slope in this area the shaft must have been shallow, probably less than a meter in depth. The entryway, also only partly preserved, was 0.47 m. wide. The chamber, with straight wall on the doorway side and elliptical around the sides and back, had a maximum diameter of 2.07 m. and a minimum diameter of 1.75 m. The chamber yielded

19 complete pottery vessels, one basalt stone jar, and two broken pots. The latter had been missed by a robber pit dug into the center and northwest area of the chamber which had sliced through the usual disarticulated bone pile in the center, a mat underneath the bone pile, and the floor of the chamber (fig. 3).

Although the robber pit had disturbed much of the stratigraphic evidence, a balk maintained through the center of the chamber suggested two distinct burial phases, the earlier belonging to EB IA and the later to EB IB (fig. 2). Near the doorway and in areas on the side undisturbed by the robber pit was a 0.20 m. thick layer of sandy soil mixed with gravel and flints. The robber pit made it impossible to tell whether this sandy soil extended over the rest of the chamber; it did not appear at the back edge. Beneath the sandy layer a clay layer, cracked on the surface from silting, extended over what remained of the chamber. Several cm. below this layer the first outline of pottery vessels appeared, the floor of the chamber being ca. 0.20 m. lower than the clay surface. All the vessels except one were either on or slightly above the floor, along with mat impressions, and one long bone cut through by the pit (fig. 3). The evidence is not conclusive but it seems likely that the sandy layer belonged to a second phase of the tomb after siltation of the bones and pottery of the first phase had occurred. Support for this interpretation may be found in the position of a large bowl (P 20) cut in half by the robber trench. This bowl was discovered 0.20 m. off the floor at the same level as the bottom of the sandy soil. In addition, a study of the sherds collected from the robber debris around the chamber has shown that they belong to EB IB. Line-group painted sherds sufficient to restore an entire jar were recovered. However, the pottery from the silted clay layer was typical EB IA in form. A similar reuse of an EB IA tomb in EB IB is found at Jericho in Tomb A 13 (Kenyon 1960: 48-49).

Tomb F 2

Three small trenches were opened 6 m. to the east of F 1 in a search for further tombs (figs. 1, 23). The third trench, 1 x 2 m., yielded the outline of a chamber tomb along with traces of a robber trench. What again was undertaken as a salvage operation turned up one of the significant finds of the season (fig. 4).

Clearance of the tomb revealed a rounded chamber with a flat side on the north. Neither a definite shaft outline nor doorway was discovered.

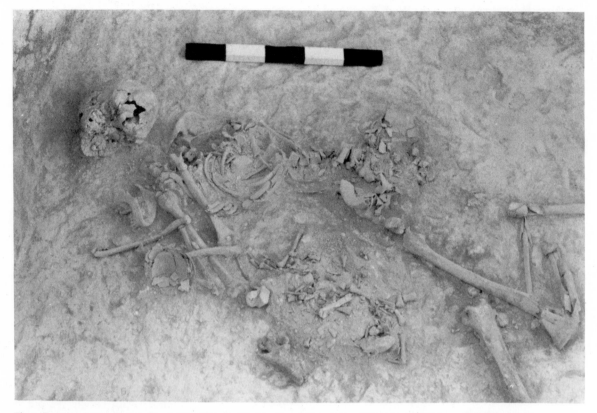

Fig. 4. Female adult skeleton in Tomb F 2 at Bâb edh-Dhrâᶜ with remains of 15 and 5 month old children at the front and back sides of skeleton; figurine is at bottom of picture.

An articulated female adult skeleton was oriented east-west on the chamber floor with the head facing north. The bones of a 5-month-old child were found next to the upper portion of the adult remains, the latter having tiny skull fragments cradled in her hand. A second child, 15 months old, was positioned near the waist of the adult. A few cm. north of the second child lay an unbaked clay figurine (figs. 4, 27). Only broken fragments of pottery appeared in the tomb. A large robber pit had been cut across the southwest portion of the chamber. From the floor to the probable roof line, which was only partially discerned, the chamber was filled with clay, dessicated chalk, and stones of cobble and pebble size. If pottery had been present, it was wholly cleared away by the robber pit.

In spite of the absence of whole pottery, fragments from the robber pit and chamber belonged to EB IA. In addition, the clay figurine is exactly parallel to 7 examples found by Lapp in EB IA shaft tombs (Lapp 1968a: 7). In contrast to F 2, the earlier figurines were found in disarticulated bone piles in which no child bones were positively identified. On the other hand, articulated burials

were the exception in EB IA tombs excavated by Lapp. Tomb A 83 from the earlier excavations, however, contained a close parallel to F 2, having an articulated female skeleton with at least one child. This EB IA tomb was cut into the lower slope of a small wadi, with its entrance on the high side of the slope. It had a shaft lined with aggregate stone and plaster, along with a downstep into the chamber. Like A 83, F 2 showed signs of a possible shaft on the higher side of the slope, as well as a stepped-down area, but the lower outlines of the latter were mostly destroyed by the robber pit. The sherds, the figurine, and the parallel with Tomb A 83 all support the conclusion that F 2 was an EB IA tomb.

Area F 3

Several additional small trenches between F 2 and F 1 yielded evidence for domestic occupation. The area was designated F 3 (figs. 1, 23). Here a mud brick wall was discovered in the section and then found to extend for 1 1/2 m. to the east (fig. 5). On both the east and west ends the wall had been cut by robber pits. In the part excavated, the wall stood 7 courses high and 2 rows wide. The brick size was ca. 0.15 x 0.30 m. The courses were bonded, and the mortar joints were staggered, with alternate bricks being placed lengthwise across the width of the wall. The wall was built up against an artificial vertical bench in the marl and bonded to the bench with a thick clay mortar (fig. 5). The bonding was strengthened by boring holes into the chalk and marl and filling them with mortar. Considerable mud brick debris north of the wall suggests that the wall was originally much higher and above ground.

The dating of this wall is problematic. Although a floor surface with a fire pit cut through the floor was discovered at the west end of the wall, with associated pottery dating to EB I, work had to be suspended at the end of the season before a sufficient area could be cleared for positive dating. The debris north of the wall, including mud brick and large boulders, contained pottery ranging from EB I to III. All the pottery in the area was domestic, much of it consisting of large vats and cooking pots. The proximity of EB I tombs to the domestic occupation constitutes a problem, since the normal pattern in this period is for tombs to be located away from the settlement. At some sites, however, underground dwellings and tombs are found together. The Lisân marl of this area provided a natural place not only for tombs but also for occupation, while the elevated terrain overlooking the wadi below would have made it suitable and even ideal for settlement.

If the EB I date proves to be correct, it would suggest that the first settlers at Bâb edh-Dhrâᶜ, along with burying their dead, built mud brick structures partly below and above the surface. A survey of the slope leading down to the lower terraces near the Wadi Kerak revealed further evidence of this sequence. Here there are remains of more mud brick walls exposed by erosion, along with large quantities of EB I domestic pottery. The first settlement of the site may well have been on this western slope opposite the shaft tombs.

The EB II-III Fortifications and Settlement

Four new fields were opened within and contiguous to the town site itself (figs. 1, 22-24).

Fig. 5. Area F 3 at Bâb edh-Dhrâᶜ, looking south, showing the cut natural Lisân marl with mud bricks mortared against cut.

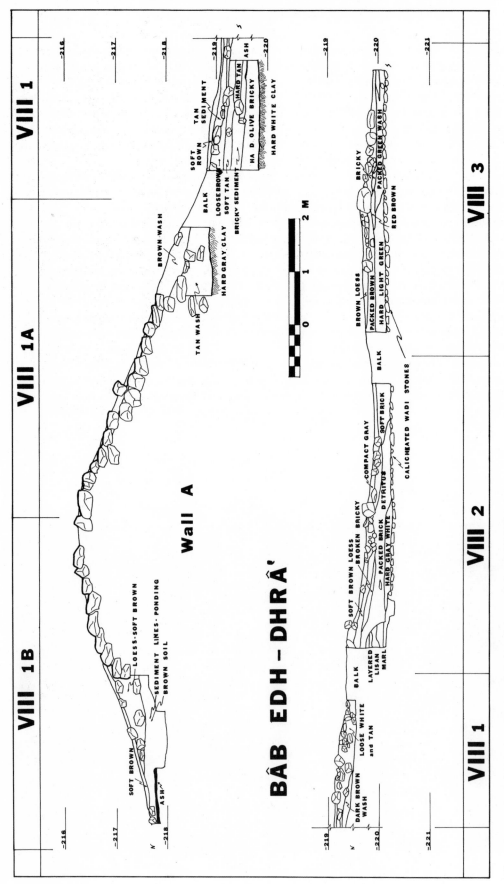

Fig. 6. East section of Field VIII on the south side of the town site of Bâb edh-Dhrâᶜ.

Three of these (Fields VIII, XI, and XIII) were devoted to clarifying the wall system and possible accompanying towers or gate, and the fourth (Field XII) to exploring domestic or industrial remains, along with occupational surfaces, on the interior of the town.

Wall A (Field VIII)

The designation Wall A continues the nomenclature of the earlier excavations of Lapp, who examined this wall in a trench on the east side (Field II). It is distinguished from Wall B, a mud brick wall discovered below Wall A on the east side by Lapp. Wall A refers to the stone defensive wall which rings the site and which has been visible in part to various explorers during the present and probably also previous centuries.

During the 1975 season it was decided to investigate these fortifications on the south (figs. 1, 22). The chief reason for this decision was that the large area lying beyond Wall A to the south is heavily concentrated with wall remains (fig. 25). The goal was to cut a trench which would serve to tie

Wall A stratigraphically to the occupation south of the town. Field VIII was opened with 5 squares, beginning from ca. 3 m. north of the interior side of Wall A and extending southward to ca. 19 m. from the exterior of Wall A. This same trench may be expanded in a future season to obtain a complete section connecting with the EB IV occupation in the area farther south of the town.

On the south Wall A was only moderately well preserved. A face could not definitely be established on the exterior, although an interior face was possibly determined, but again in a quite unstable condition. Wall A at this point is mostly near or above the surface, and this suggests that what is presently standing is mostly foundational material. Despite the absence of definite faces, the wall cannot have been much more or less than 7.25 m. wide at its base. As can be noted in the east section of Field VIII, there was a layer of wasted mud brick in Squares 1, 2, and 3 (fig. 6). Above this mud brick were large fallen stones of the type found in the wall. The stratigraphy suggests that the wall at one time had a superstructure of mud brick which collapsed and was pulled downhill. Subsequently the

Fig. 7. Wall A as exposed in Field VIII at Bâb edh-Dhrâᶜ; the transverse face of a "segment" is just to the left of the meter stick.

Fig. 8. Wall 38 just outside town in Field VIII at Bâb edh-Dhrâ^c; stones with caliche to the left of wall.

foundation stones eroded on top of the washed bricky debris. We may thus propose tentatively that Wall A was constructed of a foundation of stones, with its upper courses of brick. There was clearer evidence of this kind of construction in the building excavated on the northeast in Field XI (figs. 10-11).

An important result of the work in Field VIII was the light it threw on the design of the fortifications. Squares 1, 1A, and 1B were laid across the wall, and it so happened that the trench was through one of the "segments" or joints of the wall on the south (fig. 7). The sectional construction was noted by Lapp in the 1965 season (Lapp 1966: 561; 1969: 9, n. 14), and seems to have been observed already by Albright as a distinguishing feature in the eastern wall (Albright 1926: 59). During the season of 1975 the surface remains of the wall were traced around the entire site wherever they were visible, and at least 7 other joints were observed.

Two problems arise about this method of construction. The first is the technology of the sectional construction itself and the directional procedures followed in laying Wall A. One explanation is that the builders of the wall may have worked consistently in a clockwise direction, stopping at intervals to lay a transverse face perpendicular to the main orientation, such as the one found in Field VIII. Following upon the completion of this face, construction would continue in a clockwise direction with more

randomly laid layers of stone, until a further face was founded. However, a second explanation is also possible. It seems that the face of each section might more appropriately have been laid first and that the wall builders worked backward in a counterclockwise direction from each face. The strength of this explanation is that it would seem to be advantageous to begin construction by laying the face initially rather than moving up to the latter as the finishing element. If the second explanation is accepted, it would mean that the wall construction moved in two directions simultaneously, the overall orientation being clockwise, while the segments were worked on in a counterclockwise direction. This is a problem which may be clarified in future investigation.

The second problem regarding the Wall A construction is that of the function of the sectional design. It is possible that such wall segments were intended to minimize the stress factor. Since the rift valley and the Dead Sea region in particular are subject to earthquake, it is possible that the wall builders planned with such disasters in mind. The Early Bronze Age wall at ^cAi seems to have used a similar construction and this wall was actually found damaged in one place, probably by earthquake (Callaway 1969: 10-11, fig. 7).

A further feature was discovered concerning the sectional construction. In examining surface remains of Wall A around the site, it was noted that

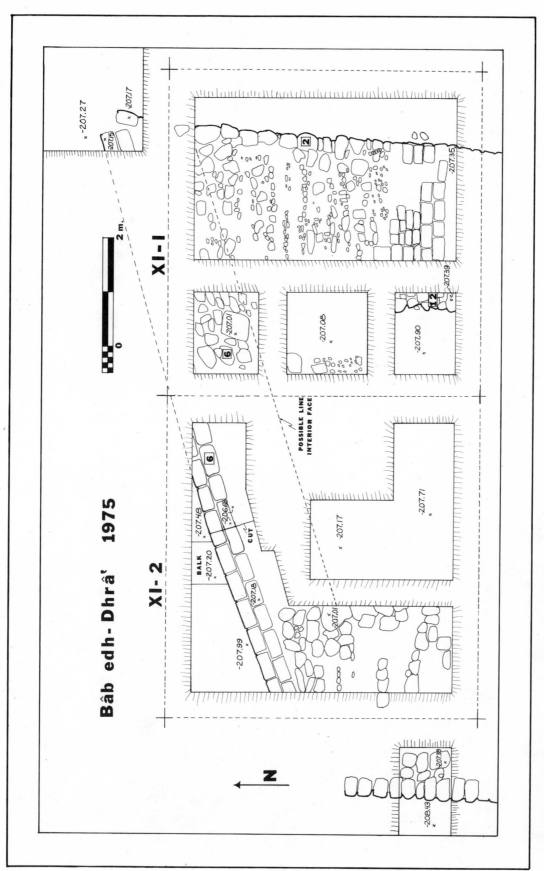

Bâb edh-Dhrâ' 1975

XI-1

XI-2

N

Fig. 9. Plan of "Northeast Tower" in Field XI at Bâb edh-Dhrâ'.

sections often differ from each other in the core material employed for a segment. Thus on the east side one segment was made of limestone taken from the hills east of Bâb edh-Dhrâᶜ, while an adjacent segment was made from a different type of stone. This feature suggests that the labor force itself was divided according to groups responsible for a particular segment. Further study of such data may result in the formulation of a working hypothesis regarding social organization during the EB II-III period. The carefully planned clusters of charnel houses in the cemetery provide an interesting parallel for the same period.

In comparing the results of this season's work on Wall A with those from the 1965 campaign, it should be noted that no remnants of the earlier mud brick Wall B were found below Wall A in Field VIII. The section shows that the footing of Wall A was laid directly on a sterile layer of hard white or gray clay. There also was no clear evidence in this field of how the town came to an end. Mud brick detritus among the stones in Squares 1A and 1B contained many charcoal flecks which might point to burning. The ashy layer (Locus 5) north of Wall A (fig. 6)

may also indicate burning, although it could belong to occupational usage of the area. The manner in which the EB II-III town came to an end is dependent on evidence from other areas.

In Square 3 south of Wall A a part of a wall (Wall 38) constructed of boulder-size stones was uncovered (fig. 8). Pottery associated with this wall dates it to EB III, and thus it was from the town period. Since one stone appears to have been a threshold stone, the wall stub may contain the entrance to a domestic or industrial building. Adjacent to the wall can be seen a field of cobbles embedded in a crust of caliche. Geological investigation suggests that this was a natural formation caused by capillary action or runoff in this area south of the town. The significance of this for the environmental history of the site is apparent and will be discussed in the final publication containing the geological report.

The Northeast Tower (Field XI)

The northeast area was selected for exploration because of two prominent stone walls running

Fig. 10. Mud brick exterior wall, Wall 6, of "Northeast Tower" in Field XI at Bâb edh-Dhrâᶜ, looking southeast; bricks can be seen in trench and to left of meter stick.

Fig. 11. Mud brick on top of stone in the "Northeast Tower" of Field XI at Bâb edh-Dhrâᶜ, looking east.

parallel along a north-south axis 13 m. apart (figs. 1, 22, 24). Erosion had exposed both walls, particularly towards the interior of the town. Squares 1 and 2 were laid out on the high point of the ridge before it slopes toward the Wadi Kerak on the north and the town interior on the south. Excavation uncovered a large structure with stone foundation and mud brick superstructure (fig. 9).

The east wall, Wall 2, was at least 0.70 m. wide. A mud brick platform or superstructure covered at least part of this wall. Some of the rectangular bricks can be seen on the plan at the southeast end adjacent to and covering Wall 2 (fig. 9). These bricks were only partially removed during the 1975 season and it may be that they rest upon the core of a wider wall, with Wall 2 being the exterior and Wall 12, uncovered in a small trench to the west, being the interior parts of a single wall.

The north wall, Wall 6, formed an acute angle with Wall 2. The northern wall contained a stone foundation and mud brick superstructure, the latter preserved at its highest point to three courses. The average width of this wall was 1.90 m. Outside Wall 6 and against it was a mud brick skin wall or casing. The latter was still standing to a height of eleven

courses as can be seen just left of the meter stick in fig. 10. This exterior wall was discovered in two phases. The earlier phase of the wall made use of smaller brown mud bricks found in the lower five courses. These were separated from the later upper six courses of very hard white mud brick by brown brick detritus, tightly compacted without clear mortar lines (fig. 10). An occupational level associated with the lower courses was sealed by fallen mud brick debris. A second occupational level related to the upper courses was found in a black ash line against the wall.

The small part of wall uncovered west of Square 2 was founded on the natural Lisân marl (fig. 9). In the area exposed the foundations followed the elevation of the slope, moving from two courses at the north end to four courses at the south. Farther down the slope to the south six courses had been exposed by erosion. Mud brick detritus outside the wall was similar in composition to the white brick of the second phase of Wall 6, suggesting again a stone foundation with brick superstructure.

The interior of the building was only partially cleared. Wall 12, a stone wall three courses high, was exposed in Square 1. The top stones of this wall were nearly at the same elevation as those of Wall 2 to the east and it had the same north-south orientation. The possibility has already been mentioned that this wall might have been the inner face of a 3 m. wide wall. A cross-wall, Wall 5, built of mud brick three rows wide and preserved three courses high, ran east-west from Wall 2 to and above Wall 12. Between the mud brick and the stones of Wall 12 were traces of wooden poles, following the mortar lines. This may indicate a type of construction found also at ᶜAi, where pole impressions were interpreted as belonging to reinforcement in the building of the wall (Callaway 1972: 48, pl. 5:2). Inside Wall 12 to the west the mud brick debris yielded sizable amounts of EB III pottery. This area appears to have been part of an interior room.

On the same level as Wall 5 a mud brick platform extended over Wall 2 to the east and Wall 6 to the north. This platform may be part of a superstructure built over the core between Walls 2 and 12. Wall 5 would then be a cross segment to strengthen the main wall. When the platform was removed, several lines of pebble-size stones appeared. These lines appeared along the mortar lines of the brick above and may have served the same function of reinforcement, and perhaps leveling, as the wooden poles. Their precise meaning, however, is enigmatic. The same phenomenon, with larger stones, occurs under the mud brick on the west side (fig. 11), although the stone lines are not as clearly marked here.

Although Wall 6 appears to be in line with the city wall to the east, a small trench in the northeast suggested that the structure may be disengaged. Surface traces of the town wall actually disappear 40 m. to the east. This fact has led to the present interpretation that the structure is a free-standing tower.

The West Trench (Field XIII)

The West Trench was opened south of Field IV of Lapp's excavations in order to begin a more intensive exploration in the area beyond Wall A west of the town (fig. 1). Two factors led to the choice of this area for investigation. One was the large number of fallen stones and fired bricks on the surface, suggesting that structures might be found nearby. A second was the location, just east of Area F. Below Wall A on the west is a gently sloping shelf which drops gradually to the Ghôr el-Mazraᶜ and the Wadi Kerak below. From this point there is a commanding view of the Lisân peninsula. This

would appear to be a natural side of the town to fortify in a special way, and it was conjectured that a main access to the city, including a gate, may also have existed on this side.

The trench of the 1975 season consisted of a 3 x 6 m. area to the west of Wall A. Since excavation in this field was not begun until mid-season, it was decided to limit this part of the work to a trial trench to be pursued more extensively in a future season. Although no definite structures were discovered, the debris was found to be of greater depth in this area (between 1.5 and 2 m.) than anywhere else on the town site thus far explored. The nature of this debris also indicates that remains of structures might be expected to appear in the adjacent area.

The stratigraphy of the West Trench was instructive. The surface layers were of loess and contained numerous fallen stones along with occasional kiln-fired bricks. Below the surface was a layer of bricky debris with many stones and fired bricks, about 0.75 to 1 m. in depth, and in turn a 0.50 m. deposit of what the geologist termed "mass wastage of mud brick wall with chunks of clay" (Locus 6). The latter rested on a surface on which were many fallen stones and some square kiln-fired bricks of the type seen in fig. 12. These bricks were well made, measuring on an average 0.20 x 0.20 x 0.07 m. They were pink to orange in color and extremely hard. In addition to the bricks, part of a wooden beam was uncovered on the same surface (fig. 12), the part exposed measuring 0.55 m. in length and 0.13 m. in width. The full length of the beam was not determined since it continues into an area left unexcavated. The wooden piece was unburnt and may have been used in the ceiling of a structure or as part of a door, either as a pivot beam for a leaf or as a bolt for locking. The wood was removed for analysis and carbon 14 dating, but neither result is as yet available. The presence of wood of this size at Bâb edh-Dhrâᶜ is striking in light of the site's environment today.

The direction of the fall of the debris in the West Trench was downslope from northeast to southwest. This suggests that if structural remains have not completely eroded, their vestiges may appear just northeast of this trench. With the exception of one locus containing a small amount of EB IB wares, all pottery from the West Trench dated to EB II-III. Not a single piece of EB IV pottery was present, indicating that the horizontal stratigraphy on the west end of the town is similar to that on the south. The town was used exclusively during EB II and III, while the EB IV peoples chose areas away from the town for settlement.

The Town Interior (Field XII)

The chief reason this area was selected for investigation was to begin excavation in a relatively undisturbed part of the town (figs. 1, 22, 23). Since the surface was approximately on the same level as the top of Wall A, there seemed to be promise of depth of debris in this field. Traces of walls on the surface also suggested a major structure might be present.

One square, Square 2, was opened in the area a week after the season began. Square 1 was reserved for a future season. Three weeks after the beginning of the season, following the completion of Field IX, the area was expanded to include three more squares on an east-west line north of Square 2.

The stratigraphy in Square 2 consisted of the usual desert pavement, large amounts of mud brick debris just below the surface, two clear occupational surfaces, and a bed of natural channel gravel which was found to wind through the area in a northwesterly direction. Architectural features included a stone walkway and sections of stone and mud brick walls which need further definition as to their extent and purpose.

While it is premature to attempt conclusive proposals on phasing in this field, some preliminary observations may be made. A platform or walkway six stones wide and running in a north-south direction perpendicular to Wall A belonged to the latest occupational phase (fig. 13). This walkway was one stone deep and ca. 8.50 m. of its length was exposed. On the south it terminated 5 m. short of Wall A, being interrupted at this point by a bed of channel gravel. Since there was no definite border on the south and since several stones follow in the same line farther to the south, there is a possibility that the walkway may originally have continued over the gravel. North of Field XII the same walkway may be followed 12 m. down the slope toward the interior of the western wall in the direction of a depressed basin area. The walkway may thus have been intentionally planned to connect this lower area with the higher area just within the southern wall.

In Square 2 a mud brick wall one course wide and one course deep was uncovered. It extended for 3 m. and can be seen in fig. 14 just to the right of the gravel deposit. Since the gravel abuts this wall it may have served as a retainer. The relation of the mud brick wall to the natural gravel deposit is similar to what Lapp found on the east end, where the foundations of the mud brick Wall B were laid on natural gravel (Lapp 1966: 560). A second wall,

made of stone and oriented east and west, was found adjacent to the brick wall on the north (fig. 14). A surface associated with it on its north side contained EB III pottery. This wall appeared underneath the walkway of the late phase.

Square 5 had two occupational surfaces separated by 0.10 m. of debris throughout most of the square. Both surfaces were earlier than the walkway. No architectural features appeared in this square, however. To the west of the walkway a

Fig. 12. Square 1 in "West Trench" of Field XIII at Bâb edh-Dhrâᶜ, looking down and to west; kiln-fired brick on bricky debris is behind meter stick, and wooden beam is at lower left.

mortar and quern were found *in situ* on the earliest surface. Nearby were large amounts of seed material, including cedar seeds, which were collected for analysis. Squares 6 and 7 also contained small remnants of mud brick wall, positioned in relation to the channel gravel as in Square 2.

The association of the mud brick walls and the natural gravel is the most significant feature of Field XII. The gravel appeared 0.10 m. below the surface in three of the squares excavated. At one place it was found to be at least 1 m. deep. It was apparently contained by walls on both the south and north ends of Field XII. The mud bricks were white and very hard, similar to those encountered in Field XI.

The channel gravel seems to follow a northwesterly path toward a large caved-in area underneath and on both sides of the western town wall. Aerial

Fig. 13. "Walkway" 6 stones wide near surface in Field XII at Bâb edh-Dhrâᶜ, looking south; inner line of town wall is a few meters farther south.

Fig. 14. Field XII on southwest interior of town site of Bâb edh-Dhrâᶜ, looking west; bricky debris with burn is above meter stick and "walkway" is to right; channel gravel abuts mud brick wall toward left of picture with stone wall to right and below "walkway."

photos taken during the 1975 season show that considerable drainage has occurred from the caved-in area in the direction of the basin just inside the western wall. Since geological investigation showed that the channel gravel was a natural bed with larger pebble-size stones at the bottom, becoming smaller on the top, the interpretation follows that the gravel provided a natural system for drainage (Helms 1975: 29). The cave-in below the western wall raises the possibility that similar natural channels within the town may have been responsible for the collapse and subsequent erosion of the northern wall into the Wadi Kerak.

EB IV Settlement

The Northeast Settlement Area (Field X)

During the 1973 survey Field X was singled out as a prime target for excavation (figs. 1, 22). Several wall lines were evident on the surface, along with a heavy concentration of EB IV sherds. A collection of the latter was included in the report of the survey (Rast and Schaub: 1974). The area is located

northeast of the town and is separated from the latter by a deep wadi which may have been formed more recently than the Wadi edh-Dhrâᶜ or the Wadi Kerak. One of the main objectives of the expedition, to obtain stratified data for the EB IV period, was centered in this field.

Four squares were opened along an east-west line following a ridge which slopes gently toward the wadi on the south and more steeply toward the Wadi edh-Dhrâᶜ on the north (fig. 15). To the west of the area excavated is a knoll of Lisân marl which had been cut for a structure on its southwest side. Beyond this knoll to the west considerable occupation during EB IV must have occurred, judging from the large amount of pottery and signs of flint working in this area.

Four phases of occupation were distinguished in the stratification of Field X. The earliest phase was found only in the eastern half of Square 2, but it continued throughout Square 3 and into Square 4. Occupation began here when the natural Lisân marl was cut and leveled for the construction of a large building which may have been only partially

Fig. 15. EB IV settlement in Field X at Bâb edh-Dhrâᶜ, looking east; late phase stone wall on left; mud brick walls of structures were at upper end of picture.

Fig. 16. Burned room, possibly a kitchen, from the early phase in Field X at Bâb edh-Dhrâᶜ, looking southwest; corner of mud brick walls is to right of meter stick; flat hotplates are lying in burn.

cleared. It included three well-defined mud brick walls laid on a gravel footing above the marl bedrock, enclosing an area 2.50 x 3.50 m. Traces of a fourth wall, completing a rectangular building, were problematic because of erosion on the north side.

The mud bricks from this building measured on an average 0.22 x 0.44 x 0.10 m. They were laid lengthwise across the width of the wall. Mortar traces were not found between the courses, but this may have been caused by erosion. A mud brick bench with smaller bricks measuring 0.20 x 0.35 x 0.10 m. was inside the west wall. To the east of this bench was a mud brick platform associated with a large burn area contained by mud brick walls (fig. 16). The ash in this burn area was 0.35 m. deep at some points. Beneath the ash a group of round, flat plates came to light on a gray marl surface (fig. 16). The plates were made of coarse ware, with many large grits, similar to cooking pot ware (fig. 17). They may have served as "hotplates," being used for items placed within the fire. From its contents and debris, this room may have served as a kitchen. Many seed remains were recovered for analysis from this burn level.

Sealing this early phase occupation was a thick layer of compacted mud brick debris varying from 0.15 to 0.25 m. in depth. Above this layer was a fill layer between 0.10 and 0.30 m. thick, apparently used to level off the area after the brick walls had collapsed. Above the filled in area and also outside the latter, especially to the west, evidence came to light of a second phase, which seems to have been limited and brief. Only one architectural fragment was associated with this phase, a stone wall two courses wide on the same line as the west wall of the early phase structure.

Above this second phase occupation the area was leveled along the ridge. Low spots were filled in with gravel while a wall one stone wide was laid in an east-west direction. After a brief occupation associated with this wall, a second similar wall was laid 2.50 m. to the south, following the same east-west line for 10 m., then veering off to the southeast. These two phases were distinguished as the third and fourth phases respectively. Mud brick debris on top of occupation layers associated with these walls indicated that they had mud brick upper courses.

The purpose of the walls in these last two phases became a bit clearer through a study of the aerial photos taken during the 1975 season. These showed that a long wall extends east from the city for ca. 200 m. where it makes a right angle turn northward and then disappears due to the erosion of the wadi

Fig. 17. Flat "hotplate" from Field X at Bâb edh-Dhrâᶜ.

between Area X and the town. Outside of Field X the continuation of the wall may be seen farther to the east. It appears that these walls served to close off this area east of the town during EB IV. Since the surface survey of this eastern area brought to light large quantities of vat and store jar sherds, along with mortars and querns, it is likely that this area was a large industrial section. The lengthy wall would have served to mark off the area, protecting it from unnecessary intrusion. It is also possible that this wall served to facilitate catchment of water in the extensive agricultural land east of the town site. It will be seen below that this entire eastern area, once thought to have been used for tombs and burials, was more likely put under intensive cultivation. The late phase walls in Field X, then, represented a small portion of the efforts to capitalize on this region.

A contribution of particular importance from Field X is the well-stratified pottery sequence from EB IV, treated in a preliminary way in a special section below.

The Southern Settlement Area (Field IX)

Along with Field X this area was productive of

Fig. 18. EB IV settlement in Field IX south of town at Bâb edh-Dhrâ⁽ looking north; rectangular house with doorway is in right foreground with roadway to left of house; town wall and Field VIII are in background.

occupational and architectural features dating to the latest usage of the site (figs. 1, 22). The surface was covered with stone litter, representing the eroded remains of walls, as well as numerous broken mortars and querns. Lines of walls were visible on the surface and some were traced in the ground survey of the area (fig. 25). Sherd concentration was also frequently heavy on the surface (fig. 25).

The accumulation of occupational debris in Field IX was very shallow, averaging little more than 0.35 m. before bedrock, in the form of Lisân marl, *huwwar,* or channel gravel, was encountered. The best recorded section was that of the east balks of Squares 5 and 6. Here, as well as over most of the area, the surface was described by the geologist as desert pavement, created as the wind carried away the fine particles of soil, leaving scattered wall stones and pebbles to jostle each other, forming a compacted surface (fig. 18). The walls in Field IX were rarely more than one course deep, and this single course of foundation stones was also impacted in the naturally created pavement. Directly below this hardened surface remains of living surfaces could be determined, although severe erosion had occurred here. In the east balk of Squares 5 and 6 a layer of broken brick and ashy white soil ca. 0.20 m. in depth was traced just below

Wall 12 of one of the latest buildings. This debris, which was also found in Square 2, might suggest that mud brick structures stood earlier in the same area.

Field IX provided plans for several structures. At least two buildings came to light, and these were most likely domestic structures (fig. 18). In the photograph three of the four foundation walls of a building can be seen in the right foreground, the eastern wall being outside the picture. The building was rectangular in shape, its doorway being off center, probably in the open space in the southern wall. To the left of this structure was a street or pathway, visible where the meter stick is lying. Again, to the left of the meter stick, the eastern end of a similar house can be seen. Sometimes these domestic buildings shared a common wall as, for example, the long wall on the eastern side of the street (Wall 6 of Square 3 and Wall 5 of Square 6) which seems to have served as a wall for at least two houses as well as a border wall for the street.

The rectangular, broad-room plan of the Field IX structures is significant. This is the style of construction most typical of the EB II and III periods (Ben-Tor: 1973), and the Bâb edh-Dhrâᶜ charnel houses fit the type for the EB II-III period. What is noteworthy is that the Field IX buildings are to be dated to EB IV on the basis of the pottery.

Fig. 19. Aerial view of charnel houses excavated in cemetery of Bâb edh-Dhrâᶜ, including A 55 of the 1975 season.

Fig. 20. Charnel House A 55 at Bâb edh-Dhrâᶜ, looking northwest; doorway with robbed-out flanking monoliths, but with threshold stone intact, is at upper center left; intense burn was in northeast section.

This would point to an interesting continuity in architecture between the EB II-III urban peoples and their EB IV successors.

That these structures were used for occupation is clear not only from the living surfaces, which contained domestic pottery, but also from various fire pits, sometimes found on the interior and sometimes on the exterior of the buildings. One fire pit (Locus 7 of Square 2) was lined with a semicircle of stones and another (Locus 14 of Square 6) contained a considerable accumulation of burned debris, in which was discovered an intact bowl. Usually these burn areas were simply defined loci within the floor surface. Samples for flotation were gathered from these loci, and in one area unidentified animal bones were also present (see the report below).

The pottery of Field IX makes it possible to assign these structures to EB IV, with some lower layers appearing to represent a slightly earlier ceramic horizon, perhaps in late EB III. As in the case of Field X, the work in Field IX shows that the EB IV period at Bâb edh-Dhrâᶜ consisted of a sedentary population, no longer related to the earlier town area, but clearly founding its own planned building complexes.

The Cemetery

A 55 (Charnel House)

The objectives of the 1975 season did not include extensive work in the cemetery south and southwest of the town. Several tombs were explored, and the recently disturbed chamber of D 1, partly excavated in 1967, was cleared out. This material will appear in the final report. The main work in the cemetery concentrated on the excavation of Charnel House A 55 (fig. 19). The clearance of this funerary building brings to 11 the total of such structures which have been excavated: 9 were examined under Lapp's direction, 1 under Fawzi Zayadine, and the present one. There were two reasons why this example was chosen for excavation. First, its location was known from the 1967 season, when its southwest corner was reached in excavating the adjacent circular EB IB funerary building (A 53). Since the stratigraphy of this area of the cemetery was closely examined at that time, it was decided that the excavation of A 55 could complete the picture. Second, the possibility that a good collection of bones and skulls would be forthcoming from this building would advance the work of the physical anthropologists.

The excavation of a charnel house in the cemetery normally follows three steps: (1) determining the location of such a funerary building; (2) clearing the exterior to determine the extent and shape of the structure, while leaving balks against the exterior to maintain the stratigraphic relation to the surrounding area; (3) excavating the interior and its contents, along with obtaining plans and section data. The first step was self-evident in this case. The second step established as expected the stratigraphic relation between A 55 and the earlier A 53; several layers of naturally formed soil covering the remains of A 53 were found to have been cut vertically in order to lay the walls of A 55. This picture is in line with the differences in the pottery of the two tombs.

The charnel house itself was rectangular in design, measuring approximately 4.80 x 2.80 m. The doorway was set off-center toward the northern end of the west wall (fig. 20). In studying the charnel

houses excavated by Lapp, it has been noted that as a general rule they were built up against a hilly area in the cemetery, with their doorways always in the wall on the lower side of the slope. In order to accomplish this a section of the hill had to be cut out and leveled, the back wall of the building then being laid to the rear of this cut. Fill was thrown into the gap between the exterior of the walls and the vertical cut. Usually this fill contained sherds and it is noteworthy that sherds taken from the fill of A 55 contained pottery of the type found in the early shaft tombs of EB IA. Such evidence is supportive of the dating of these earliest tombs at Bâb edh-Dhrâᶜ.

The bricks of A 55 were some of the hardest discovered thus far in any of the charnel houses, a factor perhaps to be attributed to the materials from which they were made. An analysis is being made of the composition of one of these bricks. They were sun-dried, rectangular in shape, some of them measuring ca. 0.45 x 0.30 x 0.08 m., although there was variation. The structure was entirely of mud brick except for the doorway, which had a single stone slab as a threshold. Apparently the two flanking monoliths at the doorway, usually found in

Fig. 21. Southeast exterior corner of Charnel House A 55 at Bâb edh-Dhrâᶜ; mud bricks are laid in staggered fashion.

the charnel houses, were robbed in antiquity (fig. 20). The exterior face of the walls was noteworthy. The bricks were not laid in a vertical face, but were rather stepped and slightly battered (fig. 21). On the other hand, the interior face, although difficult to trace, seems to have been smooth and vertical. Given the poor condition of the wall on the interior, it was impossible to determine whether a header-stretcher method was used in this structure as in several excavated by Lapp. It does seem clear that the mud bricks were not all laid in the same direction and thus some sort of alternating system was employed.

On the interior the burials were entirely covered by a deep layer of mud brick debris from the collapsed walls of A 55. This brickfall was especially notable on the east. Several whole bricks were embedded at this point and, according to geological analysis, this could hardly have occurred through natural erosion. The walls, therefore, must have been pushed over intentionally. Within this deposit of bricky debris 7 leaf impressions adhering to bricky pieces were retrieved and saved for further study.

Below the layer of brick fall burials began to appear. These consisted of heaps of bones with skulls laid nearby. There were few indications of articulation, a feature conforming exactly to burials in the charnel houses excavated earlier. A layering of burials was clearly present, so that later burials were apparently placed over earlier ones, but the burials were extremely jumbled and difficult to separate. There was a tendency to place burials in groups in particular areas of the tomb. These locations were traced on the plans of the charnel house. The heaviest concentrations of burials and pottery were along the four walls of the building, with lessening amounts toward the center. Successive articulated burial, with consequent pushing back of earlier remains, seems doubtful, however, since few of the burials farther from the walls showed signs of articulation either. Altogether the number of burials, based on skull count, was about 60. The more than 170 pottery vessels ranged from the very earliest part of EB II through EB III, with a small number of vessels just opposite the doorway being EB IV. The floor of the tomb was mostly cobbled with somewhat larger stones than those found in other tombs by Lapp. However, on the east and south sides there were spaces against the walls lacking cobbling.

A feature of special importance was the burning adjacent to and opposite the doorway. It was entirely missing in the south half of the charnel house. This burning was not an early feature of the tomb's use, but belonged to its latest phase since it reached up to the highest levels and even resulted in some of the latest burials and tomb items being burned. Small pieces of cloth analyzed as *Linum* were discovered in this burn, and they are no doubt similar to material found in several of the charnel houses by Lapp.

The interpretation of this burning is a problem. That cremation seems out of the question is indicated by the confined nature of the burn as well as by the analysis of the bone and skull material (see the report by Finnegan). Another possibility would be that the tomb was intentionally burned, and this would appear to be a more plausible explanation. In this case the burn could be taken with the evidence of the mutilated brick walls to support the explanation that the cloth material, which was purposely spread over the building at the doorway side, was set on fire, and that the walls were also pushed in at this time. We may find a clue concerning the further problem of who might have been responsible for such happenings in the latest pottery from A 55. This consisted of several vessels of EB IV type, parallel to the pottery from the latest shaft tombs at Bâb edh-Dhrâᶜ (Schaub: 1973). These vessels were on the uppermost part of the burial remains opposite the doorway, and they also showed signs of burning. The latest people to occupy the site, namely the EB IV people, may have defaced A 55 deliberately. It is also possible that these were the same people responsible for the end of the EB II-III town site, but this is a problem which needs further study at the town site itself.

A parallel situation in some of the charnel houses excavated by Lapp supports this interpretation. Of the nine charnel houses excavated earlier, three were found to be burned like A 55. In studying the pottery of these charnel houses, it is evident that the latest pottery (EB IV) is uniformly found in those buildings which were burned. The other six buildings were apparently out of use by the time of late EB III when the last burials were put in prior to the burning of the tomb. Such a pattern suggests a premeditated act of destruction within the EB II-III cemetery complex, at least against that part which was still being used late in EB III.

Cairn Tombs

Although not concentrating extensively on tomb excavation, the 1975 expedition did attempt to

Fig. 22. Aerial photo of town site of Bâb edh-Dhrâ^c, looking northwest, showing fields excavated in 1975; wadi separating Field X is visible on right; Wadi Kerak bends to northwest in front of town and flows to the Ghôr.

Fig. 23. Aerial photo showing west end of town site at Bâb edh-Dhrâ^c, looking south; recent roads were cut above Area F; Field IX, unmarked, is at left of picture; entire area to west and south of Field IX contains remains of occupation.

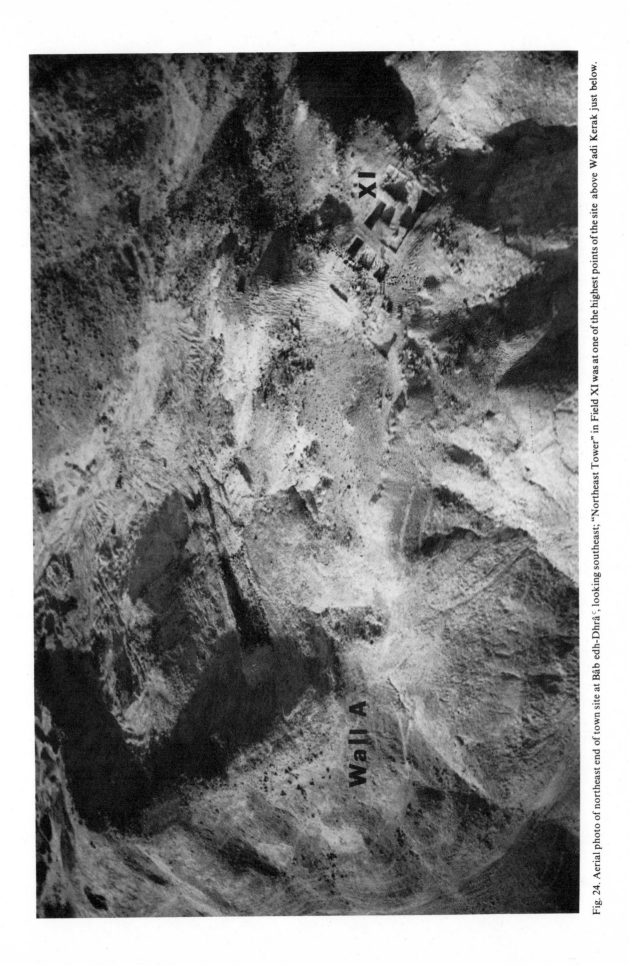

Fig. 24. Aerial photo of northeast end of town site at Bâb edh-Dhrâʿ, looking southeast; "Northeast Tower" in Field XI was at one of the highest points of the site above Wadi Kerak just below.

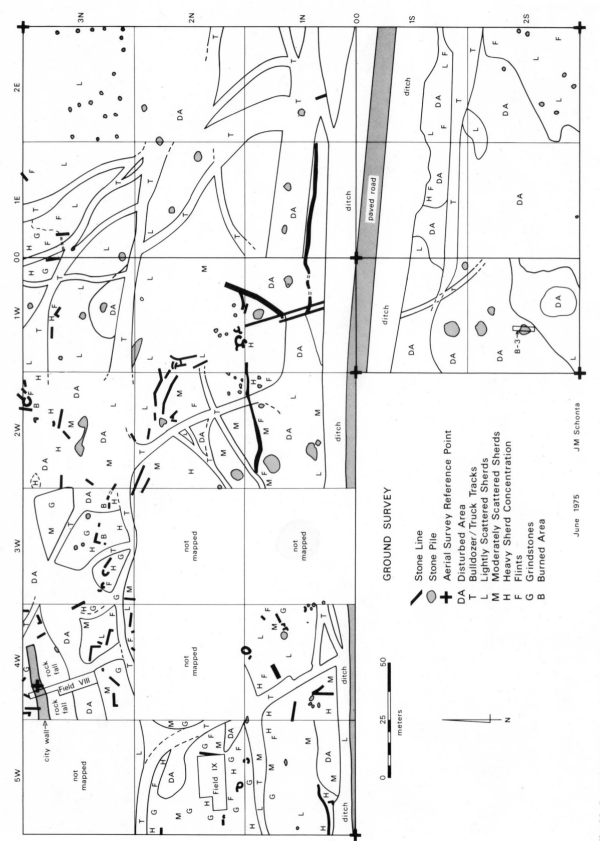

GROUND SURVEY

- ╱ Stone Line
- ⬭ Stone Pile
- ✛ Aerial Survey Reference Point
- DA Disturbed Area
- T Bulldozer / Truck Tracks
- L Lightly Scattered Sherds
- M Moderately Scattered Sherds
- H Heavy Sherd Concentration
- F Flints
- G Grindstones
- B Burned Area

June 1975   JM Schonta

Fig. 25. Ground Survey map of area south and southeast of town site of Bâb edh-Dhrâ[c], Field VIII and town wall is in 4W.

Fig. 26. Dagger from Tomb D 1 (Reg. No. 017).

clarify the problem of cairn tombs at Bâb edh-Dhrâᶜ, customarily associated with the EB IV phase. Since the discovery of the site in 1924 cairn tombs have been singled out as a prominent burial type at Bâb edh-Dhrâᶜ. Albright noted the many small circles of stones, averaging ca. 4 m. in diameter, around the edges of the fortress to the east and west and identified these as cairns (Albright 1924: 6; 1926: 59; 1944: 4; Mallon 1924: 442, fig. 22; 444, 449-50). Lapp also reported encountering four cairns during his excavation (Lapp 1968a: 10), two of which were in the cemetery area southwest of the town and were excavated (A 1, A 2), but he does suggest that this was a difficult phase at the site. During the present season three of these stone heaps were opened. One was cleared in the large open field to the east of the town site, and two were excavated south of the latter. All three turned out to be sterile. This discovery leads to the conclusion that many of these stone piles around Bâb edh-Dhrâᶜ seem to have been something other than tombs. It appears more likely that to the east of the site, where agricultural usage was heavy, judging from the numerous flints used for harvesting, the stone heaps were simply left over from clearing the land for farming. Just how old the stone heaps are and whether they go back to the Early Bronze period is an open question at this point. On the Ground Survey map (fig. 25), the stone circles are simply listed as random heaps, and it is noteworthy that large numbers of recently bulldozed tracks reflect exactly the same intent of clearing the land for cultivation.

The preliminary results of this exploration help to delimit more precisely the burial area at Bâb edh-Dhrâᶜ. The large open land area to the east of the site was apparently a cultivation zone, although some tombs, such as several tholoi (B 1, B 2) excavated by Lapp, were found in the southern part of the area. Similarly, to the south of the town site the cemetery proper does not appear to have extended any closer to the town than ca. 200 m.

Aerial Photography and Ground Survey

The comprehension of the function and significance of the Bâb edh-Dhrâᶜ site in and for the life patterns of the populations of the Early Bronze Age necessitates obtaining the widest environmental perspective possible. Such studies are particularly critical for this site. The environment in this case includes that immediately around the site itself and ultimately the entire southern Ghôr. Aerial photography provides an expansive outlook, especially for post-season study, and can often suggest the context in which components known from the ground are to be understood. Ground survey has the advantages of a close-up tabulation of patterns and data discernible on the surface. The two taken together can lead to fulfilling objectives for understanding the broad implications of a site and its history.

With the cooperation of the Department of Antiquities of Jordan, the 1975 expedition was able to obtain a permit to photograph from the air the essential areas surrounding the site. A twin-engined plane and pilot were supplied by the Royal Academy of Aeronautics in Jordan. Photographs were shot by Robert H. Johnston from a side door while the plane was in a banking position. Three are presented in this preliminary report (figs. 22-24), and others will be included in the final report.

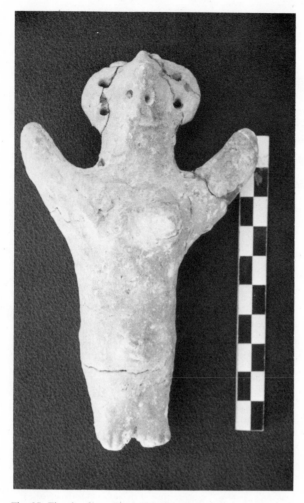

Fig. 27. Figurine from Tomb F 2 (Reg. No. 016).

The Ground Survey was carried out by Jeannine M. Schonta and was restricted to the area south and southeast of the town site. Plotting was on a 50 m. grid, employing a system of triangulation to determine relative points. The map made as a result of this survey (fig. 25) indicates the heavy settlement outside the town site to the south and east. It will be helpful for selecting areas for future investigation, and it has already been useful in indicating occupational concentrations and zones marked off for cultivation. The expedition will continue the ground survey in future seasons, with the goal of a complete map of the environs of the site.

Objects from the 1975 Season

Among the items recorded as objects during the 1975 season were two with special significance, which are here reported in a preliminary way.

Copper Dagger (fig. 26)

In clearing the disturbed southern chamber of D 1, left unexcavated at the end of the 1967 season (Lapp 1968c: 92-93), a copper dagger (Reg. No. 017) was discovered. It was moderately well preserved, with corrosion and oxidation rather advanced and with warping in the center. A piece of cloth was adhering to one side, the analysis of which has not been completed at this writing. Since the burials in D 1 were wholly disturbed by robbing of the chamber since 1967, it was not possible to plan the relation of the dagger to the burial and other objects in the tomb.

The dagger measures 0.25 m. in length, 0.03 m. in breadth, and 0.01 m. in width at its broadest and widest points. Three rivets were still preserved, and a fourth was broken off. There appears to be a slight midrib or thickening of the center.

This riveted dagger is especially interesting because it is the first found at Bâb edh-Dhrâᶜ in a late shaft tomb. Four other daggers of this type were found in charnel houses excavated by Lapp, two in A 41 and two in A 51. The latter are being prepared for publication by Alix Wilkinson. As noted above in the discussion of A 55, these were two of the charnel houses which had been burned and which also had some of the latest pottery in them, datable to the very end of EB III or early EB IV. Preliminary examination has also shown that the pottery from D 1 is from the latest phase of EB III and may already reflect the beginning of EB IV. This dagger may be dated accordingly. As a representative of this period it parallels similar EB III and IV daggers from a number of sites, a selection of which would include examples from Jericho Tomb F 5 (Kenyon 1960: fig. 66:3), Tell en-Naṣbeh Cave Tomb 7 (McCown 1947: pl. 104:1), Megiddo Tomb 1101 B Lower (Guy and Engberg 1938: fig. 171:1, pl. 86:4), and the recently published burial cave Tomb 1 at Azor (Ben-Tor 1975: 22-3, 26, pl. 22:1, fig. 12:4).

Figurine (fig. 27)

The figurine from Tomb F 2 (Reg. No. 016) is of unbaked clay containing tiny limestone grits. The color is light gray with a slight bluish tint (2.5Y N7/). It measures 0.126 m. in height, 0.08 m. from tip to tip at the arms, and 0.02 m. thick at the buttocks. The left arm and two rounded segments of the head had broken off and were restored. The right breast was missing.

The distinctive features are the upraised arms, flattened circular flaps at each side of the head, each pierced with two holes, and a pinched, bird-like face with two holes apparently for nostrils. The light slash below the latter may indicate a mouth, a feature found on several similar figurines from the earlier excavations. The feet are separated by a slight cleavage at the base, and three incised lines on each foot suggest toes. On the rear the buttocks are pronounced, possibly representing in some form a steatopygous motif. A pinched lump of clay on the frontal side could indicate a male organ, thus making the figurine hermaphrodite, but comparison with several of the figurines discovered by Lapp suggests rather that pregnancy is represented.

A number of parallels containing some of the same features may be cited from approximately contemporary cultures. The bird-like facial features are common in figurines found as far away as West Pakistan (Mellink and Filip 1974: fig. 101a, c). They are found also in Mesopotamia (Parrot 1956: pl. 68:440, 50) and Egypt (Mellink and Filip 1974: figs. 195-97). Figurines of the Naqada I period in Egypt are interesting to compare since they have rather stub-like upswept arms (Petrie and Quibell 1896: pl. 59:6). They also contain steatopygous features but lack pierced ear flaps. The latter, however, are particularly distinctive of north Mesopotamian figurines, which also normally have the arms crossed upon or pressed against the breast and legs together (Pritchard 1943: 52; Albright 1939: 108; May 1935: 29). That the Bâb edh-Dhrâᶜ figurine is closer to the north Mesopotamian type is suggested by an early 3rd millennium B.C. example which has pierced ear flaps, legs separated, and arms extended (Parrot 1961: fig. 16a). Later examples from Tell Asmar dated to 2100-2000 B.C. are identical in most details except that the legs are found together (Parrot 1961: fig. 300).

Stylized plague figurines from the 2nd millennium B.C. with arm projections and pierced ear flaps appear to be direct descendants of this type (Lapp 1964: 41; 1969: 45, fig. 30). Albright's suggestion that the arm projections are silhouettes of elbows with the hands presumed under the breasts may have validity, but a figurine in the round from the ᶜAmuq shows the same short arms definitely extended (Braidwood and Braidwood 1960: fig. 368:5).

None of the parallels cited, however, include all the features, especially pregnancy, of the Bâb edh-Dhrâᶜ example. The distinctive features of this figurine must be studied further, including the context in which it was found, that of burial, in this case the burial of a mother and two children.

Summary

Since Bâb edh-Dhrâᶜ is essentially a single major period site, its depth of debris is quite shallow. Nonetheless, occupation at the site stretched over nearly a full millennium during the Early Bronze Age. In addition, although the EB II-III town proper occupied an area of ca. 9 acres, the boundaries of the site extend much farther. The 1975 season found heavy settlement at least 200 m. farther to the east outside the town and there are similar indications to the south and west. To be added to this are the areas used for burial and the extensive cultivation land.

Future investigation includes plans for the following. If the EB I settlement, which seems to be appearing on the west end of the town, becomes substantiated, we will have evidence for a period of fundamental importance. It may become possible to reconstruct details of the evolution from EB I life patterns toward an urban concentration associated with the town site. More work should consequently be done to trace this EB I settlement pattern and the transition to the new period of the town. At this point we know only a minimum about the design of the EB II-III town. Future investigation should have as a priority the extension of the Field VIII trench into the interior of the wall, the further clarification of Fields XI, XII and XIII, and the opening of several new fields within the town site, with the goal of ascertaining its layout. Such data may help to show the degree to which the EB II-III town people operated according to a differing social structure than their EB I predecessors or EB IV successors. The EB IV occupation itself needs to be explored more extensively since the data from this period discovered during 1975 are the first substantial evidence of this kind to appear at the site.

Along with these, the cemetery remains, especially the human remains, the usage in antiquity of the surrounding cultivation areas, the abundant worked flint remains and buildings in which this industry was carried out, as well as the hydrology of the region including the possible channeling and damming of water from the wadi and spring for agricultural purposes, all need further study. As Field VIII has shown, the site also promises significant geological results, including data on climate and rainfall amounts affecting the Dead Sea basin. Finally, the objectives regarding this site can only be fully achieved when the results from Bâb edh-Dhrâᶜ are coordinated with those from the related but as yet unexcavated Early Bronze Age sites of the southern Ghôr.

BIBLIOGRAPHY

Albright, W. F.
1924   The Archaeological Results of an Expedition to Moab and the Dead Sea. *Bulletin of the American Schools of Oriental Research* 14: 2-12.
1926   The Jordan Valley in the Bronze Age. *Annual of the American Schools of Oriental Research* 6: 13-74.
1939   Astarte Plaques and Figurines from Tell Beit Mirsim. Pp. 107-20 in *Mélanges syriens offerts à M. René Dussaud* = Bibliothèque archéologique et historique 30, Vol. 1. Paris: Geuthner.
Albright, W. F.; Kelso, J. K.; and Thorney, J. P.
1944   Early Bronze Pottery from Bâb ed-Drâᶜ in Moab. *Bulletin of the American Schools of Oriental Research* 95: 3-10.
Ben-Tor, A.
1973   Plans of Dwellings and Temples in Early Bronze Age Palestine (Hebrew). *Eretz Israel* 11 (I. Dunayesvsky Memorial Volume): 25, 92-98. Jerusalem: Israel Exploration Society.
1975   Two Burial Caves of the Proto-Urban Period at Azor 1971. *Qedem* 1: 1-54.
Braidwood, R. J., and Braidwood, L. S.
1960   *Excavations in the Plain of Antioch, I: The Earlier Assemblages, Phases A-J.* Oriental Institute Publications 61. Chicago: University of Chicago.
Callaway, J. A.
1969   The 1966 ᶜAi (Et-Tell) Excavations. *Bulletin of the American Schools of Oriental Research* 196: 2-16.
1972   *The Early Bronze Age Sanctuary at ᶜAi (Et-Tell).* London: Quaritch.
Guy, P. L. O., and Engberg, R. M.
1938   *Megiddo Tombs.* Oriental Institute Publications 33. Chicago: University of Chicago.
Helms, S. W.
1975   Jawa 1973: A Preliminary Report. *Levant* 7: 20-38.
Kenyon, K.
1960   *Excavations at Jericho, Vol. I: The Tombs Excavated In 1952-4.* London: Harrison.
Lapp, P. W.
1964   The 1963 Excavation at Taᶜannek. *Bulletin of the American Schools of Oriental Research* 173: 4-44.
1966   Bâb edh-Dhrâᶜ. In Chronique Archéologique. *Revue Biblique* 73: 556-61.
1968a   Bâb edh-Dhrâᶜ, Perizzites and Emim. In *Jerusalem through the Ages.* The Twenty-Fifth Archaeological Convention October 1967. Jerusalem: Israel Exploration Society.

1968b   Bâb edh-Dhrâᶜ Tomb A 76 and Early Bronze I in Palestine. *Bulletin of the American Schools of Oriental Research* 189: 12-41.
1968c   Bâb edh-Dhrâᶜ. In Chronique Archéologique. *Revue biblique* 75: 86-93.
1969   The 1968 Excavations at Tell Taᶜannek. *Bulletin of the American Schools of Oriental Research* 195: 2-49.
1970   Palestine in the Early Bronze Age. Pp. 101-31 in *Near Eastern Archaeology in the Twentieth Century: Essays in Honor of Nelson Glueck,* ed. J. A. Sanders. Garden City, NY: Doubleday.
McCown, C. C.
1947   *Tell en-Naṣbeh I: Archaeological and Historical Results.* Berkeley and New Haven: The Palestine Institute of Pacific School of Religion and the American Schools of Oriental Research.
Mallon, A.
1924   Voyage d'exploration au sud-est de la Mer Morte. *Biblica* 5: 413-55.
May, H. G.
1935   *Material Remains of the Megiddo Cult.* Oriental Institute Publications 26. Chicago: University of Chicago.
Mellink, M. J., and Filip J., *et al.*
1974   *Frühe Stufen der Kunst.* Propyläen-Kunstgeschichte, Vol. 13, ed. Kurt Bittel. Berlin: Propyläen-Verlag.
Parrot, A.
1956   *Le Temple d'Ishtar.* Mission Archéologique de Mari 1 = Bibliothèque archéologique et historique 65. Paris: Geuthner.
1961   *Sumer.* Trans. S. Gilbert, J. Emmons. The Arts of Mankind, ed. André Malraux, G. Salles. New York: Golden.
Petrie, W. M. F., and Quibell, J. E.
1896   *Naqada and Ballas 1895.* British School of Archaeology in Egypt and Egyptian Research Account and Publications, No. 1. London: Quaritch.
Pritchard, J. B.
1943   *Palestinian Figurines in Relation to Certain Goddesses Known through Literature.* New Haven, CT: American Oriental Society.
Rast, W. E., and Schaub, R. T.
1974   Survey of the Southeastern Plain of the Dead Sea, 1973. *Annual of the Department of Antiquities in Jordan* 19: 5-53, pls. 1-11.
Schaub, R. T.
1973   An Early Bronze IV Tomb from Bâb edh-Dhrâ ᶜ *Bulletin of the American Schools of Oriental Research* 210: 2-19.

Selected Pottery from Bâb edh-Dhrâᶜ, 1975

Robert H. Johnston
Rochester Institute of Technology, Rochester, NY 14623
R. Thomas Schaub
Indiana University of Pennsylvania, Indiana, PA 15701

Pottery from Charnel House A 55 (R. T. Schaub)

The study of the pottery from Charnel House A 55 is only in its initial stages. Some representative types are found in figs. 1-2, and parallels are listed with the figures. Most of the types, such as the round-bodied juglets (fig. 1:1, 2, 6b) and the flat-based juglets (fig. 1:5a, 5c, 6a, 6c, 7), appear in the earlier sequence of the Jericho tombs (Tomb A 127 and early phases of Tomb D 12), but not in the later tombs (Tombs F 2, 3, 4). The piriform juglets (fig. 1:3, 4, 5b), however, are common in the later tombs at Jericho (Tombs F 2, 3, 4), as well as in Tomb D 12 at the same site. It should be noted that all of the A 55 juglets that have been reconstructed to date, with the exception of a badly fragmented stump base of a large jug, are either round-bodied or have flat bases. No pointed bases have been found. The juglets thus appear to be predominantly EB II forms.

The bowls, platters and small saucers are also best paralleled by EB II deposits, including the stratified material of ᶜAi and Arad. The distinctive carinated form (fig. 2:11) is common in the EB II phases at ᶜAi and Arad and is also found in Tomb A 127 at Jericho. The lamps with four pinched spouts (fig. 2:12) have their best published parallels in EB III contexts, but the form is also known in EB II.

The painted bowl (fig. 2:14) has a close parallel in Tomb D 12 at Jericho. Hennessy notes that decoration similar to that found on the jar base in fig. 2:8 is typical of EB III at Jericho and elsewhere. It occurs in Tomb C at ᶜAi. Bowls with decoration similar to fig. 2:15 are present during EB IIIB at Jericho.

A preliminary study of the pottery forms suggests that A 55 was used over an extended period of time from EB II into EB III, with the predominant use being in EB II. A few EB IV forms, found in the upper debris level of the building, are to be associated with the latter's destruction.

Pottery from Field X

It has often been suspected that sites in Transjordan might hold the key to the transitional ceramic development between EB III and MB I. Surveys in Jordan and limited excavations at sites like Ader, Iskander, and ᶜArôᶜer have pointed to the strong probability of that supposition. A preliminary study of the late forms from the 1975 season is of special value in this respect. Fields IX and X, domestic or industrial areas outside the EB II-III town, offered excellent stratified sequences through late EB III and into EB IVB.

To illustrate this sequence a selected pottery series from loci of Phases 1-4 of Field X is presented in figs. 3-5. The forms are arranged according to locus, beginning with pottery from earlier loci and moving to the later. Phase 1 is represented by figs. 3:1-4:36. Figs. 4:37-5:61 include some loci which are mixed, but which generally belong to Phase 2. Phase 3 is found in figs. 5:62-70 and Phase 4 in figs. 5:71-82.

The preliminary nature of this report precludes exhaustive study of either forms or ware. However, the effort can be viewed as the beginning of a study which will be continued in detail in the final publication. The ware types described below are indicated by Roman numerals next to each form in the drawings (figs. 3-5). Parallels from other Palestinian and Transjordanian sites are listed opposite the pottery figures.

Large Vats

Wide vats are found in Phases 1 and 2. That they were absent in Phases 3 and 4 is not conclusive at this point. The vats are often strengthened at the rim by thickening that is decorated with thumb impression (figs. 3:1, 5:61) or with extended ledge handle (fig. 3:26). Two of the examples (figs. 3:26,

5:61) also have a diagonal band of clay connected with the rim band. The Phase 2 examples (figs. 4:56, 5:61) have coarse combing on the exterior. The double-ledge form of fig. 4:56 is distinctive but not the only example since many similar forms were found in the ground survey. A close parallel to this form with similar pointed rim was found in Level XII at Beth-shean.

Medium to Wide Bowls

The bowl forms range from simple, medium-sized bowls to large, deep hole-mouth forms. Medium to large platter bowls, ranging from 20 to over 40 cm., predominate. Simple dishes (figs. 4:40, 43) are far from distinctive since they are found throughout the Early Bronze Age in both stratified contexts and tombs. The EB III-IV parallels suggest that these dishes usually have flat bases.

Among the platter bowls the wide bowls with incurved rim (figs. 4:58, 59) appear to be related to an EB IIIB form at Jericho (Hennessy 1967: pl. 9:87), although they lack the sharp carination of the Jericho forms. Similar forms are common in EB III at Ader, Jericho Tomb A, and Lachish, but earlier parallels could also be cited (De Vaux 1947: fig. 5:4). The vessel wall of the rolled rim bowls, rounded in figs. 3:2, 13, 29; 4:44, 52-3, 55, or pointed in figs. 3:12, 4:41, is also curved in, but a sharp instrument has been used to form an inner lip. Dever has concluded that the rounded or pointed rolled rim extends through the entire period from EB I to MB I (Dever 1973: 42, 44). Although the examples he cites for pointed rims from Tell el-Faᶜah (N) are all sharply angled up from the wall of the vessel, his judgment concerning the continuity of the form in the Early Bronze Age seems well founded. Examples of earlier rolled rims may be cited from Phases II-V at ᶜAi (Callaway 1972: figs. 16:17, 19; 26:22; 45:6) and the ᶜAmuq valley in Phase G (Braidwood and Braidwood 1960: figs. 202:1, 2, 4; 203:1). The later Early Bronze Age forms appear to have more upright walls with flat bases, so that only fully reconstructed vessels can help to clarify the diagnostic value of the form. The same may be said for the flat rim bowls which have a more upright upper wall (figs. 3:3, 4, 11; 4:32, 45, 54). The flat rim in fig. 5:74 belongs to a much deeper bowl.

Thickened flat rims which are concave on the interior (figs. 3:14; 4:33, 42) are also found on deep bowls with steep, curved sides. The same form, turned in and sloping inward, is found at Lachish on hole-mouth jars (Tufnell 1958: pls. 62:290; 63:333) and on spouted bowls (Tufnell 1958: pl. 58:107-8).

It should be distinguished from a similar rim associated with shallow bowl forms. The Bâb edh-Dhrâᶜ examples are upright in stance, while the Lachish examples are turned in.

The thickened rim bowls in figs. 4:60 and 5:81 are similar to hammer rim forms, which have a long history in the Early Bronze Age (Dever 1973: 44, n. 11) but these do not have the rounded surface of the more typical knob rim of EB III (Hennessy 1967: 15, pl. 10:97).

A major difference in bowl forms occurs in Phases 3 and 4 with the appearance of the inverted rilled-rim bowls (figs. 5:62-65, 67-71, 73, 75-76, 78-79). Dever has noted that the ribbing is the most distinctive feature, since downsloping rims appear through the Early Bronze Age (Dever 1973: 46). The relation of the rim to the exterior rills is noteworthy, and the form could profit from an analysis of its construction. The folded-over form appears twice without rills (figs. 5:71, 78) and a sloping rim without thickening occurs with rills on smaller bowls (Rast and Schaub 1974: fig. 1:24).

The importance of these rilled-rim bowls has often been noted (Dever 1973: 47). Albright observed that they were distinctive in Phase A at Ader (Albright, Kelso, and Thorley 1944: 6, n. 8) although they also appear in Phase B (Cleveland 1960: figs. 14:5, 15-17, 26). They were found in Strata I-F, and especially in H-G, at Tell Beit Mirsim (Albright 1932: pls. 4:1-3, 7-11; 5:26-34) and also seem to appear in Stratum J (Albright 1933: pl. 1:7, 9). Rilled-rim bowls are prominent in Level VIB at ᶜArôᶜer, at Iktanu in Phase I, and especially at Jebel Qaᶜaqir. At Bâb edh-Dhrâᶜ they have been associated with tombs (Schaub 1973: 15, fig. 7:19) and have appeared on the surface (Rast and Schaub 1974: 14, fig. 1:19-24). Their importance for the relative chronology is noted below.

Hole-mouths, Jars, Cups, Plates

Among the teapot forms, the thin, sharply everted rims of Phase 1 (figs. 3:6, 30; 4:34) are distinct. Made of fine thin ware, they differ from the forms of Phases 3 and 4, which also have ribbing on the shoulders (fig. 5:66, 82). Simple, tapered rims, again on thin-wall vessels, are also found in Phases 1 and 2 (figs. 3:7, 15; 4:49, 57). Fig. 3:7 is burnished and fig. 4:49 has a red slip. The latter, along with fig. 4:57, are probably teapots, but the large diameter of fig. 3:15 suggests that this form belongs to a large hole-mouth. Hole-mouth jars with square cut (figs. 3:8, 20-21), rounded (figs. 3:9, 4:35), and bulbous (fig. 3:18-19) rims are also present in Phase 1. The distinctive folded over rim of a large hole-mouth is a common form at Arad in Stratum II. Deep hole-mouth bowls, often with a spout at the rim, are also represented in Phases 1 and 2 (figs. 3:17, 24, 25; 4:36, 47-48).

The jar rims presented here are quite fragmentary (figs. 3:10, 27-28, 37; 4:50-51). It is noteworthy that two of the forms have combing, and the sharp angle of fig. 3:28 is similar to the distinctive jars of MB I although the ware is different. Fig. 4:50 could be a ring stand, but the combing and the ridge at the break suggest a large store jar.

The small bowl or cup with everted rim and incised lines on the shoulder (fig. 5:77) from Phase 4 has a yellow slip similar to that found on slightly larger bowls with everted rim at ᶜArôᶜer. The form is quite close to the cups of Jebel Qaᶜaqir.

Relative Dating

The dating of Phase 1 as the earliest phase in Field X is bolstered by the comparative forms, as well as by the absence or presence of certain features in the ceramic repertory. In general, the pottery forms are most closely comparable to the late EB III deposits at Lachish, Jericho, Beth-shean, Tell Beit Mirsim, and the ᶜAmuq valley, with features showing continuity with the earlier Early Bronze Age strata at Tell el-Farᶜah (N) and Arad. Some of the closest parallels are with the tomb groups of Tomb 351 at Jericho and Tombs 1101 B Lower and 1102 Lower at Megiddo. On the other hand, a relationship to Ader B, ᶜArôᶜer VIb, Khirbet Iskander, and Iktanu I, particularly in flat and rolled-rim bowls, is present. That Phase 1 of Field X is prior to these latter deposits may be argued by the total absence of rills or ribbing on bowls or teapots. That it is slightly later than the late EB III deposits may be argued by the absence of sharply-angled inverted rim forms, which are still present in Jericho C-A (Hennessy 1967: pls. 9-10), ᶜAi Phase VIII (Callaway 1972: figs. 75:2, 3, 6, 8, 11; 77:9-10, 12; 78:5-7; 80:1-2), at Lachish in the same period (Tufnell 1958: pls. 58:87; 60:198; 63:306, 322; 64:344), and Tell Beit Mirsim in Stratum J (Albright 1932: pl. 1:24, 27; 1933: pl.20:35-40). At Bâb edh-Dhrâᶜ inverted-rim platter bowls are common in the charnel houses, although only one example is found in the latest charnel house, A 20, and in the latest phases of the town site.

The positive parallels from late EB III contexts, the continuity in form with EB IV pottery, and the absence of inverted rims, on the one hand, and rilled

bowls, on the other, argue for positioning Phase 1 between late EB III and EB IV. Whether this phase should be assigned to EB III or IV will depend on the overall interpretation of the site and its cultural stages. It is certain, in any case, that Phases 3 and 4 of Area X are to be associated with Ader B-A, ᶜArôᶜer VI b-a, Iktanu I-II, and the Bâb edh-Dhrâᶜ Tombs A 52 and A 54. A series of Carbon 14 dates presently being processed should provide additional data for the absolute dating of Phases 1-4 in Field X.

Preliminary Ware Descriptions of Field X Pottery (R. H. Johnston)

The following ware descriptions were assigned in the field while doing a rough sorting and analysis of the various colors and fabrics. The size of inclusions was determined by using Wentworth's Size Classification Scale (Shepard 1968: 118). The color ranges were noted using the Munsell Soil Color Charts. It will be necessary to define these wares more precisely in the laboratory and to relate these findings to the typology of the site. This can be prime research since few studies such as this have been done with excavated material from the Early Bronze Age. Clays have been collected from the area of the site and future tests will be made using those clays, and comparisons made between clay samples fired under time-temperature-atmosphere controlled sequences and excavated material. These preliminary classifications, then, are the simple initial designations of Bâb edh-Dhrâᶜ material and the beginning of a thorough study of this material excavated during the 1975 season.

Combed Ware (I)

Combed ware is a range of pottery that relates to the surface treatment of the ware. While some combed ware is coarse, the combing technique is used at Bâb edh-Dhrâᶜ over a range of pottery. The combing was done with a notched wood, gourd, or sherd comb, probably a wooden one. The combing marks appear to follow random patterns creating an overall effect. The measurements presented here are taken from center to center of the grooves in the combed impression, using a vernier caliper. Further study will be needed to ascertain the reasons for combed ware. It is, of course, a forming and finishing technique, but probably has other ramifications in terms of vessel usage. The combing varies in the width of the combing marks generally as follows:

(a) coarse   0.53 cm. (center to center of grooves)
(b) medium   0.3 cm. (center to center of grooves)
(c) fine   0.19 cm. (center to center of grooves)

Burnished Ware (II)

Burnished ware at Bâb edh-Dhrâᶜ is defined as those wares that bear a low luster as the result of polishing the leather-hard clay with a smooth tool of stone or bone. As one rubs the surface with the polishing tool the surface is compacted and a micro layer of clay is brought to the surface to give a dull sheen. Sometimes the strokes are allowed to stand out in certain areas, producing a pattern burnish. At times the pottery is covered all over with a thin layer of fine clay called slip. Sometimes the slip might be of another color as, for example, red slip over a buff clay. This slip layer can be burnished to a sheen or left simply as a coating layer. Burnishing is a technique that takes considerable time and may have been employed on vessels that had a special usage. It would also be applied to a vessel made of rough clay to provide a more attractive surface. Burnished pottery at Bâb edh-Dhrâᶜ fits all the above criteria. There are burnished pieces, both slipped and unslipped, and there are a variety of examples of pattern burnish.

Salmon Buff Ware (III)

Salmon buff ware (color range: 7.5 YR 6.5/3) is perhaps the most common ware at Bâb edh-Dhrâᶜ It comprised 47.6% of Field X ware and 48% of Field VIII ware. Salmon buff clay is a medium fine clay; when well-fired at 800-900° C oxidation, it provides a fine utilitarian ware. It is strong and much less fragile than coarse ware. It would be porous enough for water bottles, allowing water to remain cool by the slow process of evaporation. It also would resist abrasion that might result from daily usage. It is typical of clays used by village potters in many parts of the Middle East. The ware is grit-tempered with small (ca. 0.16-0.09 cm. or smaller) pieces of limestone, quartz, and sand. The body is fairly dense and is well fired. The sherds have a hard sound when struck. Some of the largest pottery found at Bâb edh-Dhrâᶜ falls into this category of ware.

Coarse Ware (IV)

A common ware at Bâb edh-Dhrâᶜ, perhaps the second most common, this appears to be a utility ware for "cook pot" use. The sandy, coarse clay is very low-fired, ca. 700-750° C, and contains large inclusions of limestone, quartz, and some tiny traces of mica. Some of the inclusions are very large (1.35 cm., 0.90 cm., and 0.50 cm.). The clay appears to have a high degree of porosity which generally increases the resistance of fired pottery to thermal shock, since the grains in a porous mass have more freedom of movement than those in a dense mass. Also the thermal stresses and thermal shock are relieved in a porous mass where there are numerous air pockets. Porous pots can stand sudden changes that would shatter more dense pieces. Coarse ware would be easier and quicker to fire and could be removed from a simple firing into the cooler air. The ware would be most suitable for heating over a simple camel thorn fire. Much of the Bâb edh-Dhrâᶜ coarse ware has a combed outer surface. Combing with a coarse comb would help smooth and refine the coarse clay vessel in the firing stages, and the ridges would make the pieces easier to handle. Some of the coarse ware sherds examined showed carbon black on the inside and outside.

Red Ware (V)

Red ware (color range: 2.5 YR 5/6) is again a medium coarse fabric, tempered with fine to medium grains, and with a surface of reddish clay. This surface seems to be a layer of colored slip washed on the salmon buff clay. The surfaces are full of lime pops caused by the decomposition of calcium carbonate at ca. 800° C range, leaving calcium oxide which takes up moisture to form calcium hydroxide. The hydration increases the volume of the material, exerting pressure and "popping" the surface which can destroy the entire vessel. The red ware forms a much smaller percentage of excavated material and it will be interesting with further study to note the shapes of vessels in red ware and to study the relationship between vessel, usage, and clay fabric.

Cream Ware (VI)

Cream ware (color range: 10 YR 8/2) is a yellow-buff clay body with very fine to medium inclusions. It is well fired under oxidation atmosphere and very hard. Further study will probably indicate that cream ware is of the same clay as salmon buff ware and several other wares. The high lime-iron bearing clays used by Middle Eastern potters fire through a range of from brown-black at very low temperatures (600-700° C) to salmon buff at mid range (850-900° C, under oxidation conditions), to yellow, cream, or white at the high range (1000° C). Further study needs to be made to note the porosity of these sherds and to relate the apparent porosity to the color designations. It will also be interesting to relate the local clays sampled and process them through temperature, time, and atmosphere controlled firing tests.

Gray Ware (VII)

This ware (color range: 7.5 YR 6.5/1) is about the same density as salmon buff ware except that the entire sherd is gray in color throughout the body. This color is usually the result of a reduction atmosphere in the firing which produces a ware that becomes vitrified at a lower temperature than pottery fired in an oxidation atmosphere. If temperatures are in the 800-900° C range and in a reducing atmosphere, ferric oxide will be reduced to ferro-ferric oxide, coloring the clay gray. If reduction is severe enough, ferric oxide is formed, which acts as a strong flux.

Gray ware would appear again to be a utilitarian ware tempered by medium coarse to very coarse material such as limestone, quartz, and sand particles. Further study needs to be done on this ware under laboratory conditions that will involve thin sectioning and re-firing tests.

Speckled Ware (VIII)

This fabric is the most interesting at Bâb edh-Dhrâᶜ and will need further study. It seems again to be related to the salmon buff ware and in fact has a similar color range. The mottling or spotting could have been produced by reducing iron compounds on the surface during part of the firing of the pieces, and then oxidizing the surface in the later stages of firing. This ware will need thin section study and mineral analysis in addition to the other laboratory tests. It will also be interesting to relate this ware to typology and usage.

Red Yellow Ware (IX)

Again, this color designation and fabric sorting index appears to be the result of firing a high iron-bearing, lime clay. It could be the result of specific temperature-atmosphere-time variables and only lengthy study in the physical testing laboratory will shed more light on its nature. Red yellow ware, as several others, including cream ware, gray ware, and speckled ware, form only 1% of the excavated

Bâb edh-Dhrâᶜ material at this time. It is quite likely that firing variables will explain some of these differences and perhaps after study the number of ware classifications can be reduced.

Ware Statistics (R. H. Johnston and R. T. Schaub)

During the rough sorting of the wares a count was kept of diagnostic and body sherds, according to locus in all areas. A comparative study of two areas, Fields VIII and X, is found in Table 1. The final report, based on laboratory analysis, will include a breakdown in all areas of the separate wares according to phase.

The percentage amounts in Table 1 represent the ratio of each ware to the total number of sherds found in the square or field. The smaller amount of sherds from Field VIII reflects the nature of this area, outside the town walls and not associated with extensive occupation.

On the basis of the comparative types, the loci of Field VIII are predominantly EB II-III. The sherds of Square X.3 are mostly late EB III and those of Squares X.1, 2 are EB IV. Keeping in mind the limited nature of Field VIII, some tentative indications may be drawn from the statistics.

(1)   The predominance of salmon buff ware in all three areas supports a basic continuity in pottery traditions from EB III into EB IV. Some radical changes in typology, however, should not be overlooked as, for example, the change from high shouldered jars and jugs with stump or pointed bases of EB III to the low tangent and flat bases of EB IV.

(2)   The low percentage of red ware and of burnished pottery in all areas would appear to call for a reassessment of this feature, which has often been noted as perhaps the most distinctive aspect of Early Bronze Age ceramics.

(3)   The high percentage of coarse ware in Square X.3 and of combed ware generally in Field X is most likely related to the domestic and industrial use of this area.

(4)   The higher percentage of red and speckled wares in Field VIII, only sparsely represented in Field X, suggests an important area of study for understanding the transition and differences between EB III and EB IV.

TABLE 1

WARE STATISTICS IN FIELDS VIII AND X

Wares	X.3	X.1,2	X.1,2,3	VIII
I	280 (13.5%)	69 (6%)	349 (10.8%)	15 (3%)
II	104 (5%)	43 (3.8%)	147 (4.5%)	20 (4%)
III	852 (41%)	680 (59%)	1532 (47.6%)	203 (48%)
IV	790 (38%)	296 (26%)	1086 (33.7%)	97 (21.5%)
V	39 (2%)	44 (3.8%)	83 (2.6%)	55 (12%)
VI	1 (0.04%)	3 (0.26%)	4 (0.3%)	3 (0.6%)
VII	8 (0.4%)	3 (0.3%)	11 (0.7%)	3 (0.6%)
VIII	0 (0%)	8 (0.7%)	8 (0.7%)	46 (9.6%)
IX	0	0	0	0
Total Sherds	2074	1146	3220	478

BIBLIOGRAPHY

Albright, W. F.
    1932   *The Excavation of Tell Beit Mirsim in Palestine. Vol. I: The Pottery of the First Three Campaigns.* Annual of the American Schools of Oriental Research 12.
    1933   The Excavation of Tell Beit Mirsim. IA: The Bronze Age Pottery of the Fourth Campaign. *Annual of the American Schools of Oriental Research* 13: 55-127.
    1944   Early Bronze Pottery from Bâb ed-Drâᶜin Moab. *Bulletin of the American Schools of Oriental Research* 95: 3-10.
Amiran, R.
    forth- *Early Arad: The Chalcolithic Settlement and the*
    coming *Early Bronze City.* Jerusalem: The Israel Exploration Society.
Braidwood, R. J., and Braidwood, L. S.
    1960   *Excavations in the Plain of Antioch, I: The Earlier Assemblages, Phases A-J.* Oriental Institute Publications 61. Chicago: University of Chicago.
Callaway, J. A.
    1972   *The Early Bronze Age Sanctuary at ᶜAi (Et-Tell).* London: Quaritch.
Cleveland, R. L.
    1960   The Excavation of the Conway High Place (Petra) and the Soundings at Khirbet Ader. *Annual of the American Schools of Oriental Research* 34-35: 79-97.
Dever, W. G.
    1973   The EB IV-MB I Horizon in Transjordan and Southern Palestine. *Bulletin of the American Schools of Oriental Research* 210: 37-63.
Fitzgerald, G. M.
    1935   The Earliest Pottery of Beth-Shan. *Museum Journal* 24: 5-32.
Garstang, J.
    1932   Jericho: City and Necropolis. *Annals of Archaeology and Anthropology* 19: 8ff., 19ff., 38ff.
    1935   Jericho: City and Necropolis. *Annals of Archaeology and Anthropology* 22: 143-84.
Guy, P. L. O., and Engberg, R. M.
    1938   *Megiddo Tombs.* Oriental Institute Publications 33. Chicago: University of Chicago.
Hennessy, B. J.
    1967   *The Foreign Relations of Palestine during the Early*

Bronze Age. London: Colt Archaeological Publications.
Kenyon, K. M.
    1960   *Excavations at Jericho. Vol. I: The Tombs Excavated in 1952-54.* London: Harrison.
    1965   *Excavations at Jericho. Vol. II: The Tombs Excavated in 1955-58.* London: Harrison.
Marquet-Krause, J.
    1949   *Les fouilles dᶜAy (et-Tell) 1933-1935.* Bibliothèque archéologique et historique 45. Paris: Geuthner.
Olávarri, E.
    1969   Fouilles à ᶜArôᶜer sur l'Arnon. *Revue biblique* 76: 230-59.
Parr, P. J.
    1960   Excavations at Khirbet Iskander. *Annual of the Department of Antiquities of Jordan* 4-5: 128-33.
Prag, K.
    1974   The Intermediate Early Bronze-Middle Bronze Age: An Interpretation of the Evidence from Transjordan, Syria, and Lebanon. *Levant* 6: 69-116.
Rast, W. E., and Schaub, R. T.
    1974   Survey of the Southeastern Plain of the Dead Sea, 1973. *Annual of the Department of Antiquities of Jordan* 19: 5-53, pls. 1-11.
Schaub, R. T.
    1973   An Early Bronze IV Tomb from Bâb edh-Dhrâᶜ. *Bulletin of the American Schools of Oriental Research* 210: 2-19.
Shepard, A. O.
    1968   *Ceramics for the Archaeologist.* Washington: Carnegie Institution.
Tufnell, O.
    1958   *Lachish IV: The Bronze Age.* London: Oxford University.
Vaux, R. de
    1955   La cinquième campagne de fouilles à Tell el-Farᶜah, près Naplouse. *Revue Biblique* 62: 541-89.
Vaux, R de and Stève R. P.
    1947   La première campagne de fouilles à Tell el-Farᶜah, près Naplouse. *Revue Biblique* 54: 394-433, 573-89.
    1948   La seconde campagne de fouilles à Tell el-Farᶜah, près Naplouse. *Revue Biblique* 55: 544-80.

Fig. 1. Selected pottery from Charnel House A 55.

Number	Reg. Number	Parallels
1	103	Kenyon 1960: figs. 35:12, 37:24-25, 25:25-31
2	207	Kenyon 1960: figs. 25:22, 35:1-7, 37:18
3	118	Kenyon 1960: figs. 35:28, 37:42, 46:38-42, 52:39, 60:31-38
4	140	Kenyon 1960: figs. 52:40-41, 61:1-7, 68:15
5a	102	Kenyon 1960: figs. 25:14-15, 34:19-27
5b	116	Kenyon 1960: figs. 37:43, 46:43-45, 52:42-6, 61:8-10, 68:17
5c	181	See 1:5a
6a	185	Kenyon 1960: figs. 25:13-15, 34:19-27, 37:8-12
6b	158	Kenyon 1960: figs. 25:22, 35:1-4
6c	157	See 1:6a
7	115	Kenyon 1960: figs. 25:12, 34:14-16, 37:8; Tufnell 1958: pls. 58:98-100, 60:206; Hennessy 1967: pls. 39, 40

1

2

3

4

5

6

7

Fig. 2. Pottery from Charnel House A 55.

Number	Reg. Number	Parallels
8	209	Hennessy 1967: pls. 7:75, 8:82b, and p. 23
9	138	Amiran: pl. 24:20; Garstang 1932: pl. 6:6, 9; Kenyon 1960: figs. 36:21, 44:15, 16
10	188	Callaway 1972: figs. 27:2-6, 36:6, 10-17, 44:14, 16, 18-19, 60:7, 9, 12, 68:1; Kenyon 1960: fig. 38:14; Amiran: pl. 52:19; Tufnell 1958: pl. 61:260
11	190	Callaway 1972: figs. 35:8, 16, 18-23; 44:6, 7; Amiran: pls. 13:31, 22:59, 52:12; De Vaux and Steve 1948: fig. 6:10-11; Garstang 1932: fig. 8:9; 1935: pl. 30:20; Kenyon 1960: fig. 25:3
12a,b	192,136	Kenyon 1960: fig. 67:14; Garstang 1932: pl. 28:15; Marquet-Krause 1949: pls. 70:658, 78:2123; Hennessy 1967: pl. 8:79; Garstang 1935: pl. 29:10, 11; Fitzgerald 1935: pl. 4:23
13a	139	Kenyon 1960: figs. 23:3, 4, 38:1; Amiran: pls. 52:14, 22:56, 60, 61; Callaway 1972: fig. 68:1; Garstang 1935: pl. 31:17
13b	191	Kenyon 1960: figs. 43:3, 4, 57:1
13c	101	Kenyon 1960: figs. 43:20, 51:6-8, 12, 57:6-7; Amiran; pls. 22:32, 40, 52:6
14	113	Kenyon 1960: figs. 36:1, 43:13-15; Garstang 1932: pl. 8:11
15	110	Kenyon 1960: fig. 33:3; Garstang 1935: pl. 31:28; Hennessy 1967: pls. 8:80, 9:86

8   9

10

11

12

13

14

15

Fig. 3. Selected pottery from Phase 1 in Field X.

Number	Parallels
1	Cleveland 1960: fig. 14:1; Olávarri 1969: figs. 3:1, 5:11; Prag 1974: fig. 7:6; Tufnell 1958: pls. 65:381, 66:349; Callaway 1972: figs. 49:14, 63:20-22; Fitzgerald 1935: pls. 1:6, 9:9
2	Cleveland 1960: figs. 13:6, 14:23-24, 15:8, 10, 12-13; Parr 1960: fig. 1:9; Kenyon 1960: figs. 36:12-13, 38:21-23, 51:16; Garstang 1935: pl. 34:5, 9, 13, 23-36; 1932: pl. 4:11, 13; Braidwood and Braidwood 1960: figs. 271:1, 269:8
3	Cleveland 1960: fig. 15:19; Olávarri 1969: figs. 1:3, 5-7, 4:1; Kenyon 1960: figs. 38:9, 43:7-8, 44:4; Garstang 1935: pl. 27:8; 1932: pl. 4:20
4	See 3:3
5	Amiran: pl. 23:12; Tufnell 1958: pls. 62:273, 63:313
6	Cleveland 1960: figs. 13:11, 14:3; Fitzgerald 1935: pls. 4:16, 20, 9:2; Kenyon 1965: fig. 72:5; Guy and Engberg 1938: pl. 6:27; Tufnell 1958: pls. 64:357, 360, 57:62
7	Callaway 1972: figs. 62:8, 11, 14, 18, 75:7, 76:18; Amiran: pl. 42:12; Garstang 1935: pl. 33:7; 1932: pl. 3:13
8	Cleveland 1960: fig. 14:7, 14, 19, 21; Garstang 1935: pl. 28:24, 30; Prag 1974: fig. 3:18; Amiran: pls. 46:7, 47:2, 48:4, 5, 8, 10, 13, 14, 19, 23; 49:14; Tufnell 1958: pl. 56:5
9	Amiran: pls. 46:5, 47:5, 49:1, 12, 17, 43-44, 50:4, 7, 20, 23, 54:2; Tufnell 1958: pls. 63:315, 318, 64:354; Guy and Engberg 1938: pl. 7:5, 8, 12
10	Cleveland 1960: fig. 15:21; Garstang 1935: pl. 28:7; Tufnell 1958: pl. 58:118, 124; Callaway 1972: figs. 61:10, 12-19, 68:10-11; Amiran: pl. 53:4-7
11	See 3:3
12	Cleveland 1960: figs. 13:1, 6, 14:11, 24; Olávarri 1969: fig. 1:4; Kenyon 1960: fig. 57:32-33, 37; Garstang 1935: pl. 34:9; Tufnell 1958: pl. 63:325
13	See 3:2
14	See 3:5
15	See 3:7
16	Kenyon 1960: figs. 35:45, 37:54; 1965: fig. 69:4; Guy and Engberg 1938: pl. 6:29
17	Tufnell 1958: pls. 60:192-93, 61:263-64, 64:358, 65:388; Hennessy 1967: pl. 8:83; Amiran: pl. 42: 1, 3, 7; Kenyon 1960: figs. 47:8, 62:8; Garstang 1932: pl. 7:11; Olávarri 1969: fig. 5:15
18,19	Cleveland 1960: fig. 14:2, 10, 22; Garstang 1935: pl. 28:25-29; Tufnell 1958: pls. 64:356, 65:384, 387, 390; Callaway 1972: fig. 63:3-9
20,21	See 3:8
22	Amiran: pl. 21 passim; Garstang 1932: pl. 1:15
23	Cleveland 1960: fig. 13:15, 18; Tufnell 1958: pls. 58:108, 62:274, 64:351; Albright 1933: pl. 1:3
24,25	See 3:17
26	See 3:1
27	Cleveland 1960: fig. 15:15; Olávarri 19 9: fig. 3:2, 8; Kenyon 1960: figs. 53:1, 47:2, 3; Garstang 1932: pl. 5:9-19; 1935: pl. 27:10; Amiran: pl. 53:5, 17; Tufnell 1958: pls. 61:256, 63:314, 319, 336, 65:385, 389, 391A; Guy and Engberg 1938: pl. 7:2, 3, 13
28	Cleveland 1960: fig. 13:13; Prag 1974: fig. 5:19; Tufnell 1958: pl. 60:227
29	See 3:2
30	See 3:6
31	See 3:16

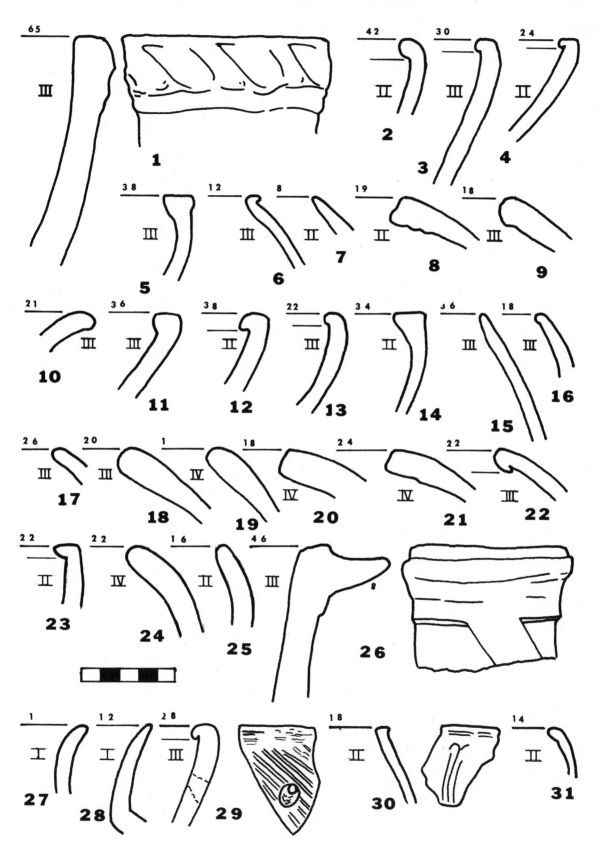

Fig. 4. Selected pottery from Field X at Bâb
         edh Dhrâᶜ: Phase 1 (32-36), Phase 2 (37-60).

No.   *Parallels*

32   See 3:3

33   See 3:5

34   See 3:6

35   See 3:9

36   See 3:17

37   See 3:27

38   Tufnell 1958: pls. 58:92, 63:324, 65:369

39   Callaway 1972: figs. 64:1, 77:5, 11;

       Garstang 1932: pl. 4:2; Guy and Engberg

       1938: pl. 7:9

40   Dever 1973: fig. 3:1-3; Olávarri 1969:

       fig. 2:5

41   See 3:12

42   See 3:5

43   See 4:40

44   See 3:2

45   See 3:3

46   See 3:23

47   See 3:17

48   See 3:17

49   See 3:7

50   Amiran: pl. 55:1

51   Cleveland 1960: fig. 14:6; Olávarri 1969:

          fig. 2:13-17

52   See 3:2

53   See 3:2

54   See 3:3

55   See 3:2

56   See 3:1

57   See 3:7

58,   Cleveland 1960: fig. 15:23; Garstang 1932:

  59   pl. 4:10; Tufnell 1958: pls. 58:77,

          59:139-40, 60:190, 64:341, 65:370;

          de Vaux 1955: fig. 14:35

60   Olávarri 1969: fig. 1:22; Garstang 1932:

          pl. 4:18-19; Kenyon 1960: figs. 38:9,

          11, 43:7; Tufnell 1958: pls. 65:381,

          379, 62:275

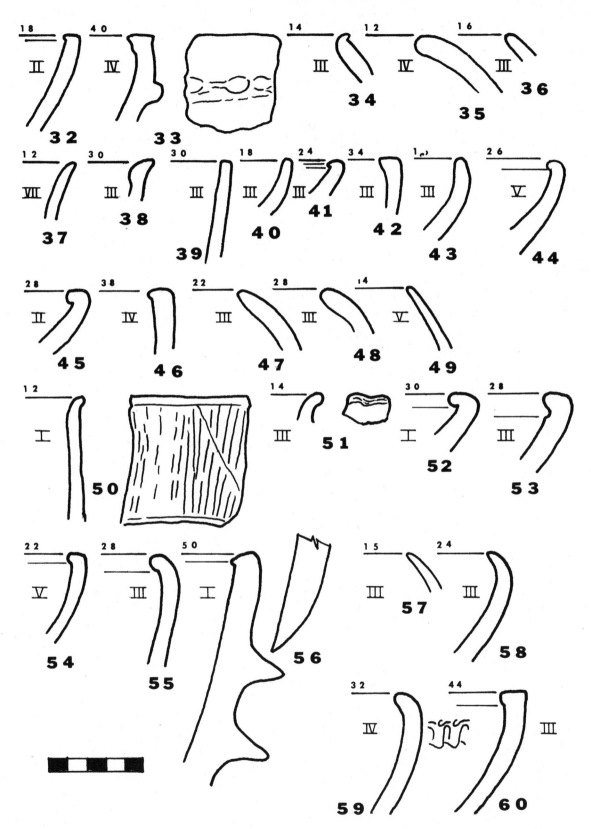

Fig. 5. Selected pottery from Field X: Phase 2 (61),
         Phase 3 (62-70), Phase 4 (71-82).

Number   *Parallels*

61   See 3:1

62   Cleveland 1960: figs. 13:4, 8, 14:15, 26, 15:5, 7,
               9; Parr 1960: fig. 1:10, 11; Olávarri 1969: figs.
               1:8, 10-13, 15-21, 4:4-9, 12; Prag 1974: fig.
               3:22-3; Dever 1973: fig. 3:15 and pp. 45-47; Guy
               and Engberg 1938: pl. 6:19

63-65   See 5:62

66   Schaub 1973: figs. 6:14, 8:23; Parr 1960: fig. 1:16

67-71   See 5:62

72   Parr 1960: fig. 1:14

73   See 5:62

74   Tufnell 1958: pls. 64:351, 62:276

75-76   See 5:62

77   Olavarri 1969: fig. 4:14, 18

78-79   See 5:62

80   Cleveland 1960: figs. 13:9, 14:16; Schaub 1973: fig.
               6:12

81   See 4:60

82   Olávarri 1969: figs. 2:1-4, 5:1-5; Prag 1974: fig.
               4:11; Schaub 1973: figs. 6:5, 7:17; Dever 1973:
               fig. 3:21

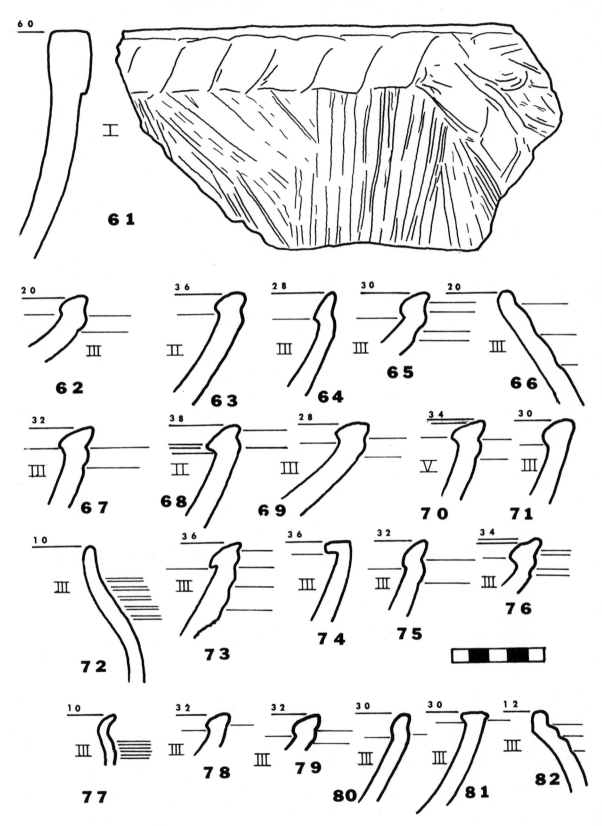

Faunal Remains from Bâb edh-Dhrâ^c, 1975

Michael Finnegan
Kansas State University, Manhattan, KS 66506

The faunal remains from the 1975 excavations at Bâb edh-Dhrâ^c can be divided into two main groups: first, the human remains which were excavated at various cemetery sites (A 55, B 3, D 1, E 1, F 2, and F 3); second, remains which were primarily animal from Fields VIII to XIII. Within each field human and animal remains were bagged separately and returned to the laboratory at Kerak. Each day the bones from the previous day were analyzed. The bones were grouped according to ungulate, mammal (large or small), or a specific type of animal such as sheep, goat, or donkey. Special attention was given to butchering marks. Following the field analysis, the bone material which displayed enough of the gross morphology to be identified, particularly at the distal and proximal ends of the bone, was packed for shipping. Bone which was identified but was not unique was discarded, whereas bone which was identified and at the same time unique was shipped for further analysis.

In general, any human bone containing promise of morphological identification was packaged for shipment to the osteology laboratory in the United States. This preliminary report is based on the field analysis and the study of a small number of groups which arrived at the laboratory in time to be included.

Animal Bone Remains

Table 1 shows the distribution of bone types from the various areas and squares. Locus and basket numbers, as well as the phase to which the material belonged, will be given in a more complete discussion in the final report.

Approximately 90% of the bone could not be identified in the field. Of this, however, approximately 10% to 15% of the bone can be determined under laboratory conditions. The largest group of identifiable remains were those of sheep and goat, where the criteria of Boessneck (1969) and Boessneck, Müller, and Teichert (1964) were used. Taxonomically these are *Ovis aries* and *Capra hircus*. Also, the domestic donkey, *Equus asinus,* was readily identifiable. The general distribution of these animals can be seen in Table 1.

Other animals suspected in various areas of the site include the camel (dromedary), *Camelus dromedarius,* and one from the gazelle group, either *Gazella dorcasor* or *Gazella gazella*. Smaller animals are also identifiable at the site, including one of the cat species, most probably the domestic cat, *Felis catus,* the domestic dog, *Canis familiaris,* the hyena, *Hyaena hyaena,* and a number of representatives from the order *RODENTIA.*

Bird bones were not differentially identified at this site, and only two bones were found which would suggest a possibility of birds. In each case the material was extremely fragmented. Reptiles, however, are seen, and from limb bones we suspect a lizard and a turtle, with the families of each unidentified. Also, a few fish vertebrae were seen. The family of fish remains unidentified and the suspicion is that the fish remains may have been intrusive in the site F 2.

Summary of Material by Field

In Field VIII both sheep and goat were identified, with both large and small mammal bones in abundance, but unidentified.

Field IX has both sheep and goat, as well as donkey in Square 6, with Squares 5 and 7 producing only unidentifiable bones. An ungulate tooth which appeared to be permineralized was found in Square 7.

Field X is an interesting area because of the amount of material that came from here. As seen in Table 1, Square 3 contained the greatest number of samples; Square 1 was second, and the lowest number of samples was obtained from Square 2. In

TABLE 1. ANIMAL BONE DISTRIBUTION BY SAMPLES FOR FIELDS AND SQUARES.

Field	Square	No. of Samples	Field Designation	KEY		
				*	=	Cooked?
				Hu	=	human
VIII	1(A)	1	UD, M	HT	=	human tooth
	2	4	sh			
	3	7	UT, M, lm, UDM	UD	=	unidentified
IX	5	12	UT, UDM, lm, M	M	=	mammal
	6	6	UT, sh-gt, Bo, *, D	sm	=	small mammal
	7	5	UT, UDM UT-permineralized	lm	=	large mammal
X	1	38	UDM, sh-gt, UT, Hu, sm, HT, Sh-gt, Bo, lm split medulary (intentional), sh, SR (lizard), gt, SMT (rodent)	sh	=	sheep
				gt	=	goat
				sh-gt	=	sheep or goat
	2	21	UD, lm, sh-gt, Hu, UT, M, Bo, sh, gt	Bo	=	burnt, oxidized
	3	56	UDM, UT, sh-gt, Bo, lm (Juvenile), M, BR, gt, sh, D, Hu, gt (ulna, worked and broken)	BR	=	burnt, reduced
				D	=	Donkey
				UT	=	ungulate tooth
XI	1	4	sh, gt, UT, D	SR	=	small reptile
	2	2	lm, UD, UT, M			
XII	2	3	UD, M	SMT	=	small mammal tooth
	5	2	UT, UD, M, Bo			
	6	3	UT, UD, M	UDM	=	undetermined mammal
XIII	1	15	UD, UT, sh, gt, Bo			

TABLE 2. HUMAN BONE DISTRIBUTION.

Area B3 Human

D1 Mostly Human, sh-recent

E1 Human

F1 Human, mostly with: UDM (butchering marks), tibia lm (camel), UT, sh, gt, sm (Rodent), bone tools, and artifacts

F3 sh, gt, UDM, lm, D, UD (butchering marks)

A55 Human bone, no animal bone observed. Human bone, some was burned-oxidized, half was reduced, suggesting that the bone had not been cremated, but met with a subsequent fire.

each of these squares, we can identify sheep and goat, with other types of ungulate teeth. Square 1 also shows reptile bones, which we suggest as being lizard, along with a number of unidentified rodent bones. A shaft of a sheep or goat femur had been split, exposing the medullary cavity, and the breakage looked intentional for the retrieval of the marrow. Burned bone was found in Squares 1, 2, and 3, with the burning being an oxidation rather than a reduction type of firing. This suggests the bone might have been involved in open fire cooking where the bones were free to oxidize, rather than being fired in a refuse pile where often the bone material is reduced. However, there were some bones from Square 3 that had been reduced. Also in Square 3 some donkey and human material was found, and a goat ulna which had been worked and subsequently broken was also found. A human tooth came from Square 1.

Of the two squares in Field XI, the first contained sheep, goat and donkey, with the second square showing only unidentified mammal, both large and small.

Three squares in Field XII (2, 5, 6) produced unidentifiable bone and teeth. Square 5 did produce some bones which had been burned and oxidized, rather than reduced.

Finally, in Field XIII, only Square 1 produced material, but 15 samples came from that square. The material is a combination of unidentified mammal, ungulate teeth, and identified sheep and goat. Some of the bone was burned and oxidized.

From the rough breakdown of bone material, animal types, and sample numbers, we get some insight into the use of various areas within the squares. The incidence of burned bone, sheep and goat, and other unidentifiable pieces may help to suggest use areas in the future. The worked goat ulna will also help to determine space utilization.

Human Remains

Human remains were found in A 55, a charnel house southwest of the town site. It provided at least 60 skeletons, although the skeletons were completely mixed. Much of this material was burned, but since the bone was oxidized rather than reduced, it may be that the burning came at a later time and that these individuals had not been cremated at the time they were put into the charnel house.

In addition to A 55, Tomb B 3 produced human remains suggesting 1 or possibly 2

individuals. Tomb D 1 contained 6 individual skeletons, 4 of which were mostly articulated but disturbed. Tomb E 1 had a single human burial, probably female. The bone was extremely fragmentary, as was most of the bone from this area. Area F was subdivided, with F 1 showing a number of bone fragments and an upper right third molar. Nothing was deduced about this skeletal material in the field.

A great quantity of material came from F 2. Besides human material, unidentified mammal bone showing butchering marks was recovered, and the left tibia of a camel was identified. Small rodent bones were also found in association with the burial, but these may have been intrusive. The main burial of F 2 was a young female seemingly cradling in her arms a 5 month old child, with a 15 month old child's skeleton lying nearby.

F 3 may not be a burial, in that few identifiable pieces of human bone were recovered. Most of the bone was unidentified mammal, but some portions of sheep, goat, and donkey were identifiable. The donkey also displayed butcher marks on the metapodial.

Although pathologies, anomalies, and other conditions of the bone have not been discussed, these features and others will be analyzed in the osteology laboratory for a future report. Objectives are to assess the demographic relationships of the Early Bronze phases in terms of sex, stature and age differences. Data on pathologies have already been noted in Tomb D 1. This tomb produced bone displaying a possible carcinoma, as well as osteomyelitis. Two bones from A 55 display mended fractures. The dental condition will be analyzed in detail, but from preliminary analysis it seems that no dental caries are present. The dental attrition on the occlusal surfaces was extensive.

The few bones that were measured *in situ* for stature estimation produced the following results. The female femur from F 2 was 40.3 cm., which, when applied to stature formula reconstruction yields a stature of 153.6 cm. A femur from A 55, sex unknown, yields a stature of 166 cm., while from D 1 a femur of a male measuring 49.5 cm. suggests a stature of 180.37 cm. This might indicate that stature was increasing during the Early Bronze period, but more examples must be tested before any conclusions can be drawn.

Because of the condition of the material, we do not anticipate being able to generate a full set of metric data on these earlier human remains. However, we will be able to employ, even given the fragmentary state of the remains, the non-metric analysis which has been efficient and fruitful in osteological analysis in recent years. The final report, therefore, should include adequate analysis of demography, pathology and non-metric, quasigenetic relationships among the 4 phases of the Early Bronze periods, both at the Bâb edh-Dhrâᶜ site and at other nearby sites representing similar time periods.

BIBLIOGRAPHY

Boessneck, J.
    1969   Osteological Differences Between Sheep (*Ovis aries Linné*) and Goats (*Capra hircus Linné*). Pp. 331-58 in *Science in Archaeology*, ed. D. R. Brothwell and E. Higgs. New York: Praeger.

Boessneck, J.; Müller, H.-H.; and Teichert, M.
    1964   Osteologische Unterscheidungsmerkale zwischen Schaf (*Ovis aries Linné*) und Ziege (*Capra hircus Linné*). *Kühn-Archiv* 78: 1-129.

Preliminary Analysis of the Plant Remains from Bâb edh-Dhrâ[c], 1975

James B. Richardson III
University of Pittsburgh, Pittsburgh, PA 15213
David McCreery
Pittsburgh Theological Seminary, Pittsburgh, PA 15206

Introduction

The Dead Sea and the lower Jordan Valley have been classified by Zohary (1952, 1962) as a distinctive phytogeographic zone designated Sudano-Deccanian. This region is represented by thirty species of trees and shrubs classed under *Zizyphus spinachristi*. The presence of *Acacietum albidae* in a few areas, including the Wadi Kerak, is suggestive of a former period of higher humidity and vegetation cover, which has been restricted due to dessication or man's interference. This is further substantiated by Vita-Finzi's (1966) study of the alluvial sediments in the Wadi Hasa, south of Wadi Kerak, that indicates that cooler and more humid conditions prevailed prior to ca. 2,000-4,000 B.P.

The modern rainfall isohyet for the central and lower Jordan Valley is less than 50 mm. annually. If the indications that the past climate of the Dead Sea was more moist in antiquity are valid, the agricultural potential of the Wadi Kerak and neighboring regions would have been greater.

Techniques of Recovery

Water flotation was used to recover botanical remains from the six fields of excavation and the three burials from which 184 samples were secured for analysis.

The flotation techniques employed at Bâb edh-Dhrâ[c] during the 1975 season were necessarily limited in scope due to the unavailability of sophisticated equipment, as well as the shortage of water and personnel needed for a large scale operation. All soil samples had to be transported 30 km. to Kerak since there was no water source at the site. Even in Kerak water was in short supply and it was necessary to adopt strict conservation measures. Soil submitted for flotation was generally restricted to samples which, in the judgment of the respective square supervisors, looked promising. Thus most of the samples came from ash layers or layers in which obvious plant or animal remains were detected during the course of excavation. The sampling was selective, but representative soil samples from all fields of the excavation were floated, whether or not they looked promising.

The flotation apparatus itself was constructed from local materials, supplemented by wire mesh of different gauges. The main flotation chamber was a 40 gal. barrel. The second major piece of equipment was a cylindrical bucket. The bottom of the latter was replaced by galvanized window screen which was tightly stretched and held in place by metal striping secured around the outer edge of the bucket and supported by metal strips across the bottom of the bucket.

The flotation procedure was quite simple and could be carried out by one person, although a two-man operation was much more efficient. The 40 gal. barrel was filled with from 15 to 20 gals. of water, after which the screen-bottomed bucket was inserted into the barrel and submerged in the water. The soil sample was then gradually introduced. By moving the bucket back and forth in a circular motion, the fine dirt sifted through the window screen and collected at the bottom of the barrel, while all large stones, sherds, artifacts, bones, and other organic material which would not float, were caught by the screen. Lighter organic material floated to the surface and was retrieved with a common kitchen strainer. The remaining material was collected with a very fine brass sieve with 100 ga. wire gauze.

The size of the samples varied from a few cups of

soil up to five buckets, the average sample being about one-half of a bucket. After the processing of each sample, the flotation barrel was emptied and thoroughly cleaned in order to avoid contamination by material from different loci. The samples were allowed to dry overnight and then packaged.

The technology and the recovery procedures were similar to Struever's (1968) initial experiments in flotation in Illinois. Due to limited water resources, froth flotation was impractical.

The flotation samples contained numerous plant remains and exhibited large quantities (over 50 specimens of each species) of cultivated grains, olives, grapes, and lentils. The following is a list of the plants identified to date:

> Emmer wheat *(Triticum dicoccum),*
> grains and spikelet forks
> Barley *(Hordeum vulgare)*
> Bread or Club wheat *(Triticum aestivum* or *compactum)*
> Grape pits *(Vitis vinifera)*
> Olive pits *(Olea europoea)*
> Lentils *(Lens esculenta)*
> Dates *(Phoenix dactylifera)*

When the analysis is completed, oats, chickpeas, cedar seeds, and various wild plant species, including *Chenopodium species* and *Crucifera,* used as famine food presently, may ultimately prove to be present.

The list above does not contain any surprises, for it has been well established that these items were under cultivation during the preceding Chalcolithic period. The Chalcolithic sites of Teleilat Ghassul, north of the Dead Sea, Tell Abu-Matar, and Ḥorvat Beter near Beersheba, all contain cereal grains, olives, and dates, dating to between 3,600-3,300 B.C. (De Vaux: 1966, Zaitchek: 1959) and the 3rd millennium B.C. Bronze Age levels at Lachish include the same plant complex as Bâb edh-Dhrâᶜ (Helbaek: 1958).

Conclusions

The Wadi Kerak is the main fresh water source in the vicinity of the site and must have played a key role in the agricultural system of the Bâb edh-Dhrâᶜ community. The wadi may have been dammed to impound the water flow for agricultural purposes. The fine alluvium that built up behind the checkdams would have made the Wadi Kerak suitable for cultivation. The contained water could also have been used to maintain plant production outside of the wadi proper. The only evidence for the use of dams in the wadi dates to the Roman period, the Early Bronze Age dams having been destroyed probably by erosion and periodic flooding.

The method of water flotation has been responsible for the recovery of plant remains that reflect the economy of this Bronze Age society, and when the final analysis is completed we will have a clearer picture of the agricultural component to the Bâb edh-Dhrâᶜ economic base.

BIBLIOGRAPHY

Helbaek, H.
  1958 Plant Economy in Ancient Lachish. Pp. 309-17 in *Lachish IV: The Bronze Age,* by O. Tufnell. London: Oxford University.

Struever, S.
  1968 Flotation Techniques for the Recovery of Small-Scale Archaeological Remains. *American Antiquity* 33: 353-62.

Vita-Finzi, C.
  1966 The Hasa Formation: An Alluvial Deposition in Jordan. *Man* 1: 386-90.

Vaux, R. de
  1966 Palestine during the Neolithic and Chalcolithic Periods. Pp. 498-538 in *The Cambridge Ancient History*[3], Vol. 1, Part 1, eds. I. E. S. Edwards, *et. al.* Cambridge: Cambridge University.

Zaitchek, D. V.
  1959 Remains of Cultivated Plants from Ḥorvat Beter (Beersheba). ᶜ*Atiqot* 2: 48-52.

Zohary, M.
  1952 Ecological Studies in the Vegetation of the Near Eastern Deserts. I: Environments and Vegetation Classes. *Israel Exploration Journal* 2: 201-15.

  1962 Plant Life of Palestine. *Chronica Botanica.* New Series of Plant Science Books, No. 33. New York: The Ronald Press.

Textile Remains and Basketry Impressions from Bâb edh-Dhrâ[c], 1975

J. M. Adovasio, R. Andrews, and M. R. Carlisle
University of Pittsburgh, Pittsburgh, PA 15260

Introduction

In the present context, the term textile is reserved solely for loom-woven cloth, while basketry encompasses several distinct kinds of items including rigid and semi-rigid containers or baskets proper, matting and bags. Matting includes items which are essentially two dimensional or flat, while baskets are three dimensional. Bags may be viewed as intermediate forms because they are two dimensional when empty and three dimensional when filled. As Driver (1961: 159) points out, these artifacts may be treated as a unit because the overall technique of manufacture is the same in all instances.

Specifically, all forms of basketry are manually woven without any frame or loom.

There are three major kinds or sub-classes of basketry which are generally mutually exclusive: twining, coiling, and plaiting.

Twining denotes a sub-class of basket weaves manufactured by sewing stationary (passive), vertical elements or warps with moving (active), horizonal elements called wefts. Twining techniques may be employed to produce containers, mats, bags, as well as fish traps, cradles, nets, clothing, and other "atypical" basketry forms.

Coiling denotes a sub-class of basket weaves manufactured by sewing stationary, horizontal elements (foundation) with moving vertical elements (stitches). Coiling techniques are used almost exclusively in the production of containers, and very rarely, bags. Mats and other forms are seldom, if ever, produced by coiling.

Plaiting denotes a subclass of basket weaves in which all elements pass over and under each other without any engagement. For this reason, plaited basketry is technically described as unsewn. Plaiting may be used to make containers, bags, and mats as well as a wide range of other non-standard forms.

Twining is the only sub-class of basketry represented among the finds of the 1975 season at Bâb edh-Dhrâ[c].

Analytical Procedures

Due to the highly friable condition of the textile fragments from Bâb edh-Dhrâ[c], the usual pre-analysis cleaning procedures (Adovasio: 1974) were not employed. Rather, the specimens were simply visually scrutinized with a seven-power hand lens or a variable power stereoscopic microscope to insure recognition of the construction technique employed.

The basketry impressions from Bâb edh-Dhrâ[c] were examined second-hand from detailed photos prepared in the field.

All textile specimens, as well as the photographed impressions, were measured with a Helios needle-nosed dial caliper, and all measurements were recorded in the metric system.

Criteria of Classification

The impressions representing identifiable basketry or textile techniques were allocated to two structural types according to procedures and utilizing terminology outlined in Emery (1966) and Adovasio (1974, 1976). It should be noted that the term "type" is herein used solely as a classificatory device. Whether or not these types reflect fixed mental templates of the Bâb edh-Dhrâ[c] weavers is a question best left to others more conversant with such matters.

The two types established by the aforementioned procedures are presented below by major form category (i.e. textiles or basketry) with numerical prefixes.

Textiles

Type I: Balanced plain weave: single warps and wefts.

Number of specimens: 48.

Technique and Comments: This is the simplest of all textile techniques. Single warps and wefts of generally equal size pass over and under each other in a 1/1 interval. Each warp and weft element passes over and under successive warp units, and each successive weft reverses the procedure of the one before it. All warps that lie above one passage of the weft lie below the next passage and so on. The number of warp and weft elements per cm. is equal, hence, the assignation of the term "balanced" to this type. The few extant side selvages in this assemblage are of the continuous weft variety, while end selvages are of the 180° type. All specimens are unmended and undecorated and appear to represent portions of cloth fabrics of unknown configuration.

This structural type may be divided into a series of six sub-types based on the composition of the vertical and horizontal sets of weaving elements. While it is certain that one set of elements represent warps and the other wefts, it is impossible to verify which are which in the general absence of selvages. Since it is highly unlikely that all of these sub-types would appear in a single cloth, it must be assumed that they represent portions of at least six different items. The six sub-types are listed below in descending order of frequency with pertinent measurements appended.

Sub-type 1: One ply, Z spun elements with two ply, Z spun, S twist elements.

Number of specimens: 21.
Measurements:
    Range in diameter of Z spun elements, 0.25-0.59 mm.
    Mean diameter of Z spun elements, 0.44 mm.
    Range in diameter of $Z\frac{s}{s}$ elements, 0.31-0.75 mm.
    Mean diameter of $Z\frac{s}{s}$ elements, 0.49 mm.
    Range in twists per 0.25 cm., $Z\frac{s}{s}$ elements, 3-6.
    Mean twists per 0.25 cm., $Z\frac{s}{s}$ elements, 4.6.
    Range in angle of twist, $Z\frac{s}{s}$ elements, 38°-68°.
    Mean angle of twist, $Z\frac{s}{s}$ elements, 46.7°.
    Range in Z spun elements per 0.25 cm., 3-6.
    Mean Z spun elements per 0.25 cm., 4.4.
    Range in $Z\frac{s}{s}$ elements per 0.25 cm., 3-5.
    Mean $Z\frac{s}{s}$ elements per 0.25 cm., 4.1.

Sub-type 2: Mixed one ply, Z spun; two ply, S spun, Z twist and three ply, S spun, Z twist elements with mixed one ply, Z spun; two ply, S spun, Z twist, and three ply, S spun, Z twist elements.

Number of specimens: 11.
Measurements:
    Range in diameter of all elements, 0.26-0.74 mm.
    Mean diameter of all elements, 0.42 mm.
    Range in twists per 0.25 cm., multiple ply elements, 2-8.
    Mean twists per 0.25 cm., multiple ply elements, 5.45.
    Range in angle of twist, multiple ply elements, 15°-75°.
    Mean angle of twist, multiple ply elements, 50°.
    Range in elements per 0.25 cm., 4-8.
    Mean elements per 0.25 cm., 4.62.

Sub-type 3: Two ply, S spun, Z twist elements with two ply, S spun, Z twist elements.

Number of specimens: 6.
Measurements:
    Range in diameter of elements, 0.35-0.50 mm.
    Mean diameter of elements, 0.43 mm.
    Range in twists per 0.25 cm., N.A.
    Mean twists per 0.25 cm., N.A.
    Range in angle of twist, N.A.
    Mean angle of twist, N.A.
    Range in elements per 0.25 cm., 4-8.
    Mean elements per 0.25 cm., 4.62.

Sub-type 4: One ply, Z spun elements with three ply, S spun, Z twist elements.

Number of specimens: 2.
Measurements:
    Range in diameter of Z spun elements, 0.50-0.54 mm.
    Mean diameter of Z spun elements, 0.52 mm.
    Range in diameter of $Z\frac{s}{s}$ elements, 0.41-0.50 mm.
    Mean diameter of $Z\frac{s}{s}$ elements, 0.46 mm.
    Range in twists per 0.25 cm. $Z\frac{s}{s}$ elements 5-6.
    Mean twists per 0.25 cm., $Z\frac{s}{s}$ elements, 5.5.
    Range in angle of twist, $Z\frac{s}{s}$ elements, 38°-48°.
    Mean angle of twist, $Z\frac{s}{s}$ elements, 43°.
    Range in Z spun elements per 0.25 cm., 4-5.
    Mean Z spun elements per 0.25 cm., 4.5.
    Range in $Z\frac{s}{s}$ elements per 0.25 cm., 4.
    Mean $Z\frac{s}{s}$ elements per 0.25 cm., 4.

Sub-type 5: Two ply, S spun, Z twist elements with mixed one ply, Z spun; two ply, S spun, Z twist and three ply, S spun, Z twist elements.

Number of specimens: 1.
Measurements:
    Range in diameter of all elements, 0.47-0.54 mm.
    Mean diameter of all elements, 0.51 mm.
    Range in twists per 0.25 cm., multiple ply elements, 2-3.
    Mean twists per 0.25 cm., multiple ply elements, 2.5.
    Range in angle of twist, multiple ply elements, 24°-45°.
    Mean angle of twist, multiple ply elements, 34.5°.
    Range in elements per 0.25 cm., 4.
    Mean elements per 0.25 cm., 4.

Sub-type 6: One ply, Z spun elements with mixed

one ply, Z spun: two ply, S spun, Z twist and three ply, S spun, Z twist elements

>*Number of specimens:* 1.
>*Measurements:*
> Range in diameter of all elements, 0.31-0.49 mm.
> Mean diameter of all elements, 0.40 mm.
> Range in twists per 0.25 cm., multiple ply elements, 8.
> Mean twists per 0.25 cm., multiple ply elements, 8.
> Range in angle of twist, multiple ply elements, 45°.
> Mean angle of twist, multiple ply elements, 45°.
> Range in elements per 0.25 cm., 5.
> Mean elements per 0.25 cm., 5.

Raw Materials: All weaving elements are composed of a vegetal fiber which appears to be *Linum* spp. However, positive identification is not presently available.

Provenience: Charnel House A 55, Group 20, bones and pottery.

Basketry

Type II: Open, simple twining, weft type unknown.

Number of specimens: 3 (minimum).

Technique and Comments: Plain (?) twined weaving over single warps. In all cases weft rows are apparently spaced at regular intervals to expose warps. Warps are unspun single elements while the type and composition of the wefts are unknown. No side or end selvages are represented. All specimens are undecorated, unmended and appear to be portions of large mats.

Measurements: Not available.

Raw Materials: Warps appear to be longitudinally split reeds, genus/species unknown, while the source of the fiber used for Type II wefts is unknown.

Provenience: Floor of Tomb F 1.

Internal Correlations

Technology, Form, Function

Despite the paucity of the data presented on the preceding pages, a number of observations may be made. While it is almost certain that the two structural types discussed above can scarcely be considered representative of the entire range of textiles and basketry known to the Bâb edh-Dhrâᶜ weavers, they do provide direct evidence for the production and/or use of both textiles and basketry at the site. Moreover, despite the general absence of selvages and other basic construction and finishing attributes, it is clear that all specimens represent technically well-made items and are scarcely "primary essays in the craft." The diversity of warp and weft preparation in the Type I textile fragments suggests long term antecedent development, not only for that specific technique but for the perishable industry at large.

The general regularity and narrow gauge of the weaving elements used in Type I further suggest the presence of heddle looms at the site. This would appear to be confirmed by the recovery of both spindle whorls and loom weights. The range of forms of Type I cloth produced is not and probably will not be available, due to the very fragmentary character of the extant remains. However, it is not unlikely that the Bâb edh-Dhrâᶜ collection includes portions of garments as well as burial shrouds.

The restriction of basketry to matting forms, while perhaps a factor of differential preservation, may not be altogether fortuitous. Twined and plaited matting was extensively used in both the prehistoric and historic Near East for floor, wall, table, and roof coverings, as well as for bedding; hence, recovery of this form of basketry may simply reflect the overall incidence and popularity of the technique in question.

Raw Materials

Only two fiber sources are represented in the Bâb edh-Dhrâᶜ perishable assemblage. These include a lacustrine or fluviatile reed of unknown genus or species and a plant tentatively identified as *Linum* spp. The use of longitudinally split reeds for the production of matting is consistent with construction practices reported from other Near Eastern sites and is not unexpected in the present context. Reeds constitute a highly plastic and therefore much exploited construction medium, not only for the production of basketry and matting but also for various flooring and roofing needs. It may be suggested on the basis of analogy to modern Near Eastern weavers that, in addition to longitudinal splitting, considerable pre-soaking of the reeds to facilitate flexibility was an inherent part of the Bâb edh-Dhrâᶜ weavers' art.

If the identification of the *Linum* spp. from the site is corroborated, this will represent one of the earliest positively documented incidences of this fiber source in the general Syro-Palestinian area. Detailed data on the preparation and processing of the Type I fiber sources, whatever they may be, will be presented in the final report.

Chronology

The Type I textiles from Bâb edh-Dhrâ^c are tentatively dated to the mid-3rd millennium (2600) B.C., while the Type II basketry may be ascribed to the late 4th millennium (3100) B.C. In the absence of any other dated textile or basketry remains from the site, no direct data are available on the local developmental sequence of the types described above. Using comparative data from both the Old World and the New World, some tentative suggestions of general evolutionary trends in Near Eastern perishable manufacture have been made and the reader is advised to consult Adovasio *et al.* (1976) for particulars.

External Correlations

The perishable assemblage from Bâb edh-Dhrâ^c may be ascribed part and parcel to the general milieu of Near Eastern basketry and textile production, the beginnings of which lie in the late Pleistocene and early post-Pleistocene, ca. 9500-9000 B.C. The two structural types represented at Bâb edh-Dhrâ^c have been reported from a large number of Near Eastern sites and both have very great antiquity (Adovasio *et al.*: 1976), extending back to at least the mid-10th millennium B.C.

Moreover, both techniques persist into historic times and are probably represented in various sub-areas of the modern Near East. The possible affinities of the Bâb edh-Dhrâ^c textiles and basketry to other earlier, contemporary, and later Near Eastern assemblages will be detailed in the final report.

Summary and Conclusions

In retrospect, the salient attributes of the Bâb edh-Dhrâ^c textile and basketry assemblage as suggested by the foregoing analysis are:

(1) Technically well-made cloth as well as basketry in the form of matting were produced and/or used at Bâb edh-Dhrâ^c during the period 3100-2600 B.C.

(2) The relative sophistication of the cloth fragments suggests not only the use of heddle looms but also long term antecedent development of this industry.

(3) The Bâb edh-Dhrâ^c assemblage may be allocated to the general milieu of Near Eastern basketry and production, the beginnings of which lie in the late Pleistocene or early post-Pleistocene, ca. 9500-9000 B.C.

We would like to acknowledge the assistance of Mr. Peter Marone and Mr. John Padden of the Allegheny Crime Laboratory, Pittsburgh, in the material identification of the cloth specimens from Bâb edh-Drâ_c.

BIBLIOGRAPHY

Adovasio, J. M.
  1974   *Prehistoric North American Basketry*. Nevada State Museum Anthropological Papers 16.
  1976   *Basketry Technology*. Chicago: Aldine.
  n.d.   Notes on the Analysis of Textiles from Tepe Yahya. Unpublished.
Adovasio, J. M., *et al.*
  1976   Textile and Basketry Impressions from Jarmo. *Palèorient* 3.1.

Driver, H. E.
  1961   *Indians of North America*. Chicago and London: University of Chicago.
Emery, I.
  1966   *The Primary Structure of Fabrics*. Washington, DC: The Textile Museum.

The Seventeenth Campaign at Sardis (1974)

Crawford H. Greenewalt, Jr.
University of California, Berkeley, CA 94720

The seventeenth campaign of the Harvard-Cornell Archaeological Exploration of Sardis, supported by a grant from the National Endowment for the Humanities, as well as by 290 individual and corporate Supporters of Sardis and the two sponsoring institutions, took place from late June through early September, 1974. The season's projects were directed and managed by a staff of sixteen and, as in previous seasons, were assisted greatly by Turkish Government officials and private individuals (see Appendix: "Acknowledgements").

Study of materials excavated in previous campaigns (notably Hellenistic pottery and metal objects) was the primary objective and activity of the 1974 season. In addition, some modest excavation (in the Roman gymnasium-bath complex and on the Acropolis), restoration and consolidation (in the same gymnasium-bath complex), and recording of archeological material fortuitously exposed and recovered at Sardis and environs were carried out.

Fortuitous Discoveries: Sardis

The *tyche* of Sardis, generally parsimonious with favors to her devoted excavators, each season takes perverse delight in bedeviling the expedition with swarms of miserable artifacts presented by village children; although unexceptional, fragmentary, and without context, these unsolicited horrors nevertheless need to be acquired at cost, require accounting, inventorying, and photographing, and increase the expedition's responsibilities. Occasionally, to tantalize her devotees and to sustain their faith, the Lady releases a treasure from her stores (Hanfmann and Waldbaum 1970: 35-36; 1975: 118-25; Ramage 1972: 33, 35, fig. 23; Gusmani 1975: 11-24), usually in some context quite remote from the excavators' work, to emphasize that the credit is hers, not theirs. Her latest gift is an inscription of major interest for the subject of Achaemenid Persian influence in religious matters at Sardis, which appeared as a result of erosion of the Pactolus stream during the winter months of 1973-74 (at no. 42, fig. 1). The text emerged slightly above eye level and right side up, for easy reading (fig. 2). The inscribed block was noticed by two excavation guards, who notified the expedition's administrative agent, attempted to secure a photographic record, and covered the block with earth for protection and security until the expedition members arrived in June. Professor and Mme L. Robert (1975), who have prepared the *editio princeps* and a commentary to the text, IN 74.1, kindly have supplied the following summary.

L'inscription, complète en 13 lignes, a été gravée à l'époque romaine avancée, pas avant le IIe siècle de notre ère. Elle résume un document, écrit en dialecte ionien, qui était daté de la 39e année du règne d'Artaxerxes II Mnemon. Le gouverneur de la Lydie, appelé "hyparque," le Perse Droaphernès (nom iranien nouveau, mais très bien formé et de sens clair) a élevé la statue de Zeus, lequel est l'apparence grecque du grand dieu iranien Ahura Mazda. Il donne l'ordre aux néocores qui ont le droit de pénétrer dans l'adyton, serviteurs du dieu (il faut rapprocher de ses expressions *Sardis*, n. 22 [Buckler and Robinson 1932: 47-48], qui doit provenir du même lieu d'origine, sanctuaire de Zeus Polieus, que la nouvelle inscription) et qui "couronnent le dieu", de ne pas participer aux mystères de divers dieux indigènes, Sabazios, Agdistis et Ma. A cette époque tardive, on a tenu à tirer des archives un règlement perse du milieu du IVe siècle, qui voulait lutter contre un rapprochement que certains faisaient avec des dieux indigènes de l'Anatolie, en participant à des mystères. Cela est très intéressant à la fois pour la situation religieuse à Sardes au IVe siècle, pour

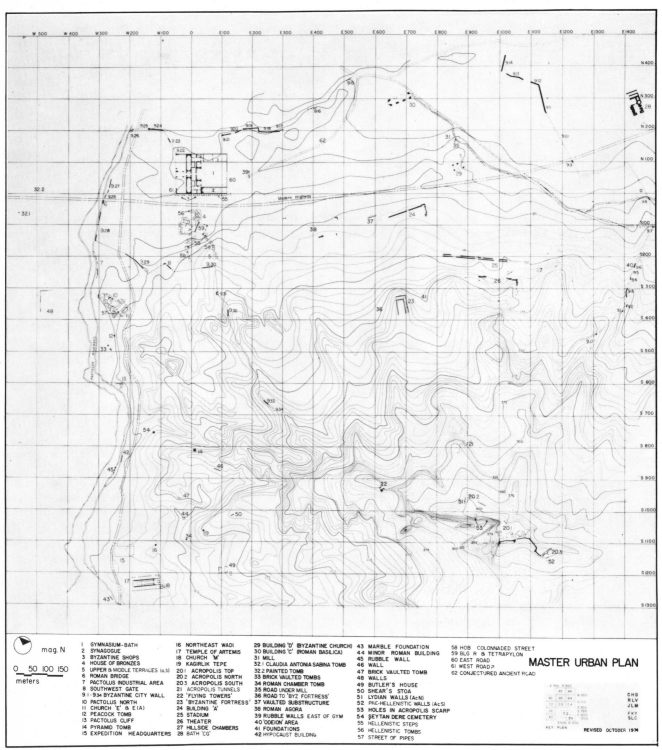

mag. N

0 50 100 150
meters

1 GYMNASIUM-BATH	16 NORTHEAST WADI	29 BUILDING 'D' (BYZANTINE CHURCH)	43 MARBLE FOUNDATION	58 HOB COLONNADED STREET
2 SYNAGOGUE	17 TEMPLE OF ARTEMIS	30 BUILDING 'C' (ROMAN BASILICA)	44 MINOR ROMAN BUILDING	59 BLG R & TETRAPYLON
3 BYZANTINE SHOPS	18 CHURCH 'M'	31 MILL	45 RUBBLE WALL	60 EAST ROAD
4 HOUSE OF BRONZES	19 KAGIRLIK TEPE	32.I CLAUDIA ANTONIA SABINA TOMB	46 WALL	61 WEST ROAD?
5 UPPER & MIDDLE TERRACES (a,b)	20.1 ACROPOLIS TOP	32.2 PAINTED TOMB	47 BRICK VAULTED TOMB	62 CONJECTURED ANCIENT ROAD
6 ROMAN BRIDGE	20.2 ACROPOLIS NORTH	33 BRICK VAULTED TOMBS	48 WALLS	
7 PACTOLUS INDUSTRIAL AREA	20.3 ACROPOLIS SOUTH	34 ROMAN CHAMBER TOMB	49 BUTLER'S HOUSE	
8 SOUTHWEST GATE	21 ACROPOLIS TUNNELS	35 ROAD UNDER MILL	50 SHEAR'S STOA	
9.1-9.34 BYZANTINE CITY WALL	22 'FLYING TOWERS'	36 ROAD TO 'BYZ FORTRESS'	51 LYDIAN WALLS (AcN)	
10 PACTOLUS NORTH	23 'BYZANTINE FORTRESS'	37 VAULTED SUBSTRUCTURE	52 PRE-HELLENISTIC WALLS (AcS)	
11 CHURCH 'E' & E (A)	24 BUILDING 'A'	38 ROMAN AGORA	53 HOLES IN ACROPOLIS SCARP	
12 PEACOCK TOMB	25 STADIUM	39 RUBBLE WALLS EAST OF GYM	54 ŞEYTAN DERE CEMETERY	
13 PACTOLUS CLIFF	26 THEATER	40 'ODEION' AREA	55 HELLENISTIC STEPS	
14 PYRAMID TOMB	27 HILLSIDE CHAMBERS	41 FOUNDATIONS	56 HELLENISTIC TOMBS	
15 EXPEDITION HEADQUARTERS	28 BATH 'CG'	42 HYPOCAUST BUILDING	57 STREET OF PIPES	

MASTER URBAN PLAN

KEY PLAN   REVISED OCTOBER 1974

1:2000

M26 U 101

Fig. 1. Site plan of Sardis.

l'existence de mystères des trois divinités nommées et pour la politique religieuse des Perses et leur souci de pureté du culte de leur grand dieu. Intéressant aussi qu'on ait jugé bon de graver ce document dans l'époque impériale.

The inscription stone is an L-shaped block of marble (figs. 3 and 4): length 1.05 m.; height 0.64 m., width of inscribed surface 0.58 m.; width of back 0.63 m.

In the following account, *right* and *left* surfaces are reported with reference to the inscribed surface as viewed by the observer; *right* and *left* surface features with reference to the surfaces concerned as viewed by the observer.

Front (inscribed) surface. At the time of discovery, uniformly covered with mortar.

Right surface. Even, smooth finish.

Left surface. At left, essentially rectangular extension ca. 0.44 m. wide, projecting ca. 0.05 m.; battered and roughly hammer dressed at top, evenly pointed at bottom. (Non-extended) right side shows anathyrosis: smooth-chiseled borders at front and top sides; center rough-punched with somewhat finer punching to left near extension. 0.21 m. in from right edge, a narrow vertical channel (ca. 0.05 m. wide and deep) extends 0.40 m. from top surface and evidently penetrated to dowel hole in under surface.

Back surface. Anathyrosis: smooth-chiseled border at left and left side of top (extending ca. 0.24 m. and increasing in width towards the right from 0.11 m. to 0.135 m.); punched/pointed center. 0.105 m. in from left edge, narrow vertical channel (ca. 0.05 m. wide and deep) extending the preserved height of block (which is broken at lower left corner) and penetrating by round hole (ca. 0.017 m. in diameter) to dowel hole in under surface.

Top surface. Anathyrosis: smooth-chiseled border 0.12 m.-0.15 m. wide) at front and left; center neatly pointed. At right side ca. 0.17 m. in from front edge, dove-tail clamp hole with clamp pin and leading. At back side ca. 0.16 m. in from left edge the same.

Bottom surface. Anathyrosis: neatly-chiseled border (0.12 m.-0.13 m. wide) at front and sides; center neatly pointed (and at time of discovery partly covered with mortar). Two square dowel holes: one completely preserved (0.08-0.085 m. square) 0.075 m. in from front surface, 0.06 m. in from left surface, and penetrated from channel in left surface; and other partially preserved (ca. 0.08 m. wide) ca. 0.07 m. in from right surface, ca. 0.03 m. in from back surface, and evidently penetrated from channel in back surface.

The inscribed surface alone, with its neat accommodation of text, might suggest that the block (recovered out of context; see below) had formed the stock of a small base or pedestal. Anathyrosis on all surfaces save the front and right, however, and the evidence for stout clamps on the top (at left and back) show that the inscribed block was designed for integration into a masonry

structure of some substance (the L-form extension serving to "key" the block securely in the structure). The smooth right surface indicates that the block occupied a corner rather than an axially-central position. The reference to the statue of Zeus in lines 4-5 suggests that the structure was a monumental pedestal which accommodated statuary rather than a building on whose walls official information was inscribed (like the Metroon at Sardis — Hanfmann 1964: 34; cf. Plutarch, *Themistocles* 31) or a wall specially designed to serve as a "notice board" for particular texts (Dow: 1961).

Buildings so inscribed were common in the Graeco-Roman world. Among several at Priene, the Temple of Athena

Fig. 2. Professor Ramage inspects inscription concerning Persian religious matters (IN 74.1).

Fig. 3. Inscription block (IN 74.1), front (inscribed) surface at right.

Fig. 4. Inscription block (IN 74.1), back surface at lower right.

Fig. 5. Section of hypocaust-unit building (from which IN 74.1 was recovered) as revealed in the east bank of the Pactolus stream.

Polais and the North or Sacred Stoa or the Agora are particularly noteworthy (Hiller von Gärtringen 1906: nos. 1, 14, 15, 16, 27, 37 (Athena Temple); 107-30 (Stoa). The bouleuterion at Miletus (Knackfuss 1908: 77-98) and the north parodos wall of the large theater at Aphrodisias (Erim 1970: 174; reference supplied by C. Habicht) served a similar function.

The off-center position of our inscription suggests that it was not the structure's most significant text (and therefore that the statue of Zeus had not been its only or most important statue?). The structure might have been a multi-statue pedestal like the Monuments of the Athenian Eponymous Heroes at Athens and Delphi, to which additions were made from time to time, (Pausanius 1.5.5; 10.10.1-2; Shear 1970: 171-76, 196-203; R. S. Stroud kindly informed the author about the monument at Delphi).

The inscribed block had been reused as building material in a wall or foundation belonging to a Late Roman building complex situated in the east bank of the Pactolus stream, about 200 m. north of the Sardis expedition compound (fig. 1, no. 42; fig. 5).

Parts of this complex have been exposed since 1960 (when mosaic paving was noticed by R. H. Whallon, Jr.) if not before; subsequent erosion of the bank has sheared off more and more of the structure, exposing successive sections in a west-to-east sequence. The remains *in situ* are totally submerged in debris and, because of inaccessibility from above and below, difficult or impossible to investigate short of excavation.

As exposed in 1974 (fig. 5), the complex appears to extend for a distance of ca. 24.25 m. in a north-south direction; some wall remains, most of them oriented at more-or-less right angles to the scarp, can be recognized. In the northern half is a hypocaust unit whose walls have foundations about 1 m. deep and whose brick pillars appear to be distributed in three adjoining chambers. Near the hypocaust floor between some pillars occur concentrations of carbonized matter. At some points the hypocaust ceiling (schist slabs) appears to remain *in situ*, at others to have collapsed. The southern part of the building displays mosaic floor paving (at ca. *119.30 a.s.l.), parts of which (as revealed in segments collapsed from a floor directly south of the wall or foundation which incorporated the inscription block) display an over-all pattern of interlocking circles in a white, blue-black, red, and yellow color scheme.

The only other fortuitously recovered antiquity from Sardis which merits remark in this report is a

Fig. 6. Mosaic paving near Allahdiyen village. Photograph by E. Gombosi.

small "altar" of marble (IN 74.2/NoEx 74.1), cylindrical in form, decorated in relief with a garland festooned in three swags over two bucrania and an eagle grasping thunderbolts, and with paterae in the spaces above the swag festoons. It is inscribed (in Greek) with a dedication by one Demetrios the son of Hermogenes to an emperor (. . . *ano kaisari*: i.e. Trajan or Hadrian?).

Fortuitous Discoveries: Allahdiyen

A visit (by the expedition's agent, T. Yalçınkaya, and government representative, A. Tulga) to the mountain village of Allahdiyen, some 10 km. southeast of Sardis, led to the discovery and recording of two Roman monuments: an inscribed pedestal and a mosaic paving. Both were found on the east side of the Salihli-Boz Dağ road, about 1 km. below and east of Allahdiyen village (near a bend in the road at "eski mektep yeri," where the villagers once had contemplated building a schoolhouse). Unfluted and torded column shafts appear in the road bed at this location, in fields immediately north of the road bend are brick and rubble ruins of Roman or Byzantine structures. The inscribed pedestal, extracted by farmers from a field adjacent to the road, had been incorporated into a dry rubble roadside wall; it has been removed to the Sardis expedition compound (IN 74.7). The text, which indicates a date before A.D. 220, was substantially complete and documented in nineteen lines the wrestling victory of an athlete from Hypaipa in games held at Sardis. The mosaic paving, which had been exposed when the road was widened, was situated a little further to the south of the pedestal

and was exposed in the scarp of the hillside at a level slightly above that of the road surface. Just underneath the exposed portion of mosaic metalling rested part of a conduit of small terracotta pipes, *in situ* (oriented approximately east-west, ca. 0.10 m. in diameter; two pipe sections observed). Only a narrow segment of the mosaic paving, ca. 2 m. long by 0.21 m. wide (figs. 6 and 7), was cleared and recorded; additional tesserae exposed further north in the scarp indicated that the paving extended in that direction. The exposed segment showed an overall geometric pattern which included a simple ivy rinceau and a roundel with partridge-like bird and stemmed flower. Two tones of yellow, blue-gray, and green (the last glass, for the flower stem) added a subtle richness to the basic color scheme of black against white with brick-red highlights. After photography and reproduction in a measured water-color facsimile, the mosaic was reburied.

Excavation: Gymnasium-Bath Complex

In the gymnasium-bath complex by the İzmir-Ankara highway, a modest but wise investment of excavation (by F. K. Yegül) yielded substantial returns in new architectural information. Near the southern end of the complex's largely-unexcavated western section ("West B"), a small trench some 11 m. north of and parallel to the south wall revealed a series of piers (of ashlar masonry), corresponding in position to those of the south wall, and a wall of rubble and brick connecting the central two piers and containing a monumental door frame, with marble jambs and lintel preserved *in situ* (between

Fig. 7. Mosaic paving near Allahdiyen village. Facsimile watercolor by E. Wahle.

W 23 and W 48, on the N 14 grid line; see plan in Greenwalt 1973b: fig. 1, p. 16); the wall appeared (to Yegül) to belong to a secondary remodeling of the interior (in the 5th century A.D.?). Between and near the piers were exposed large hunks of fallen brick arches or vaults.

> In the gymnasium-bath complex's "West Hall" (BE-H, previously BE-W; see plan, Greenewalt 1973b: fig. 1, p. 16) the brick arches of the west wall were repaired, the central pool (natatio) was emptied of debris, and a protective layer of gravel was laid down over part of the pool and room floors (the last of these projects, all of which were supervised by T. Yalçınkaya, could not be completed due to restrictions imposed in consequence of international politics).
> In the "Marble Court," recording of the second-story columns, pillars, and entablature (of the Severan pavilions) was completed (by F. K. Yegül).

Near the southwest corner of the gymnasium-bath complex's palaestra, in the (blocked) arched passageway of the north wall of the Synagogue, the expanse of intriguing Early Byzantine graffiti (Hanfmann 1964: 33) was recorded in a comprehensive drawing (by E. Wahle, with the aid of photographs taken in previous seasons and showing those parts which had since deteriorated; fig. 8). After long deliberation (with conservators P. A. Lins and J. Soulanian, Jr.), it was regretfully concluded that the graffiti had deteriorated too far to justify the elaborate measures which would be involved in attempting to preserve their surviving parts.

Reexamination of the "Byzantine Shops" and "Main Avenue" colonnade directly south of the gymnasium-bath complex (by F. K. Yegül)

suggested that the shops had been built in the 2nd or 3rd century A.D. (not, as previously thought, in Early Byzantine times) and that the original colonnade had had monumental columns similar to and only slightly shorter than those fronting the east side of the complex. The difference in column height (ca. 5.60 m. in the shop colonnade, 6.40 m. in the east colonnade) would have had to be resolved at the southeast corner of the complex, where the colonnades converged, perhaps, according to Yegül, through masking by a tetrapylon structure at the crossing of the streets known to have existed in front of the colonnades. Sometime after ca. 400 A.D., this colonnade would have been replaced by the extraordinary ensemble of miscellaneous pedestals, bases, shafts, and capitals whose remains were prominent at the time of excavation (Hanfmann 1962: 40-45) and were partially reconstructed during the 1973 season (probably with more sensitivity than in the 5th century).

Excavation: Acropolis

On the Acropolis, a small sondage was made by the two terrace walls of limestone and sandstone ashlar construction, situated high on the north slope (Ramage 1972: 15-20) to explore the possibility that a third terrace wall lay slightly below the other two. The existence of a third wall was suggested by the presence of a large L-shaped limestone block (2.80 m. long, 1.15-.90 m. wide, 0.56 m. thick), poised askew on the hillslope (and essentially resting on bedrock) some 15.50 m. horizontally distant from and ca. 7 m. below the foot of the lower

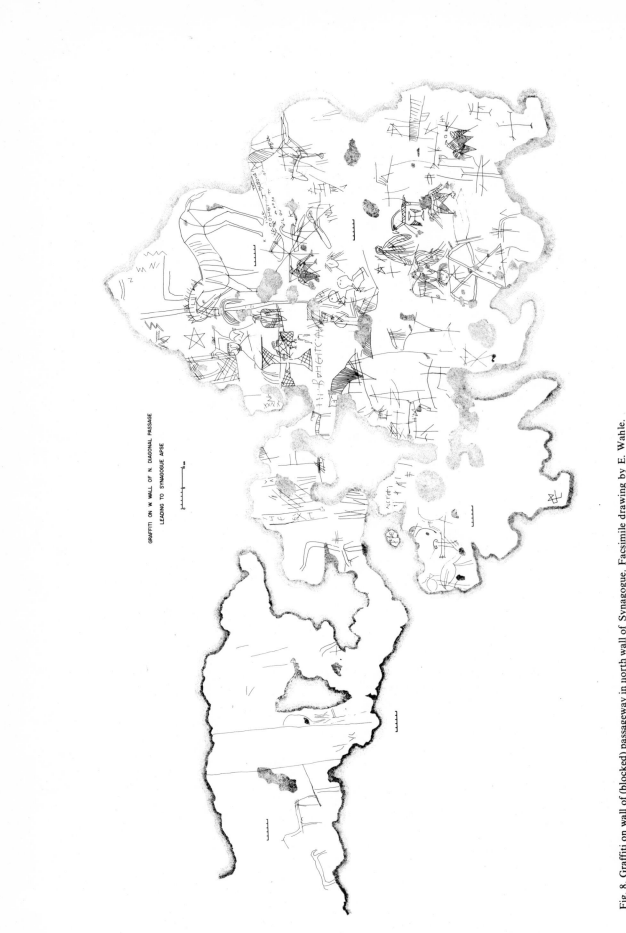

GRAFFITI ON W WALL OF N. DIAGONAL PASSAGE

LEADING TO SYNAGOGUE APSE

Fig. 8. Graffiti on wall of (blocked) passageway in north wall of Synagogue. Facsimile drawing by E. Wahle.

terrace wall ("AcN wall 1"): the material and neatly chiseled surfaces (lacking, however, drafted borders) of this block relate it to the terrace-wall masonry; while its dimensions, considerably greater than those of the terrace wall blocks, suggest that it belongs not to their superstructures but to another construction. Granted that the block has not been artificially moved (always a strong possibility on the Acropolis) and given its considerable weight and the law of gravity, such a construction might be anticipated somewhere above the block and below the lower terrace wall.

A narrow (2-3 m. wide) trench was laid out to link these two features and dug from the highest point, at the foot of the terrace wall, downward. Although the lowest part of this swath was not cleared to bedrock when work was terminated (due to restrictions imposed in consequence of international politics), sufficient clearing had been done to suggest that wall foundations would not appear in the trench.

The clearing of debris in the higher end of the trench exposed the profile of Acropolis bedrock at that point: below the terrace wall footing it plunged precipitously for a distance of ca. 1.5 m., then made a turn of ca. 90° and extended outward in a flat, slightly rising, "shelf"-like surface for a distance of 7-8 m., then dipped downward to follow an irregular incline of ca. 40° (little of this lowest part was cleared to bedrock). The even, uniform surface of the "shelf" suggests that it was artificially created. Resting directly on it was a lens of debris, apparently homogenous and some 2.0 m. deep at the easternmost part, which contained many roof-tile fragments and hunks of unevenly-fired crude brick, some marble chips, one worked limestone block resembling those of the terrace walls, three catapult balls—one inscribed I E (cf. von Szalay and Böhringer 1937: 48-54; Laurenzi 1938: 33-36; Philo, *Bellopoeica* 51.21-26; Vitruvius, *De Architectura* 10.11.3; Marsden 1971: 197-200)—and pottery fragments of 4th century B.C.-to-Hellenistic date (at least five fish-plate fragments, one palmette-stamped bowl).

The apparent homogeneity of this debris (residue from the siege operation, which would explain the catapult balls—another catapult ball [S 60.34:3030] was discovered in 1960 just below the lowest terrace wall [information from S. L. Carter]—and burnt brick?) and its direct contact with the "shelf" floor suggest to the writer that the "shelf" itself was created no earlier than the Hellenistic period, and thus several centuries after the construction of the terrace walls (for the date, Ramage 1972: 16, 19). In that case, the outer support of the "staircase" against the lower terrace wall, suggested by shallow stepped cuttings in the wall face, would have been destroyed when the bedrock was cut away to create the "shelf." The senior architect of the expedition (S. L. Carter), however, thought that the "shelf" might have been created to provide an even bedding for an outer terrace wall (to which the large limestone block belonged).

Study Projects

The following material excavated at Sardis between 1958 and 1974 was studied at Sardis in the 1974 season: Hellenistic pottery other than molded relief wares (by A. Oliver, jr.); metal objects (by J. C. Waldbaum); Byzantine glazed wares (by J. A. Scott); roof tiles and terracotta revetment plaques (by A. Ramage); stone sculpture (by G. M. A. Hanfmann, assisted by T. A. Vann); coins (by T. A. Vann, for A. E. M. Johnson and T. V. Buttrey); seals and gemstones (by T. A. Vann for R. S. Thomas); pre-Hellenistic ritual dinner sets (by C. H. Greenewalt, jr.).

Acknowledgments

The contributions of 23 foundation and individual donors made possible the support of NEH Grant RO-10405-74-319. The season's work and the publication program were also benefited by grants from the Charles E. Merrill Trust and the Memorial Foundation for Jewish Culture.

Officers of the Ministry of National Education and Department of Antiquities and Museums, notably the Department's Director-General, Bay Hikmet Gurçay, and his associates, Bay Burhan Tezcan and Bay Çetin Anlağan, showed the expedition their customary courtesy, with prompt attention and friendly, flexible cooperation in all matters. His excellency the Vali of Manisa and Kaymakam of Salihli acted with special consideration and kindness in a potentially distressing situation. Bay Hasan Koramaz, the expedition foreman, energetic and dependable as always, was again a tower of strength through the season. To these and other good Turkish friends go hearty thanks for fundamental help.

Staff members were:

G. M. A. Hanfmann (Harvard), *director*

A. Tulga (Manisa Museum), *Turkish Government repressentive*

T. Yalçınkaya (Izmir), *manager and architect for restoration*

C. H. Greenewalt, jr. (University of California), *field director*

A. Ramage (Cornell), *assistant field director and archeologist*

S. L. Carter (Huygens & Tappe, Boston), *senior architect*

F. K. Yegül (Wellesley College), *architect and archeologist*

R. L. Vann (Cornell), *architect*

T. A. Vann (Mrs. R. L.; Ithaca City Schools), *recorder*

E. C. C. Gombosi (Harvard), *photographer*

E. G. Wahle (Harvard), *draftsman and assistant recorder*

P. A. Lins (Institute of Fine Arts, New York University), *senior conservator*

J. Soultanian, jr. (Institute of Fine Arts, New York University), *conservator*

J. A. Scott (Harvard), *recording specialist for Byzantine glazed pottery and pottery analysis*

J. C. Waldbaum (University of Wisconsin), *specialist in metal antiquities*

A. Oliver, jr. (The Textile Museum), *specialist in Hellenistic pottery*

C. F. Foss (University of Massachusetts), *specialist in epigraphy and numismatics*

BIBLIOGRAPHY

Entries marked with an asterisk constitute a bibliography of the preceding campaign, as well as references not mentioned in previous reports. Where appropriate, the entries are annotated to guide the reader to the relevant reference.

Bammer, A.; Fleischer, R.; and Knibbe, D.
 *1974 *Führer durch das Archäologische Museum in Selcuk-Ephesus.* Vienna: Österreichisches Archäologische Institut. Pp. 95-97 (inscription with death sentence for 45 Sardians, Inv. # 1631).

Buckler, W. H., and Robinson, D. M.
 1932 *Sardis 7.1: Greek and Latin Inscriptions.* Leiden: Brill.

Colledge, M. A. R.
 *1974 Review of *The Dura-Europos Synagogue: A Reevaluation (1932-1972)*, ed. Joseph Gutmann. *American Journal of Archaeology* 78: 442-43.

Dow. S.
 1961 The Walls Inscribed with Nikomakhos' Law Code. *Hesperia* 30: 58-73.

Erim, K. T.
 1970 Aphrodisias. P. 174 in Archaeology in Asia Minor, by M. J. Mellink. *American Journal of Archaeology* 74: 157-78.

Greenewalt, C. H.
 *1973a Ephesian Ware. *California Studies in Classical Antiquity* 6: 91-122.
 1973b The Fifteenth Campaign at Sardis. *Bulletin of the American Schools of Oriental Research* 211: 14-36.

Gusmani, R.
 *1975 *Neue epichorische Schriftzeugnisse aus Sardis (1958-1971).* Sardis Monograph 3. Cambridge: Harvard University.

Hammond, M.
 *1972 *The City in the Ancient World.* Cambridge: Harvard University. Chap. III.3: Phrygian Gordion and Lydian Sardis, pp. 145-46 (results of recent excavations and bibliography).
 *1974 The Emergence of Mediaeval Towns. *Harvard Studies in Classical Philology* 78: 1-33. Discussion of Asia Minor, pp. 26-33.

Hanfmann, G. M. A.
 1962 The Fourth Campaign at Sardis (1961). *Bulletin of the American Schools of Oriental Research* 166: 1-57.
 1964 The Sixth Campaign at Sardis (1963). *Bulletin of the American Schools of Oriental Research* 174: 3-58.
 *1974a A Pediment of the Persian Era from Sardis. Pp. 289-302, pls. 99-104 in *Mélanges Mansel*. Ankara: Türk Tarih Kurumu.
 *1974b Sardis. In Archaeology in Asia Minor, by M. J. Mellink. *American Journal of Archaeology* 78: 124-25 and 129; pl. 28, fig. 14; pl. 29, fig. 18; pl. 32, fig. 28.
 *1974c Sardis 1973. *Anatolian Studies* 24: 53-55.
 *1974d The Sixteenth Campaign at Sardis (1973). *Bulletin of the American Schools of Oriental Research* 215: 31-60.
 *1975a Excavations and Restoration at Sardis-*1972*. *Türk Arkeoloji Dergisi* 21-22: 59-77.
 *1975b *From Croesus to Constantine: The Cities of Western Asia Minor and Their Arts.* Ann Arbor: University of Michigan.

Hanfmann, G. M. A., and Ramage, A.
 *1974 Excavations at Sardis, 1973. *American Journal of Archaeology* 78: 291.

Hanfmann, G. M. A., and Waldbaum, J. C.
 1970 The Eleventh and Twelfth Campaigns at Sardis (1968, 1969). *Bulletin of the American Schools of Oriental Research* 199: 7-58.
 *1975 *A Survey of Sardis and the Major Monuments outside the City Walls.* Sardis Report 1. Cambridge: Harvard University.

Hausmann, U.
 *1975 Review of *Studies Presented to George M. A. Hanfmann*, ed. D. G. Mitten, J. G. Pedley, and J. A. Scott; Fogg Art Museum—Harvard University Monographs in Art and Archaeology 2. Cambridge:

Fogg Art Museum / Mainz: von Zabern. In *Welt des Orients* 7: 314-20.

Hawkes, J.
*1974   *Atlas of Ancient Archaeology*. New York: McGraw-Hill. P. 144, 2 plans.

Hiller von Gärtringen, F.
1906   *Inscriften von Priene*. Berlin: Reimer.

Knackfuss, H.
1908   Das Rathaus von Milet. *Milet* I.2: *Ergebnisse der Ausgrabungen und Untersuchungen seit dem Jahre 1899*. Berlin: Reimer.

Kraabel, A. T.
*1974   Synagogues, Ancient. Pp. 436-39 in Vol. 16, *Supplement 1967-1974* of *New Catholic Encyclopaedia*. New York: McGraw-Hill.

Latte, K.
*1950   Ein antikes Gygesdrama. *Eranos* 48: 136-41.

Laurenzi, L.
1938   Projettili dell'artigliera antica scoperti a Rodi. Pp. 33-36 in *Memorie pubblicate a Cura dell'Istituto Storico-Archeologico F.E.R.T. e della R. Deputazione di Storia Patria per Rodi* 2. Rhodes: Istituto Storico-Archeologico di Rodi.

MacDonald, D. J.
*1974   Aphrodisias and Currency in the East, A.D. 259-305. *American Journal of Archaeology* 78: 280-86. Comparison of distribution of Imperial coinage at Sardis on the basis of the Princeton excavations.

Marsden, E. W.
1971   *Greek and Roman Artillery: Technical Treatises*. Oxford: Oxford University.

Meinardus, O. F.
*1974   The Christian Remains of the Seven Churches of the Apocalypse. *Biblical Archaeologist* 37.3: 69-82. Sardis, Pp. 78-80.

Metzger, H.
*1973   Campagne du 1971 au Letoon et a Xanthos. *Dergi* 20.1: 117-27. Sardis, Pp. 121, 127, fig. 14 (parallel for Church "E").

Pedley, J. G.
1974   Carians in Sardis. *Journal of Hellenistic Studies* 94: 96-99.

Pouilloux, J.
1974   Les décrets delphiques pour Matrophanès de Sardes. *Bulletin de Correspondance Hellenique* 98: 159-69.

Ramage, A.
1972   The Fourteenth Campaign at Sardis. *Bulletin of the American Schools of Oriental Research* 206: 9-39.

Ramage, N. H.
*1974   Draped Herm from Sardis. *Harvard Studies in Classical Philology* 78: 253-56.

Reynolds, J.
*1974   Review of *Letters from Sardis*, by G. M. A. Hanfmann. *Journal of Roman Studies* 64: 282.

Robert, L.
*1975   Une nouvelle inscription grecque de Sardes. *Comptes rendus de la Academie des Inscriptions et Belles-Lettres*: 306-30.

Saldern, A. von
*1975   Ein glaserner Schlangenkorb in Hamburg. Pp. 56-61 in *Festschrift für Peter Wilhelm Meister*, eds. A. Ohm and H. Reber. Hamburg: Hauswedell.

Scott, J. A.
*1975a   The Seventeenth Campaign at Sardis. *Archaeology* 28.2: 130-31.
*1975b   The Seventeenth Campaign at Sardis. *Journal of Field Archaeology* 2.1/2: 1834.

Seager, A. R.
*1974   *Archaeology at the Ancient Synagogue of Sardis, Turkey: Judaism in a Major Roman City*. Ball State University Faculty Lecture Series. Muncie, IN: Ball State University.

Shear, T. L.
1970   The Monument of the Eponymous Heroes in the Athenian Agora. *Hesperia* 39: 145-222.

Szalay, A. von, and Böhringer, E.
1937   *Altertümer von Pergamon* 10: *Die Hellenistische Arsenale*. Berlin: de Gruyter.

Vacano, O.-W. von
*1973   Forward. Pp. v-xix in G. Dennis, *Die Städte und Begrabnisplätze etruriens*. Darmstadt: Wissenschaftliche Buchgesellschaft. Comments on origin of the Etruscans and Dennis' work at Bin Tepe.

Wheeler, T. S.
*1974   Early Bronze Age Burial Customs in Western Anatolia. *American Journal of Archaeology* 78: 413-18. Reference to discoveries at Ahlatlı Tepecik and Eski Balıkhane.

Yüğrüm, G.
*1973   *Sart Harabeleri Regberi: Guide to the Excavations at Sardis*. Ankara: Türk Tarih Kurumu.

Excavations at Meiron in Upper Galilee—
1974, 1975

Second Preliminary Report

Eric M. Meyers
Duke University, Durham, NC 27706
Carol L. Meyers
Duke University, Durham, NC 27706
James F. Strange
University of South Florida, Tampa, FA 33620

The first full-scale effort at recovering the archeological history of Meiron was conducted during the summer of 1974 (previous seasons—Meyers, Meyers, and Strange: 1974). Both the 1974 and 1975 campaigns were carried out under the supervision of Eric M. Meyers, Director; James F. Strange, Associate Director; and Carol L. Meyers, Field Archaeologist, and conducted under the auspices of the American Schools of Oriental Research and its Jerusalem affiliate, the W. F. Albright Institute of Archaeological Research. The 1974 season was sponsored by Duke University and the Duke University Summer School. Additional support came from the Cooperative Program in Judaic Studies at Duke University and the University of North Carolina at Chapel Hill, the Department of Interreligious Affairs of the Union of American Hebrew Congregations, Hebrew Union College, and George Washington University. The 1975 campaign was supported exclusively by Duke University and the Duke Summer School in Cooperation with the Cooperative Program in Judaic Studies.

The following staff members participated in the field work: in 1974, Sara Raymond, photographer; William Lessig, draftsman; Frazier Anderson, small objects; Carolyn Strange, registrar; Richard S. Hanson, numismatist (in absentia); area supervisors included Marilyn Spirt-Lanson, John Hanks, and Anne Young in Field MI, Louise Upchurch in MV, Anne Arenstein (Zion Fellow) in MIII and MIV, Austin Ritterspach and Daniel Pienaar in MIII, and James Hodges in TI. In 1975, the staff included Richard S. Hanson, numismatist; Hendrik van Dijk, Sr., photographer; Richard H. Chandler and William W. Lawrence, architects; Freya Mechanic, small objects; Day Ricketts, registrar; John K. Hanks, conservator; Lee Maxey, formatore; area supervisors were Melanie Montgomery (Zion Fellow), MI; John Montgomery (Zion Fellow), MI; Catherine Snyder, MI; Steve Falconer, MI and MV; Sarah P. Morris, MI; Louise Upchurch (Zion Fellow), MV; Willard Hamrick, MIII and MVI; Daniel Pienaar, MIII; Michael Banks, M *Beth*; David Reese, M *Beth* (also lithics and animal bones). The authors wish to express their indebtedness to all those who made these excavations possible, especially the student workers.

Revised Chronology

In light of the extensive work conducted during these seasons (fig. 1) and based on a preliminary study of the ceramics and coins of all seasons, the following table represents a complete revision of the stratification presented in our previous report (Meyers, Meyers, and Strange 1974: 14):

Stratum I	88-1 B.C.E.	Late Hellenistic
Stratum II	1-135 C.E.	Early Roman
Stratum III	135-250 C.E.	Middle Roman
Stratum IV	250-360 C.E.	Late Roman
Stratum V	360-750 C.E.	Byzantine, Abandonment
Stratum VI	750 - 1000 C.E.	Early Arab
Stratum VII	1000-1399 C.E.	Late Arab
phase a	11th-13th century	
phase b	14th century	

The Meiron chronological table should be compared with that of Khirbet Shemaᶜ:

Stratum I	103-76 B.C.E.	Hasmonean
Stratum II	180-284 C.E	Late Roman 1
Stratum III	284-306 C.E.	Late Roman 2
Stratum IV	306-419 C.E.	Byzantine 1
Stratum V	419-640 C.E.	Byzantine 2
Stratum VI	640-850 C.E.	Arab
Stratum VII	1150-1277 C.E.	Medieval

Several observations should be made on this new schema before summarizing our findings. Stratum I occupation has left only the scantiest architectural remains, but the ceramic and numismatic data clearly point to the late Hellenistic era. Richard S. Hanson (1974: 22) has recently proposed that the Hasmonean mints attributable to Janneus indicate that he "not only subdued this area but that free Jewish enclaves survived despite the fact that the Seleucids regained some of the area." In any case, the large numbers of Hasmonean coins found at Khirbet Shemaᶜ and Meiron indicate an important aspect of Maccabean expansion, which hitherto had very little documentation. We know from recent excavations at Tell Anafa that Janneus' northern campaign brought him to the northernmost part of the Huleh valley. Whether or not Stratum I should be pushed back further into the Hellenistic period is a question to be resolved by future seasons of digging.

Stratum II has also left behind meager architectural remains, since an extensive Stratum II-IV building in the lower city (MI) has caused major disturbance in this earlier level. Fortunately, enough of this occupation has been preserved to document clearly a village of the Second Temple period. The real heyday of the Meiron community is represented by Strata III and IV, giving striking

testimony to the expansion of Jewish life in Galilee after the Bar Kochba War. From the artifactual data, this population movement is clearly attested before the middle of the 2nd century C.E. The large building complex in MI is attributable to Stratum III, with major remodeling and additions in Stratum IV. The tower in MV also was constructed during Stratum III, indicating that major building operations took place during this period.

Expansion of the settlement probably peaked in Stratum IV when the large and imposing synagogue of Meiron was erected. New private houses were also built for the wealthy (MII) and the town expanded an appreciable distance to the north, as rescue work in Meiron *Beth* has shown. Then suddenly in the reign of Constantius II a massive exodus seems to have occurred, in all probability due to the excessive taxes imposed at that time. The revolt of Gallus could not have had any repercussions in the Meiron area (conversation with Prof. S. Lieberman; for a detailed discussion of this crucial period, see Lieberman: 1945-46; 1947; the hypothesis that excessive taxation brought about the abandonment at Meiron is a result of the authors' conversations with Prof. Lieberman). The case for the abandonment of the site is made mainly on the coins and the nature of the finds in MI. All of the Late Roman coins dated after 360 C.E. either do

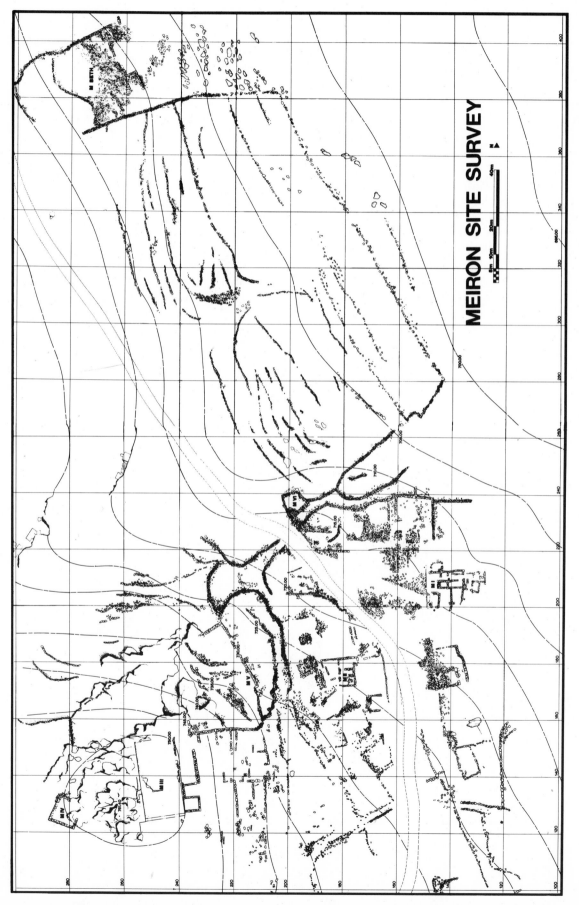

Fig. 1. Site plan of ancient Meiron, including all excavated areas; scale is 1:250.

not come from stratified contexts or come from areas which easily could have been used after the site was abandoned. No coins are dated to the 5th century and, unlike Khirbet Shemaᶜ,, the earthquake of 419 C.E. apparently played no role (Amiran 1950-51: 225; 1952: 54-55). The 306 C.E. and 419 C.E. earthquakes were responsible for destroying both Strata II and III synagogues at Khirbet Shemaᶜ. Apparently neither was an important factor at Meiron, though further work may require revision of the Meiron chronology. At present, it is not certain that the great basilica at Meiron was finished by 306 C.E. In the Byzantine period an occasional squatter seems to have been at the site and some stragglers may have lingered on after 360.

In both the early and late Arabic periods, the ruin comes to life again: there is a major rebuilding in

Stratum VI in MV, and Stratum VII is especially well attested in MIII and MIV. Due to the fact that the medieval inhabitants primarily reused older material, their architectural remains are not well preserved. The ceramic and numismatic evidence, however, is substantial. By late medieval times, Meiron had become an important pilgrimage center, but it is difficult, if not impossible, to say whether any phase of Stratum VII is related to this development.

MI. The Lower City (figs. 2-8)

Excavations at Meiron were begun in 1971 and 1972 in the field designated MI, a substantial building complex in the lower city where the construction of a Yeshiva was threatening to obliterate some ancient remains. It became clear in

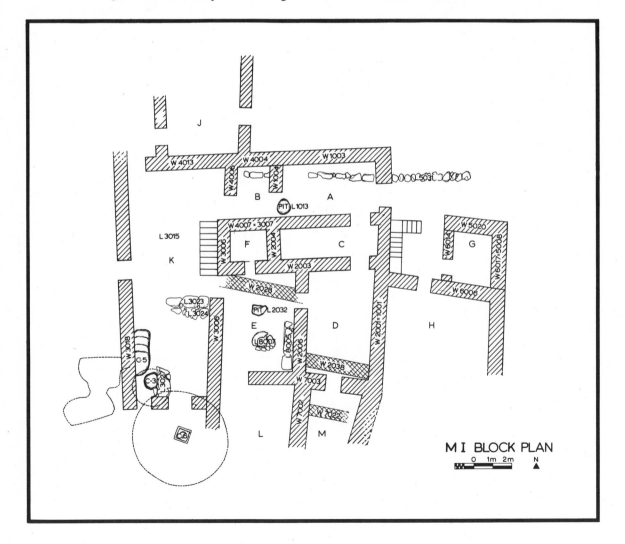

Fig. 2. Schematic block plan of MI.

Fig. 3. Photo tower shot of MI building complex, looking northeast, with main entrance at top center.

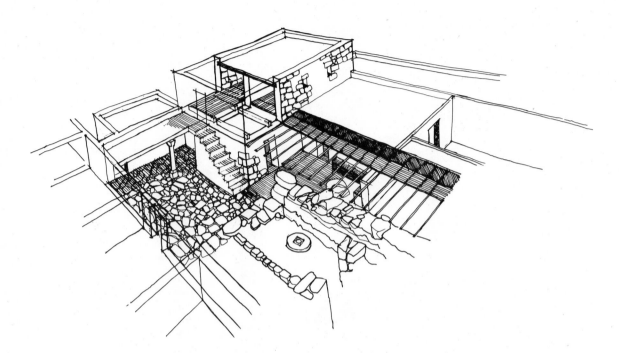

Fig. 4. Reconstruction of MI, looking northeast; prepared by William W. Lawrence.

the first two seasons that this building consisted of an extensive series of rooms, shops, courtyards, and underground chambers used over a considerable period of time, spanning the two major periods of occupation at Meiron, Strata III and IV. It also concealed the only significant architectural remains at Meiron from the smaller village of Stratum II of the Early Roman period. Therefore, in both the 1974 and 1975 seasons, a major effort was made to trace as far as possible the outlines of this building complex, the extent of the earlier materials underlying it, and the various activities carried on within it. It is a testimony to the magnitude and importance of this structure that, after four seasons of work there, its full dimensions have not yet been recovered; further excavations at Meiron must include additional work in this field.

The first two seasons in MI uncovered the main entry and core of the building in Rooms A, B, C, and F and also began to follow the spread of the building towards the south (Rooms E and D) and east (Rooms F and H) and also in the area of the large, well-paved courtyard (labeled K, or Locus 3015). Subsequent excavation has concentrated upon three objectives: following the architecture towards the south in an attempt to determine the limits of the building; digging underneath the earliest floors of this building wherever possible in order to recover information about the Early Roman—if not also Late Hellenistic—occupation at Meiron; and continuing work on the east in front of the major entrance and in the areas of Rooms G and H in an effort to clarify the main approach to the building as well as the nature of the attached rooms at the southeast.

The first two objectives were clarified by the expansion of the work which was begun in the area designated MI.2 and which had provided the major stratigraphic evidence for Strata II-V at Meiron. This included excavations in Rooms D and E, with the southerly extension in Room E, beyond the main east-west balk being called MI.8, and the southerly extension of Room D, beyond Wall 7003, being called MI.7.

Evidence of a first building from Stratum II was recovered in several places. An east-west wall in MI.7 (Wall 7022) was founded on bedrock, and the pottery from its founding levels below a badly disturbed surface (Locus 7019) associated with it was consistently Early Roman with a fair measure of late Hellenistic pottery, including a Hasmonean lamp fragment as well as a coin from the 2nd century B.C.E. Directly on bedrock the pottery was Hellenistic, representing Stratum I.

Significant architectural remains, with two phases still extant, were recovered in Room E of MI.2 and testify to the founding of the first building in the 1st century C.E. Several courses of a small east-west wall (Wall 2028), 0.62 m. wide for an exposed length of 3.50 m., were found beneath the earliest floor level of the major (second) building. Two distinct usage phases associated with this wall are represented by a flagstone surface (Locus 2033) in the earlier phase and a plastered surface (Locus 2027) in its later phase. A small plastered pit (Locus 2032), perhaps analogous to the Stratum II pit (Locus 1013) uncovered in Room A, was in use with both phases; a tabun was built upon the floor of the

second phase. The pottery under the first surface is Early Roman and thus dates the early building in this area to the 1st century. The material between the surfaces contains some Middle Roman sherds, and thus indicates a 2nd century date for the subsequent phase.

The situation in Room D to the east is more difficult to interpret. An east-west wall (Wall 2040) by orientation alone seems to go with the Stratum II remains described above. Also, the fact that it was partially dismantled and then covered over by at least the beginning of Stratum IV, unlike any other wall of the Stratum III-IV building, points to its existence in Stratum II. However, the earliest surface associated with it and with the walls perpendicular to it (though not bonded with it), Walls 2006 and 2001, seals material down to bedrock which contains Middle Roman pottery and

Fig. 5. Room E of MI, featuring a circular stone platform and stone workbench, possibly for cooperage.

at least one 2nd century C.E. coin. Thus, assigning Wall 2040 to Stratum II would mean assuming that the terrain was cleared to bedrock of any Early Roman sherds. Clarification may come in future work down to bedrock in the adjoining part of Room E.

Further information about the possible usage of this building in at least part of its Stratum II-IV existence came from the excavation of Room E. A well-tamped red clay surface (Locus 2022 = Locus 8006) of Stratum III provided a floor for a workshop area, and featured a semicircular stone platform (Locus 8007) in the center of the room and a stone workbench (Locus 8005) along its eastern wall (fig. 5). The function of these installations is not entirely clear, though it is not impossible that this area served as a cooperage for the construction of barrels needed for Meiron's well-known olive industry. An assortment of metal fittings found in the debris, along with an iron and bronze plane (maasad, fig. 6), would tend to support such a possibility. A small oven in the northeast corner might have been connected with the manufacture of

barrels. A large stone with channels cut into it from each side, found in the courtyard area outside Room A, may have been used for the bending of wooden staves to prepare them for the construction of barrels. In any case, the make-up for the floor of this workshop room contained Middle Roman pottery. The coin range, while including a number of Alexander Janneus specimens, goes up to the early 3rd century. Here, as elsewhere in MI, a Middle Roman date early in the 3rd century seems best for the initiation of the major building activities.

Excavation to the east of the building at the access to the major doorway and in the two attached rooms (G and H) on the east revealed little of Stratum II. The exception was the appearance of some large worked stone fragments, remnants of some industrial activities (olive-pressing?) which were carried on during Stratum II. Detailed information about the phasing of Strata III and IV was obtained here in areas designated MI.5 and MI.6. The original street area in front of the main doorway (into Room A) consisted of flagstones in

Fig. 6. Bronze plane (of *maasad*) with iron handle found in Room E of MI.

Stratum III. These flagstones (Locus 5040) are preserved only a few meters to the east of the entrance. In the connecting passage southward to Room H, the flagstones give way to a cobbled surface, Locus 6034.

Immediately over these two surfaces was found another set of surfaces marking a second phase of the Stratum III building. In the MI.5 street area, Stratum IIIb is represented by cobbles 5033, sealing Middle Roman pottery and confirming an early 3rd century date for these resurfacings. In MI.6, the resurfacing took the form of simple tesselation (Locus 6028 and Locus 6023), forming a courtyard area with a tabun built against the MI building and its annex, Room G.

Major structural changes signalling the onset of Stratum IV were apparent in this area of excavation. Most noteworthy was the erection of Wall 6014, bisecting the tesselated surface and forming a small room (Room H) in the courtyard (fig. 7). The threshold of the main entryway was altered by the addition of another step, raising the level of the exterior street and resulting in another layer of cobbles (Locus 5032) and a curb (Locus 5031) used as a retaining wall at the northern edge of the street. A second phase of this stratum is marked chiefly by the accumulation of living debris on the surfaces throughout, although at one point in the street a poor re-cobbling was effected and beaten earth surfaces were established in Rooms G and H, particularly in connection with an upended store jar set into the ground in Room G at the spot where the tabun stood in the Stratum III courtyard. Even though this last phase is less impressive than previous ones, the general feeling remains that considerable care was taken, with flagstone, cobbled, and tesselated surfaces, to create an entrance into the building that would withstand heavy traffic approaching the well-made doorway to Room A, which no doubt constituted the chief access to the building complex.

Excavations south of the courtyard area Locus 3015 or K, to the west of the heart of the building, failed to provide any architectural remains of the early building but unexpectedly did reveal a series of cuttings or declivities in bedrock which seem to have preceded the construction of the main building, since a dirt surface of Strata III-IV completely covered them. However, the date of these cuttings cannot be established directly since large quantities of intentional fill containing Late Roman pottery were dumped into these cavities at the time of the construction of the Strata II-IV building, including

Courtyard K.

The nature of these cuttings is of interest. There are two large cavities in bedrock which are not joined but which are immediately adjacent to each other. One of them, known as C (for cavity)-5, is an underground chamber entered by descending a series of seven rock-cut stairs and then stepping through a well-cut stone doorway (fig. 8). The interior of the chamber is covered with plaster which is still in good condition, so that some connection with water use was immediately assumed, i.e., it was a *miqveh*. Consultation with rabbinic authorities who visited the site confirmed the opinion of the excavators.

Additional confirmation came from the excavation of the other declivity (more than 2.00 m. in diameter at its bottom) known as C-3. This cavity, cleared before the discovery of the *miqveh*, was at first thought to be a small cistern because of its bell shape and its seemingly narrow mouth. However, it contained very little debris and relatively few sherds–and no whole pottery–unlike other cisterns excavated at Meiron. It was found to have no distinct mouth; its eastern wall contained a small opening leading toward the east. This last feature in itself precluded the storage of water in this cavity. The discovery of the adjacent *miqveh* has led to the suggestion that C-3 played some role in the heating of the water in the *miqveh* itself, perhaps as a warming chamber in which fires were lit to heat the walls of the adjacent bathing chambers during the cold winter months in Upper Galilee. Since the declivity had been cleaned and filled with debris in Stratum IV, there were no traces of fires or ash preserved. Recent excavation at Herodian Jericho, however, has produced several examples of these heating chambers in which clear evidence of fires was preserved (communication from Ehud Netzer, the excavator).

These two cavities were covered by an earthen surface to the south of Courtyard K, but another cavity cut into bedrock was also found in this area, dating to the main period of occupation at MI, Strata III-IV. This cavity, C-6, is in fact a cistern and is treated below.

The courtyard itself was cleared completely during the 1974 and 1975 seasons and seems to have been in continuous use during both Strata III and IV. Originally, it appeared to be part of a street (Meyers, Meyers, and Strange 1974: 8), but the recovery of its full limits showed it to be a courtyard area measuring 7.00 m. x 5.00-5.30 m. It was at least partially roofed over, judging from a posthole at its

Fig. 7. Tesselated surface of Stratum III cut by Wall 6014 of Stratum IV, forming Room G on the eastern side of the main entrance to MI.

Fig. 8. Entrance to *miqveh* (C-5) at left and C-3 or warmer (?) at bottom left; note Stratum IV blockage with wall at top of picture.

southern end and a roughly-squared pedestal set into the floor at its northern end. A simple capital was found in the debris, but no pieces of column drums were in evidence. A small probe under the floor of the courtyard, carried out by the removal of several flagstones, produced some distinctive Early Roman wares, pointing again to a possible 2nd century date for the founding of the building.

Work in the 1974 and 1975 seasons bore out the information gained in the two earlier seasons about the history of the MI building subsequent to its Stratum IV occupation. Throughout MI the story is the same. The building was abandoned (around 360 C.E.) but did not disintegrate or collapse immediately or entirely at one time. Stragglers or squatters continued to inhabit odd corners of the building intermittently during the beginning of the Byzantine period. They made no structural changes

or additions but used whatever portions of the building were in sufficiently good repair. The pottery and coins which indicate their presence fall off sharply if not completely by the beginning of the 5th century.

Therefore the remains in Field I have produced important evidence for the Early Roman and perhaps, on the basis of coinage, at least, Late Hellenistic presence at Meiron. Excavation there has uncovered one of the largest and best-preserved structures of the Middle-Late Roman period in the whole country. Because of this, the Excavation Project went to considerable length—as much as its meager resources would permit—to consolidate the uncovered walls and installations. Further work at Meiron will again include excavation in this field and it is hoped that some restoration can be undertaken.

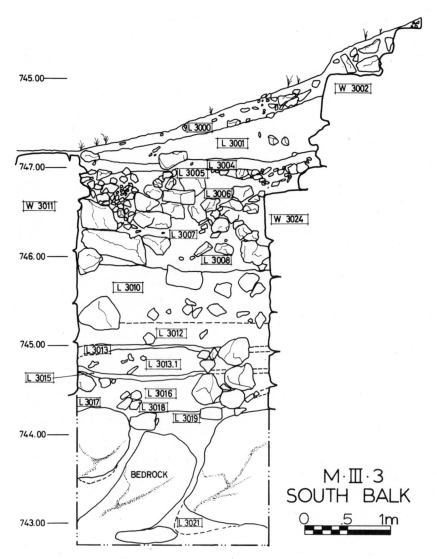

Fig. 9. South balk of MIII.3.

MIII. Soundings along the Eastern Wall of the Synagogue (figs. 9-11)

In the course of the 1974 and 1975 seasons a major effort was made to discover the total stratigraphic and architectural history of the area just east of the ancient synagogue. This part of the excavation was critical, since it was the only place left to dig; Kohl and Watzinger had cleaned the synagogue to bedrock. As a result of the work of these two seasons, the major outlines of the archeological history of this area have emerged, though it has not yet been possible to fill in the details. This history is best represented in two of the seven strata at Meiron.

Strata I, II, are III are not represented in any architectural remains, though sherds, coins, and other artifacts of these periods have been found in the soil on bedrock, beneath the major, later structures. For example, the pocket of *terra rosa* soil (Locus 3021) visible in the south balk at the bottom of MIII.3 (fig. 9) contained Early and Middle Roman pottery, but no coins.

From the evidence of the 1975 season it is now clear that the synagogue was built in Stratum IV, probably about the year 300 C.E. This is the first stratum to yield data for massive structures with pottery and coins in a clear, stratified context associated with the building of the synagogue. Previously the authors (Meyers, Meyers, and

Strange 1974: 10) had speculated that a trapezoidal building existed here. (In view of the revised chronology, caution is urged in consulting the work on C-1 at Meiron [Ritterspach 1974: 21].) During this stratum the synagogue was built along with a small building on the eastern terrace that has been designated "Annex A." This 4.90 m. x 6.00 m., two-storied structure was bonded to the eastern wall of the synagogue with Wall 1006 (fig. 10); Wall 1030 formed its northern extremity. These 50-80 cm. thick walls were built of hammer-dressed rough ashlars laid without mortar, as is true of the lower courses of the eastern wall of the synagogue.

The lower story of this structure had been packed with a series of soil and large stone fills to form a more-or-less solid mass. Great care was taken in excavation to separate the soil between the stones from that sealed underneath each boulder. The material sealed beneath the stones in question contained Middle and Late Roman pottery that occurs at this site not later than the end of the 3rd and beginning of the 4th century. This date was confirmed by the coins, which provide a *terminus a quo* of 276-282 C.E., the latest coin in the fill (Locus 1024) belonging to Probus.

Because of the thickness of the walls it is very likely that this structure had a second story. It is reasonable to suppose that the second story contained a single room, although none of the living floors survived in the extant remains because of later disturbances. Since there were no thresholds or doorjambs in the fill exterior to the synagogue and

Fig. 10. View of Annex A in MIII during excavation, looking west; note large rock fill in room and bonding of southwest corner.

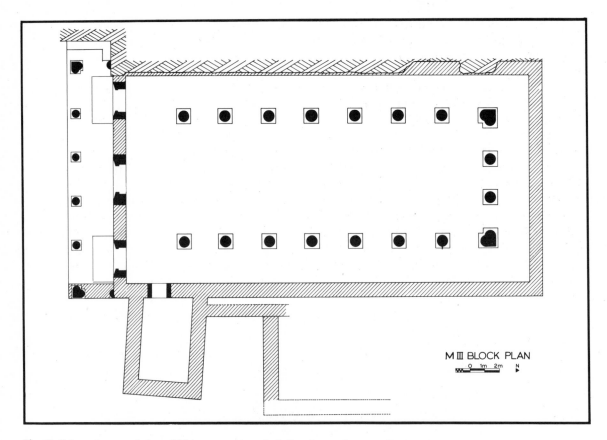

Fig. 11. Schematic ground plan of Meiron synagogue, including Annex A.

no sign of a stairway outside, it seems clear that the entrance was from inside the house of prayer itself.

It is possible that another such structure ("Annex B") will be recovered north of Annex A, since another wall (Locus 3032) extends east from the synagogue at least 4.20 m. This wall is parallel to Wall 1030, the north wall of Annex A, and is of the same character.

The final remains belonging to Stratum IV consist of a wall (Locus 3031) built up against and parallel to the eastern wall of the synagogue. The northern Wall 1030 of Annex A bonds or abuts this wall, as does the southern wall of the putative Annex B just mentioned. This north-south wall appears to strengthen the foundations of the east wall of the synagogue inasmuch as bedrock, which is found to the north and south of this point, is noticeably missing in this portion of the center of the synagogue wall. Wall 1031 is 0.50 m. wide and 4.60 m. long to the limit of the excavation at present, though it may prove to be longer in future seasons.

Stratum V is represented only in and upon bedrock between Walls 1030 and 3032. In other words, no architectural remains were found between Annex A and the possible Annex B. This suggests that this area was left open and collected water-washed and wind-blown material during the use and abandonment of the site. Likewise, Stratum VI is only represented high up in the fill of this room but so disturbed into the modern period that nothing can be said about it.

Stratum VI is the next period of major building in MIII. During this period, walls of Annex A were reused and new walls were built to form Late Arab structures of indeterminate function. Thus Wall 6003 to the south was used with Wall 1006 to the east to define the southern end of the terrace. A roughly square building was built jutting farther out into the terrace. This building was approximately 3.00 m. square without internal walls and therefore consisted of one room.

A single 0.60 m. wide wall extends north from the

middle of this square building to define the eastern limits of the terrace. This wall is pierced by a door almost 16 m. from the southeast corner of the terrace walls. The northern limit of this wall is unclear because of a modern (pre-1948) pill box that cuts the wall, but it probably cornered to the west just beyond the northeastern corner of the synagogue.

The Stratum VII occupation and architectural phases cannot be discerned completely because of modern robbing and other disturbances. The rich stratigraphic history of the single square room jutting out of the terrace is well illustrated, however, by the south balk of MIII.3 (fig. 9). Here one can see that the walls are founded on bedrock to an extant depth averaging 2.50 m. Loci 3005, 3006, 3007, and 3008 in particular seem to represent the last, abandonment phase of this complex of architecture in the late Arab period, while Locus 3010 and below to Locus 3019 represent the various uses of what is apparently a basement.

This square building does not appear to have an entrance to the south, east, or north; in all likelihood it opened onto the terrace to the west. The doorway in the western terrace wall probably opened directly onto a courtyard, where a well-paved floor was found in 1974, supporting this interpretation.

MIV. Western Medieval Tower

West of the ancient synagogue and the *wêli* built around the British triangulation point above is a roughly square tower made of somewhat irregular ashlars that average 0.40 x 0.50 m. on their faces. The tower measures 10 x 10 m. and appears to be made of stones cut for another structure, judging from the looseness of fit. A probe trench was cut against the western face of this small tower, since there was no convenient, undisturbed place within it to dig.

The probe uncovered a "floating" medieval east-west wall. That is, it did not bond or abut any other wall, and its entire length was contained within the probe. It was found to rest in and upon 13th-14th

Fig. 12. Reconstruction of Meiron synagogue, looking southwest; prepared by Richard H. Chandler.

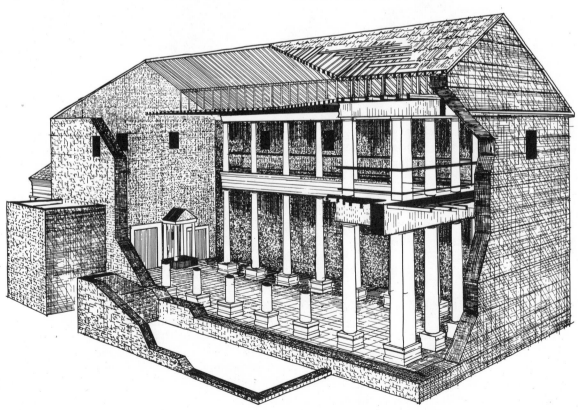

Fig. 13. Tower in MV with medieval superstructure, looking west.

century debris and therefore was part of the medieval village. Although its original function was not discernible, it seems likely that it was part of a house.

It was clear that the tower itself was founded directly upon bedrock and that the soil outside was 14th century to the bottom. While the original founding and use of the tower is not yet known, a medieval date is likely.

MV. The Tower (fig. 13-17)

Digging in the area known as the "tower" was determined by the fact that of all the standing ruins on the site, with the exception of the synagogue facade, this one was the most impressive. Commanding a spectacular view of the northern

and eastern accesses to the site, high on the middle terrace, the 6.00 m. high walls of the northeastern corner suggest a sort of defense installation or lookout. Since Josephus lists a Merō/Meroth as one of the villages fortified by him in 66 C.E. (*Life* 188; *War* 2:573), the excavation team naturally was led to speculate about a possible Early Roman date for the tower.

The field strategy adopted from the outset was to sink probes up against the tower from the outside or east (MV.1) and from within (MV.2, 3, 4, and 5). In 1974 a major effort was expended on the external probe in MV.1, where it soon became clear that the eastern wall (Locus 1002) had two distinct phases (fig. 14). Best preserved was the section above ground attributed by coins and pottery to Stratum VI, possibly even to the Ummayad period. In this section four courses of Stratum VI were preserved above ground, while the nine below the surface related to Stratum III. The later Stratum VI phase is composed mainly of field stones, but the lower courses of Stratum II origin are composed of hammer-dressed and much more carefully prepared stones. The ceramic and coin data in this trench are overwhelmingly Middle Roman down to the lowest level in which fragments of a flagstone floor (Locus 1013) were found just outside the eastern wall, perhaps a remnant of an ancient walkway outside the tower. The accumulation on this path, Locus 1010, points clearly to a *terminus a quo* of the 2nd-3rd century C.E. In the north balk Wall 1008 abuts the tower and there are indications that some outside structures were added in Stratum IV. In all, however, nothing in MV.1 permits us to move the date of construction back into the 1st century C.E.

This trench was extended westward and over Wall 1002. While the soil on bedrock produced Stratum II material, it did not connect with the lower courses or earlier phase of the tower. The soil connecting the wall (here noted as Wall 2002A) with bedrock, as well as most of the fill itself, contained sherds of Stratum III. A plastered pool here (Locus 2004 = 2007) indicated occupation within the tower proper. Nothing of Strata IV or V could be isolated in this area, but the rebuild of Wall 2002 was once again attributed to Stratum VI.

In another internal probe just to the north (MV.5) only the Stratum VI phase of the tower could be traced in the adjoining soil layers. The soil on bedrock several meters west of the tower wall, however, yielded predominantly late Hellenistic material including several sherds of Attic black ware and also some Persian and Iron II sherds. A fragment of a terrace wall in the south balk probably is to be dated to the end of Stratum I or the beginning of Stratum II. MV.3, another internal probe in the corner itself, was dug for just a short while in 1974. It was abandoned shortly after because it endangered the stability of the uppermost courses of fieldstone in the last phase of the use of the tower.

The second largest effort in MV was in MV.4, which was excavated in 1974 and 1975. In 1974 an "L-shaped" probe was sunk far to the south in the tower area, where the high debris was being retained by what we thought to be the southern demarcation wall. Thus we hoped that we could find the southeast corner of the tower here. The trench was only 1 m. wide, extending 3 m. east-west and 3 m. north-south. As it turned out, the area was much too small to provide any definitive stratigraphic information,

Fig. 14. View of MV.1 looking west, indicating two phases of tower wall; photograph by Sara Raymond.

except that the early Arab phase of the tower (Wall 4002) was not free-standing, an observation corroborated in MV.3, where shallow digging had jeopardized the stability of the northeast corner of the tower.

In 1975 a major effort was made in MV.4; the internal probe against the north-south tower wall was extended to a north-south length of 7.50 m. with a width of 2.25 m. The old east-west part of the L-shaped probe was also widened to a width of 2.25 m., forming a sort of "T." In the northern extension of the new area a large limestone kiln, Locus 4010 (fig. 17), belonging to Stratum VI was discovered. Approximately 60 coins were found in the fill which had accumulated inside the kiln, the majority of which date to the 11th-14th centuries C.E. Its diameter averages 2.50 to 2.70 m. at the top and it is preserved to a height of eight courses totalling 2.10 m. The kiln was not a free-standing structure but was sunk deep into pre-existing debris layers. It is assigned to Stratum VII on the basis of our sections (fig. 15); it is clear that the tower wall was contemporary with the kiln. Moreover, the uppermost debris layers into which and from which the kiln was sunk (Loci 4013, 4012) contained late Arabic material. The bottom floor of the kiln was thick cement just over bedrock, while the material sealed underneath the floor was Late Roman; the later context for the kiln is beyond doubt.

Excavation in the area south of the kiln also uncovered a series of walls. The cut here (fig. 16) showed clearly that the tower Wall 4002 indeed turns a right angle. The east-west wall is designated Wall 4025 and bonds to form a corner at the junction of Wall 4002. A piece of bedrock forms a sort of threshold separating the western extension of Wall 4025 from Wall 4007 where it intersects the western balk. Wall 4007 is founded on this jutting piece of bedrock at elevation 730.615 and is composed of five courses, the top two fieldstone, the

lower three hammer dressed. Wall 4025 is founded at elevation 729.335, due to the dipping of bedrock. Against the northern face of Wall 4025 a mortared pool was sunk, its eastern side being delimited by mortared Wall 4022. The mortared surface inside this pool was designated Locus 4031. This mortar was identical to that found in MV.2, Locus 2004. Middle Roman pottery was found under both surfaces and supports a Stratum III dating for the tower which, according to the evidence, was in use as a living area during this period. Further work needs to be done in the southeast and southwest corners of MV.4 where so many substantial walls intersect. The problem of dating them arises from the fact that the soil loci around them are very restricted and were disturbed by the medieval renovations.

Whether this tower ever served any defensive function is still a matter of doubt. Insofar as the settlement itself is otherwise unwalled, it is unlikely that MV would have served as the only defense station. Rather, it appears that the huge structure was erected as a central lookout at the point where most traffic coming through Meiron would have converged.

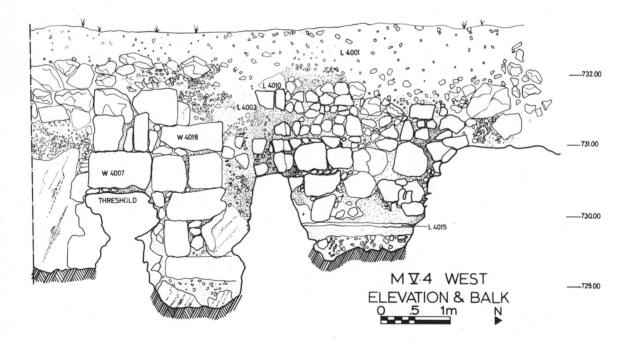

Fig. 15. West elevation and balk drawing of MV.4.

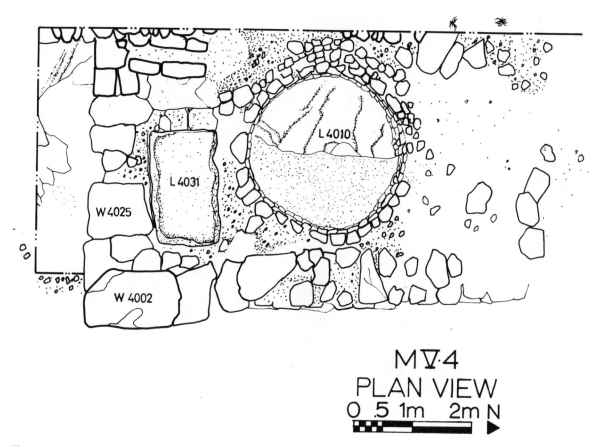

Fig. 16. Plan view of MV.4, including kiln 4010.

MVI. The Field House (fig. 18)

An area to the west of Meiron I and at about the same point on the lower slopes of the Meiron hill was selected for excavation in the 1975 season (fig. 18). Walls protruding above the surface gave the impression of a tower, smaller than but similar to the tower in MV. An L-shaped trench was laid out in the most obvious corner of this structure so that information about the two large walls (Loci 1003, 1002) forming this corner could be retrieved. Excavation to bedrock in the trench against the north-south Wall 1003 produced no evidence to substantiate a tower hypothesis. Rather, the two cornering walls were joined by two smaller walls (Loci 1005, 1009), 0.70-0.75 m. in width, forming a single small room with a poor beaten-earth floor and an entry on the west, in Wall 1005. The pottery throughout was predominantly Late Roman and suggested that the building was in use only during Stratum IV. The coins found under the only surface were no later than the 3rd century.

The northern and western walls proved to be terrace walls rather than free-standing walls. When the other two walls were added, they formed a small, shed-like structure, perhaps used as an occasional shelter when agricultural work on this terrace was in progress. The presence of household pottery as well as fragments of grinding stones also suggest that this area served some domestic function.

T-1. Tomb (fig. 19)

During the course of the 1974 season one tomb, designated T-1, was opened to study burial practices at the site, gather further information about the occupational history of ancient Meiron, and gain skeletal evidence about ancient inhabitants (Meyers and Strange: 1974). This tomb was located by surface exploration within the ancient necropolis which extends to the northeast, west, south, and southwest of Meiron.

This tomb proved to be a three-chambered

Fig. 17. Medieval kiln 4010, looking south; meter stick rests on surface 4015.

natural cave (fig. 19) enlarged and used by its owners almost wholly for secondary burial. One chamber to the southeast had suffered total roof collapse in the past and therefore was not excavated. The eastern chamber (T-1.4) was rather irregular but measured 3.00 x 4.50 m. with one niche or *kokh* (*kokh* 1) measuring 0.65 x 2.00 m. and another (6) only 0.50 x 0.35 m. The second chamber (T-1.5), on the other hand, measured 2.90 x 3.60 m. with six niches of varying dimensions: the largest (2) measuring 0.70 x 2.00 m. and the smallest 0.55 x 0.35 m. Our entrance had been cut into *kokh* 2 of the western chamber outside and above this *kokh*, which led us to discover the tomb.

Excavation inside this tomb-cave was rewarding in terms of the materials recovered, which have proved important for understanding ancient Meiron and its inhabitants. For example, we noted that the burials were almost all secondary, a fact which suggests that this burial custom was the norm. The bones were gathered in small heaps on the floors of the two chambers or placed together in small repositories carved out of the bottom of the largest niches.

Noteworthy in this regard is the fact that in the western chamber (T-1.5) in *kokh* 2 the bones of six adults and three children were found. Gathered together on the floor in the main chamber were the remains of about twelve adults and several children. In a repository in the front of *kokh* 5 were packed the bones of perhaps four adults, while *kokh* 3 contained the bones of one old person and a child. (See the report on the skeletal remains, which follows.)

Likewise, in the eastern chamber (T-1.4) the bones of about five adults and several children were found on the southern ledge. Perhaps the most interesting burial spot was *kokh* 1 in that chamber, partially closed by a wall 0.80 m. high, 0.84 m. wide, and 0.15-0.20 m. thick, made of stones and plaster. The wall was founded in part upon the floor debris of that *kokh*, which included two large adult vertebrae directly under the wall. The *kokh* contained scattered, small bones; but in the back, in a small ossuary repository, the bones of two adults were laid side by side, with the skulls in the middle. It is possible that the low wall kept the bones

gathered in the chamber from coming in contact with those within the *kokh*.

An interesting corpus of burial goods has been recovered from this tomb-cave, including several items rare or unique in tombs. In the eastern chamber (T-1.4), for instance, a fine glass juglet about 5 cm. high was recovered; it was discovered on the south ledge among the burials. In the middle of the chamber near the floor were found a small copper dipper, a stone spindle whorl, and a fine, decorated, molded glass bowl characteristic of the

Fig. 18. Top plan of MVI.1, showing field house in right corner.

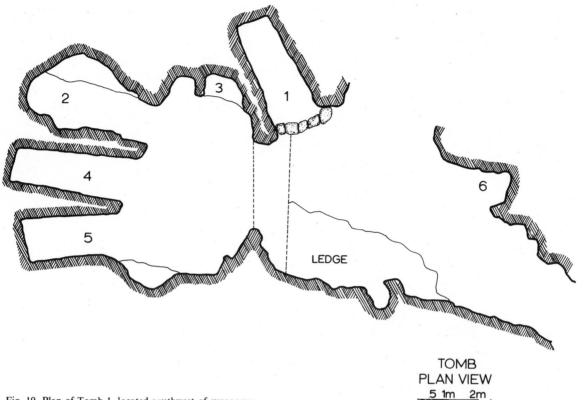

Fig. 19. Plan of Tomb-1, located southwest of synagogue.

late Hellenistic and Herodian periods.

On the other hand, in the western chamber (T-1.5), in *kokhim* 4 and 5, large iron nails came to light, perhaps implying that wooden ossuaries were originally placed there, since the *kokhim* were too short for coffins. Finally, we note that in the bone repository in the bottom of *kokh* 2 (where the bones of the six adults and three children were found) in and among the bones, a 3rd century glass flask, a bronze spoon, a stone spindle whorl, and a ceramic ink well that has parallels at Qumran were discovered.

The morphology of the tomb suggests that its original entrance was from the now collapsed southeast chamber. In other words, the entrance into *kokh* 2 of the western chamber was due to other circumstances. Perhaps, later citizens of Meiron tried to cut a new tomb and accidentally cut into this niche, since it is unlikely that entrance would require walking over earlier burials.

C-2 and C-6. Cisterns (figs. 20-22)

Two cisterns, both associated with occupation in the lower city, were excavated in the 1974 and 1975

seasons at Meiron. A cistern designated C-2, located about 50 m. southeast of the MI building complex, was dug in the 1974 season. The cistern was bisected on a north-south axis and excavation proceeded on the eastern side. The cistern is a bell-shaped cavity measuring 2.48 m. in diameter at the bottom. It is 4.55 m. deep, and a square capstone (0.76 x 0.80 x 0.28 m. high) with a circular opening (0.30 m. in diameter) covered its mouth. The somewhat irregular walls are covered with a thick plaster imbedded with sherds.

Several loci could be distinguished in the course of excavation. The top fill contained modern debris. Then a thick (0.90 m.) deposit of washed-in occupational debris containing Late Roman to Byzantine pottery was excavated. At some point in the Late Roman period a large section of plaster from the upper walls collapsed. The material sealed below this fallen plaster, going down 1.30 m. to the floor of the cistern, was very silty and contained a large quantity of Middle and Late Roman sherds, including several whole and nearly whole cooking pots of the Late Roman period (fig. 21). The cistern thus appears to be contemporary with the main MI building complex in its origin. The few Byzantine

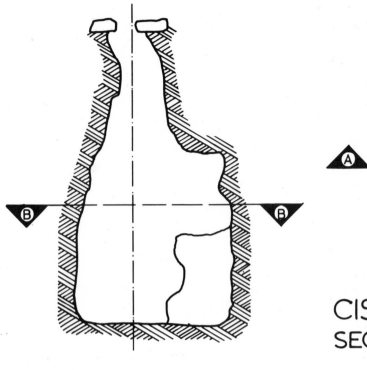

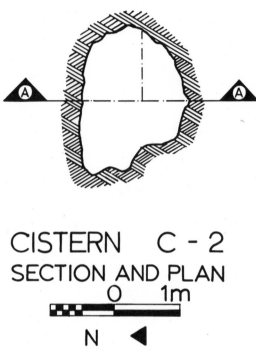

CISTERN C - 2
SECTION AND PLAN
0   1m

N ◀

Fig. 20. Plan of cistern (C-2) located south of MI.

sherds may attest to a limited continuing usage during the period of abandonment.

The designation C-6 was given to a cistern found within the limits of the MI building south of the courtyard K area. It is about a meter south of Piers 3033 and 3025 and west of Wall 3006. The capstone is square (0.76 x 0.70 x 0.40 m. high) with a round opening (0.30 m. in diameter); there are grooves worn into the sides of the opening by the friction of ropes used to lower and raise vessels. The cistern itself is a bell-shaped cavity, with the neck being built up with rocks to a height of about 0.60 m. above bedrock. Total depth of the cistern is 7.75 m., while the diameter at the bottom is 5.05 m. The walls are coated with a thick layer of plaster.

The debris at the bottom of this cistern was bisected on a north-south axis, and the material to the west was excavated. Once the bottom was reached, the rest of the debris directly below the mouth was removed. Unlike C-2, this cistern contained a fairly homogeneous soil locus from immediately below the surface debris to the bottom. The opening to the cistern had been buried in antiquity and had not, in contrast to C-2, remained open to the skies until the present day. The pottery

throughout was predominantly Late Roman, although there was also a considerable amount of Early Byzantine wares, providing evidence that the cistern continued to be used during the early abandonment period. There were also many whole or nearly whole vessels, including several lamps, buried in the accumulated debris.

M *Beth*. The Northern Suburb (fig. 1)

Excavations in the northernmost extremity of ancient Meiron were begun in 1975 at the request of the Israel Department of Antiquities because further expansion of Moshav Meiron was endangering what had hitherto been considered another and separate ruin at Meiron. The rockfall in this sector was awesome and a tremendous effort was required for brush-clearing and rock removal. As soon as it became apparent that the latest ceramic material belonged to Stratum IV, the entire area was added to the site survey plan (fig. 1).

Three areas were established in M *Beth*: MBI.1, 2, and 3. In Areas 1 and 3 an excellent cobbled pavement which had been laid over bedrock was cleared. Digging here provided evidence of an

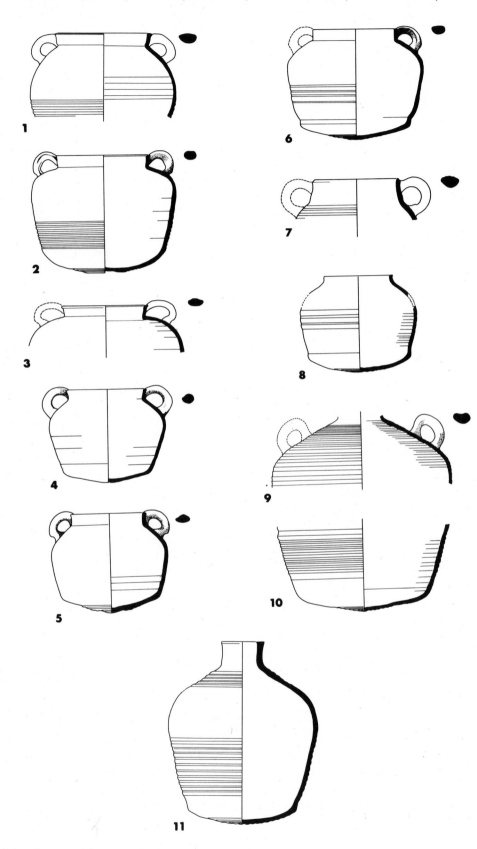

Fig. 21. Selected pottery of Stratum IV from C-2.

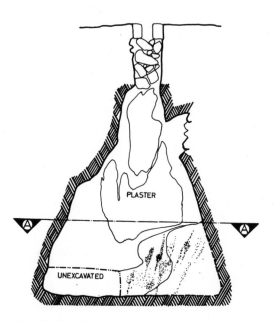

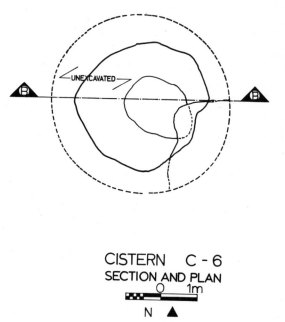

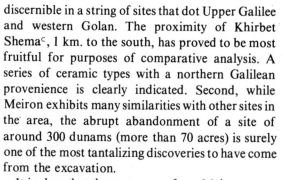

CISTERN   C - 6
SECTION AND PLAN

Fig. 22. Plan of cistern (C-6) in MI; cf. fig. 2.

access route from the east into a possible storeroom area. A tabun uncovered on the pavement, however, suggests some domestic occupation. Areas 1 and 3 comprise the southernmost area of exposure. To the north, in MBI.3, a large room was partially excavated. The surface inside this room was also a sort of cobble floor with an abundance of crushed pottery clearly destroyed by roof collapse. One doorway in the southeast corner was revealed and another one along the western wall was articulated.

Nothing uncovered in this northern sector dates to later than our Stratum IV material. Because of the terracing which surely is ancient, the structures in this vicinity made use of the natural contours. Several weeks of work, however, led to the conclusion that the area was part of the ancient Jewish village and that it probably served as storage for produce and as a secondary entrance to the settlement itself.

Conclusions

Along with the exciting artifactual and architectural remains which have come to light in the course of excavation, several important historical inferences can be drawn from the data. First, the village belongs to a cultural continuum discernible in a string of sites that dot Upper Galilee and western Golan. The proximity of Khirbet Shema^c, 1 km. to the south, has proved to be most fruitful for purposes of comparative analysis. A series of ceramic types with a northern Galilean provenience is clearly indicated. Second, while Meiron exhibits many similarities with other sites in the area, the abrupt abandonment of a site of around 300 dunams (more than 70 acres) is surely one of the most tantalizing discoveries to have come from the excavation.

It is clear that the move away from Meiron was a considered one. The rooms of the building complex of MI in the lower city were virtually stripped bare of their supplies and only a few objects were found here and there. The deterioration of the structures occurred over a long period of time and there is no evidence that the city was destroyed by invasion or earthquake. The entire population, under severe stress to meet the tax burdens, probably left during the reign of Constantius II, taking as much of their provisions with them as possible. Since taxes were in the main paid in provisions, the move would have occurred just before the collection. Some of the inhabitants may have gone to Khirbet Shema^c, where the population lingered on somewhat longer. Their tax burden may have been lower proportionately as well as actually because the population was much smaller. Others may have gone to nearby villages such as Gush Ḥalav, and still others may have gone to the Golan Heights.

The disappearance of Meiron as a major Jewish settlement of the 4th century C. E. is a poignant reminder of the very tenuous and troubled status of Judaism in the early Byzantine period. Further archeological work will be required to understand the dispersion of Jewry in Upper Galilee at the very same time that the Palestinian Talmud was compiled.

BIBLIOGRAPHY

Amiran, D. H. K.
  1950-51 A Revised Earthquake-Catalogue of Palestine I. *Israel Exploration Journal* 1: 107-20.
  1952   A Revised Earthquake-Catalogue of Palestine II. *Israel Exploration Journal* 2: 48-65.

Hanson, R. S.
  1974   Toward a Chronology of the Hasmonean Coins. *Bulletin of the American Schools of Oriental Research* 216: 21-23.

Lieberman, S.
  1945-46 Palestine in the Third and Fourth Centuries. *Jewish Quarterly Review* 36: 329-70.
  1947   Palestine in the Third and Fourth Centuries. *Jewish Quarterly Review* 37: 31-54.

Meyers, C. L.; Meyers, E. M.; and Strange, J. F.
  1974   Excavations at Meiron in Upper Galilee—1971, 1972: A Preliminary Report. *Bulletin of the American Schools of Oriental Research* 214: 2-25.

Meyers, E. M., and Strange, J. F.
  1974   Notes and News: Meiron. *Israel Exploration Journal* 24: 281, pls. 61:B, C, D.

Ritterspach, A. D.
  1974   The Meiron Cistern Pottery. *Bulletin of the American Schools of Oriental Research* 215: 19-29.

Meiron Coins: 1974–75

Richard Simon Hanson

Luther College, Decatur, IA 52101

A report of the coins is premature at this point for two reasons: (1) there are a few rare coins that we have been unable to locate in the published literature as of the present, and (2) our Islamic expert, Michael Bates of the American Numismatic Society, has not had the opportunity to study our 1975 Islamic coins at this early date [1 November 1975]. With these two omissions of bibliography and information, we beg the indulgence of the reader and present our preliminary report of the numismatic evidence, following the numerical order of excavation areas.

Meiron I.2, 3, 4, 5, 6, 7, 8

Coin type	Date (by century)	Quantity
Tyrian (Ptolemaic era?)	3rd-2nd B.C.E.	1
Seleucid	2nd B.C.E.	10
Tyrian	2nd-1st B.C.E.	2
Hasmonean	1st B.C.E.	35
Tyrian	1st B.C.E.-1st C.E.	1
Jewish	1st C.E.	3
Tyrian	1st-2nd C.E.	8
Roman Provincial and Imperial	1st-2nd C.E.	9-11
Roman Colonial: Tyre	3rd C.E.	11
Roman Colonial: Petra	3rd C.E.	1
Roman Colonial: Antioch	3rd C.E.	1
Roman Colonial: Ptolemais-Acre	3rd C.E.	1
Roman Imperial	3rd C.E.	6
Roman Imperial	early-mid 4th C.E.	28
Roman Imperial	late 4th C.E.	4
Islamic		2
Unidentifiable		7

The data for this season are similar to those for the earlier seasons at Meiron (Hanson 1974: 22-23), with one exception: the absence of anything so early as the Sidonian coin of the Persian era. It is noteworthy that the coin supply shows no break from the 2nd century B.C.E. coins minted by the Seleucid rulers through the Roman Imperial coins of the 4th century C.E. A significantly higher percentage of 4th century Roman coins was discovered at MI.8—eight out of a total of eighteen specimens—and six of these were found in Locus 8001. We have tried in various ways to account for the relatively high frequency of Hasmonean and 4th century Roman coins in the past, suggesting a greater supply of coins during those periods and/or a greater concentration of population. At this time a third possibility has been suggested to us through an article by R. Reece (1975) which demonstrates the high frequency of coin drops during periods of devaluation. He states (Reece 1975: 303) that "In the fourth century the coinage was changed often and swiftly. For this reason coin loss, and therefore coin supply, may be a much better guide to coin use, with each issue dropping quickly out of circulation." The fact that Hasmonean coins lost value after the Roman conquest may have resulted in larger numbers than usual being lost carelessly or simply discarded. Similarly, the devaluation of Roman coins that occurred in the 3rd century was not corrected by the Diocletian reforms. From that time on the populace knew that Roman coppers were worth little. It may be that with every new issue of coins the previous issues lost value and persons became careless about retaining them. (For a complete review of the types, see Carson, Hill, and Kent: 1960.)

R75475	Ae	Obv:	bust of Tyche facing right.	Tyrian, 114/5 C.E.
MBI.3	16mm			Hill (1910)
L3006	2.33g	Rev:	palm tree with inscription around ΜΗΤΡΟΠΟΛΕΩΣΙΕΡΑΣ; date in field: ΛΣ.	pl. 32: 2, 3

R74049	Ae	Obv:	laureate bust (of Germanicus?) facing right; inscription around: ΓΕΡΜΑ . . . . ΑΥΤΚΑΙC.	Roman, 19 C.E.
MI.4	17mm			
L4024	4.26g	Rev:	Victory advancing to right with shield before; inscription around: ΚΑ	

R75313	Ar	Obv:	laureate bust of Nero facing right; inscription around: ΝΕΡΩΝΚΑΙΣΑΡΣΕΒΑΣΤΟΣ.	Roman provincial 64 C.E.
MVI.1	24mm			
L1013	14.58g	Rev:	eagle facing right with thunderbolts in claws, palm branch at right, circle of dots around; at left, date: [ΗΚ] Ρ.Ι.	

R75258	Ae	Obv:	laureate bust of Nero facing right (note the Oriental character of the portrait!); inscription around: ΝΕΡΟΝΚΑΙ CΑΡ.	Roman provincial 67 C.E., minted in Gadara
MVI.1	23mm			
L1010	12.25g	Rev:	Ceres standing to left with wreath in right hand; inscription around: ΓΑΔΑΡΑ; date in the left field: LΑΛΡ.	

R75259	Ae	Obv:	bust of Antoninus Pius facing right; inscription around: ΑΥΤΚΑΙCΜΑΥΡΑΝΤΩΝΕΙΝΟC.	Roman provincial, 138-161 C.E., minted in Antioch(?)
MVI.1	24mm			
L1010	9.39g	Rev:	Tyche on horse moving left; inscription around: ΒΑCΥΛΟΥΑΝΤ . . . ΤΩΠΡΙΠΤ	

R75418	Ae	Obv:	laureate bust of Marcus Aurelius(?) facing right; inscription around: ΑΥΤΚΑΙC . . . ΑΥΡΑΝΤΩΝ.	Roman provincial, 161-80 C.E.(?), minted in Antioch(?)
MI.3	27mm			
L3031	10.13g	Rev:	Tyche on horse moving left, palm branch in left hand; inscription around: ΑΝΤ[ΙΟ]ΧΠΡΙΠΙCΡΑCΥΛΟC.	

R75345	Ae	Obv:	laureate bust of one who appears to be Commodus, facing right; inscription around: ΚΑΙCΑΡ ΛΑΥΡΟΥ.	Roman provincial, 170-92 C.E.(?), minted in Antioch(?)
MI.8	23mm			
L8004	8.17g	Rev:	goddess (Pax or Tyche) standing on pedestal with cornucopia in left arm; inscription around: ΑΝΤΠΡΙΠΙCΡΑCΥΛ.	

R75212	Ae	Obv:	bust of Septimus Severus (possibly Antoninus Pius) facing right; inscription around: . . . . . . ΑVGIMP.	Roman, 193-211 C.E. (or 138-161); the reverse type is found in Mattingly 1940: pl. 1: 7; Mattingly and Sydenham 1930: pl. 1: 3.
MI.6	16mm			
L6020.1	2.52g	Rev:	Aeguitas draped, standing left with scales in right hand, cornucopia in left; the inscription is worn away.	

ᏃᏋᎀᏮᎮ

R75475   R74049

R75313   R75258

R75259   R75418

R75345   R75212

Meiron III.1, 3

In our report on the 1971-72 seasons of work at MIII we were able to tabulate the following data (Hanson 1974: 24-25):

Coin type	Date	Quantity
Hasmonean	1st B.C.E.	1
Jewish	1st C.E.	1
Roman Imperial	1st C.E.	1
Tyrian	1st-2nd C.E.	2
Roman Colonial: Tyre	early 3rd C.E.	1
Roman Imperial	4th C.E.	4
Islamic (Mamlūk)	14th C.E.	7
European (Charles, Duke of Calabria)	1545-1608 C.E.	1

We now add to that group the following, from the 1974-75 seasons:

Hasmonean, Jewish	1st B.C.E.	2
Jewish	1st C.E.	1
Tyrian	1st-3rd C.E.	1
Roman Provincial and Imperial	3rd C.E.	3
Roman Imperial	early-mid 4th C.E.	19
Roman Imperial	late 4th C.E.	3
Byzantine	6th C.E.	1
Islamic		13

In the discussion above regarding soundings along the eastern wall of the synagogue we were able to point out that Strata I-III of Meiron are represented at MIII only by small artifacts and that the earliest architectural remains are from Stratum IV, which we date to the period 250-360 C.E. Only our 3rd-4th century Roman Imperial coins represent this period. Extraneous to it and falling into the period of Stratum V (360-750 C.E.) are three Roman Imperial coins of the period 393-95, one of which was found in 1972 at Locus 3004, the others in 1975 at Locus 3034. The single Byzantine coin was found in 1974 at Locus 8002.

Meiron IV

A limited amount of work was done at MIV in the 1974 season and in that probe we found four coins: (1) a Tyrian specimen quite likely of the 1st century C.E., unusual in that it has a Melqart bust on the obverse and spreading palm tree with ΙΕΡΑΣ beneath on the reverse, (2) a badly worn Tyrian coin with a Tyche bust on the obverse that probably dates from the 1st-2nd century C.E., and (3) two 4th century Roman coins, one of which is late.

Meiron V.1, 2, 4, 5

At MV we found a large number of Islamic coins, notably in Areas 4 and 5. The bulk of these appear to be Mamlūk. Complete tabulation of the evidence is as follows:

Coin type	Date	Quantity
Seleucid	2nd B.C.E.	5
Hasmonean	1st B.C.E.	20
Jewish	1st B.C.E.-1st C.E.	1
Roman Imperial	1st-2nd C.E.	1
Roman Colonial: Tyre	3rd C.E.	2
Roman Imperial	early-mid 4th C.E.	14
Roman Imperial	late 4th C.E.	7
Islamic (largely Mamlūk)		27
Unidentifiable		5

The pattern of distribution found here is typical for our area. We became accustomed to it in our excavations at the Khirbet Shemaᶜ site. The large quantity of Hasmonean and 4th century Roman coins suggests the interpretations noted above. Further work with the Islamic coins will redefine the picture somewhat.

Meiron VI

The material found at MVI is quite exciting from a numismatic point of view. For one thing, it seems to be the truest representation we have of the actual density of our early continuous phase of occupation

(88 B.C.E.-360 C.E.). In addition to that, it has provided us with some fine and intriguing coin specimens. Tabulated, the evidence is as follows:

Coin type	Date	Quantity
Seleucid	2nd B.C.E.	4
Hasmonean	1st B.C.E.	10
Jewish	1st C.E.	7
Tyrian (Tyche-galley)	1st C.E.	2
Tyrian (Melqart)	1st-2nd C.E.	2
Roman Provincial (Nero)	1st C.E.	2
Roman Provincial	2nd C.E.	1
Roman Colonial	3rd C.E.	3
Roman Imperial	3rd C.E.	3
Roman Imperial	early-mid 4th C.E.	7
Roman Imperial	late 4th C.E.	2
Unidentifiable		1

While there are no coins later than the 4th century, two specimens are very late in that century. The site appears to have been inhabited continuously through the entire period covered by the coins. This information raises doubts about the proposed 360 C.E. date for the abandonment of Meiron. [But note above the excavators' interpretation of the coin data, pp. 74 and 76.]

Meiron *Beth* I.2, 3

Two small probes at M *Beth* turned up a small number of coins. At MBI.2 we found a Tyrian coin (Melqart obverse, war club reverse) of the 2nd century C.E., an unclear Roman coin of the 2nd-3rd century C.E., a Roman Colonial coin (Tyre) of Elagabalus (218-22 C.E.), and an Antonianus of Probus (276-82 C.E.). At MBI.3 we found one coin in rather good condition: a Tyrian coin (Tyche obverse, palm tree reverse) of the mint year 114/5 C.E.

A number of uncommon coins turned up in the 1975 season. Some of these may be very rare, though further study is required to verify the conclusion. Just as important for our records is the fact that several of our most typical coins are now represented by good to excellent specimens. While time and space do not permit a comprehensive presentation here, a representative selection is offered (fig. 1).

BIBLIOGRAPHY

Carson, R. A. G.; Hill, P. V.; and Kent, J. P. C.
    1960 *Late Roman Bronze Coinage: A.D. 324-498.* London: Spink.
Hanson, R. S.
    1974 Preliminary Coin Report. Pp. 22-25 in Excavations at Meiron in Upper Galilee — 1971, 1972: A Preliminary Report, by C. L. Meyers, E. M. Meyers, and J. F. Strange. *Bulletin of the American Schools of Oriental Research* 214: 2-25.
Hill, G. F.
    1910 *Catalogue of the Greek Coins of Phoenicia.* Catalogue of Coins in the British Museum, Vol. 26. London: British Museum.

Mattingly, H.
    1940 *Coins of the Roman Empire in the British Museum IV: Antoninus Pius to Commodus.* London: British Museum.
Mattingly, H., and Sydenham, E. A.
    1930 *Roman Imperial Coinage III: Antoninus Pius to Commodus.* London: Spink.
Reece, R.
    1975 Roman Currency: New Thoughts and Problems. *World Archaeology* 6: 299-306.

Preliminary Report on the Human Skeletal Remains from Tomb 1

Patricia Smith

Hebrew University Hadassah Medical and Dental Schools, Jerusalem, Israel

with the assistance of

Elizabeth C. Bornemann and Joseph Zias

The skeletal remains recovered from Tomb 1 were somewhat friable, but otherwise well preserved. From the pile of disarticulated bones that were found no positive identification of individuals could be made, with one exception to be described later.

On sorting the skulls it became apparent that many parts were missing; thus, less than 100 skulls or cranial fragments were identified, while over 300 femura from 196 individuals were present. Secondary burials are often incomplete as a result of a careless or hasty collection of the bones, but the skull is nearly always present, even though some postcranial parts may be missing. The situation in Tomb 1 is therefore somewhat unusual. The age and sex distribution based on the femur as the bone best preserved is shown in tables 1 and 2. The high infant mortality together with a second mortality peak around forty and few surviving to old age is typical for primitive communities of the period (Brothwell: 1965).

Comparisons with the measurements of Second Temple populations from Jerusalem and En-gedi (Arensburg: 1973) suggest that the population at Meiron was generally shorter faced, with broader noses. The mandibles also were shorter, in keeping with the total facial structure. The inhabitants of Meiron were similar to the two contemporary populations mentioned in that they too were generally mesocranic or brachyocranic. However, they seem to differ from the individuals found in the contemporary tomb from Givᶜat ha-Mivtar, who were dolichocranic (Haas: 1970).

Also among the remains found at Meiron were two individuals whose bones were of much greater size than the others. One was represented by the bones found in Locus 4004: left scapula, ulna, right pelvis, right femur, proximal end of right tibia, and the two fibulae. The other, larger than the first, was represented by a right pelvis, left humerus (4005-6) and left tibia (1003-2) (figs. 1-4). They were both approximately 10 cm. taller than any of the other individuals at Meiron or in the contemporary populations.

Pathology

Fifteen individuals, represented at least by the vault, and twenty-one others, represented by fragments of the skull, were examined for pathological disorders and structural anomalies. Only one skull showed evidence of traumatic injury.

One male, aged 50 + (5004), showed asymmetric development of the occipital bone, with overlapping of the lamboid suture, and chronic lesions of the skull. One female skull showed asymmetry of the foramen magnum region with a reduced left hypoglossal canal. In a second skull, also female, the left hypoglossal canal was completely missing.

Two individuals showed a pronounced thickening of the cranial vault. One male was represented by the vault of the skull and frontal bone including the orbital region. The brow ridges were very prominent, and although the bone was thick, it appeared normal on the roentgen film. This individual may be associated with one of the "giants" described earlier.

The second individual, represented by two cranial

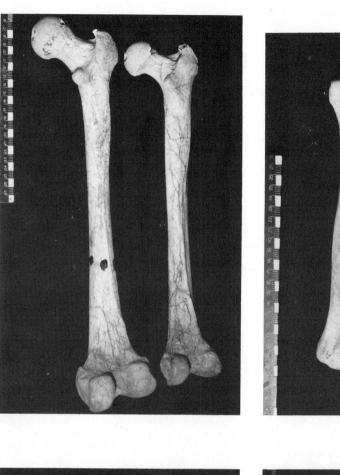

Fig. 2. Femur of one "giant," 4004 (top); normal femur, 1003-28 (bottom).

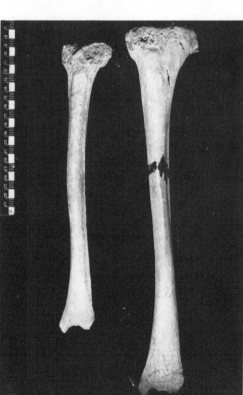

Fig. 4. Humerus of one "giant," 4005-6 (bottom); normal humerus, M8 (top).

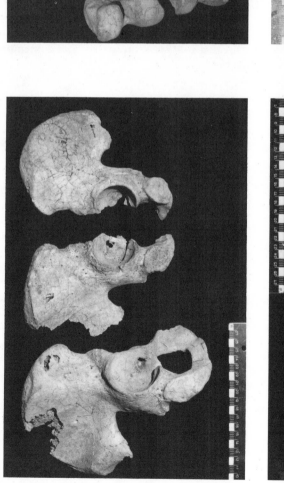

Fig. 1. Pelvises of "giants," M1 (left), 4004 (middle); normal pelvis, 4005-44 (right).

Fig. 3. Tibia of one "giant," 1003-2 (bottom); normal tibia, M7 (top).

Table 1.   Skeleton Count

LOCUS   AGE IN YEARS

Kokh	0-1	2-5	6-12	13-18			19-25			26-39			40+			Adult Age
	?	?	?	M	F	?	M	F	?	M	F	?	M	F	?	?
I	1	2		1										1		1
II	1	1	1		1								1			2
III		1	1						1				1			
IV	3		1		1										1	
V	1	1	2		1				1				1	2		
VI	3	3			1								2	2		
1003 & 2003	4	7	2		1		1	1		5	4	8	3	2	1	
4001	1	1			1					1		1				
4002	2	1										2				
4004										1						
4005	1	2	1							1	1	3	1	1	1	
4006	4	2	3								2	2				
4007	3	1										2				
4009	1	2	1									2				
4011	3	2						2	2	3	2	2				
4012	5	2	1								1	3				
5005		6	1		2				1			11			4	3
No number	2	1			2					1	3	2				
Subtotal				1	10		1	3	5	12	13	38	9	8	7	
Total	35	38	14	11			9			63			24			6

Table 2.   Mortality

	0-1	2-5	6-12	13-18	19-25	26-39	40+	Adult?
Total %	17.7	17.7	7.1	5.5	8.91	32.3	12.2	3.0
Male %	—	—	—	—	11.1	17.4	37.5	—
Female %	—	—	—	—	33.3	22.2	33.3	—

Total: Adult = 107; Sub-adult = 95.

fragments, also showed thickening of the bone, especially of the orbits, and excessive overgrowth of the superior nuchal crest.

Arthritis was found in all the vertebrae, but especially in the cervical region. The degree of arthritis varied from the early stages of lipping to very severe with fusion between the vertebral bodies. The most severe forms were found in the lumbar and cervical vertebrae.

The arthritis in the long bones was not very severe in most cases. Generally, it was represented by some lipping and in a few cases was accompanied by osteophytes. One ulna (1003-54) showed very severe arthritis proximally, possibly caused by a reaction to a distal fracture. The upper limb was affected as well as the scapula and clavicle. The fibula was the only lower limb to be affected. However, the pelvic girdle also showed arthritic changes, primarily around the auricular surface of the pelvis and the articular surfaces of the sacrum. Apart from one fractured metatarsal, arthritis was the only lesion evident in the hand and foot bones.

Anomalies of the vertebral column, aside from arthritis, included: incomplete arch formation in 1:29 atlases; double arch formation in 2:20 atlases; bifid spine in 28:82 of the cervical vertebrae; divided right foramen in 4:85 (4.7%) of the cervical vertebrae; divided left foramen in 2:85 (2.3%); both foramina divided in 5:85 (5.8%). Congenital fusion of two cervical vertebrae was also found. In the thoracic region, 35 vertebrae were deformed to the right; the dorsal spine was commonly deflected. Five of the sixteen sterna were thickened, presumably as a result of blood dyscrasias. Other signs of pathology were few. There were four bones with healed fractures: a metatarsal, a clavicle, a fibula, and an ulna. In one instance (the ulna) the absence of malposition of the fractured parts indicates that skilled fixation was applied.

Four of the thirteen intact sacra had six vertebrae instead of the usual five, and spina bifida of varying degrees was present in most of the rest examined. The high incidence of congenital anomalies of bone described — specifically spina bifida and vertebral fusions — would indicate that the population from this tomb was highly endogamous. This conclusion may apply only to the families represented at Meiron, but further investigation of the region may provide verification.

In conclusion, the population of Meiron resembles that from Jerusalem, shows little evidence of traumatic injuries, was susceptible to arthritis, and was prone to congenital anomalies of the skeletal system.

BIBLIOGRAPHY

Arensburg, B.
    1973   The People in the Land of Israel from Epipaleolithic to Present Times. Unpublished Ph.D. dissertation, Tel Aviv University.
Brothwell, D. R.
    1965   The Biology of Earlier Human Populations. Pp. 325-29 in *Science in Archaeology*, eds. D. Brothwell and E. Higgs. London: Thames and Hudson.

Haas, N.
    1970   Anthropological Observations on the Skeletal Remains from Giv^cat ha-Mivtar. *Israel Exploration Journal* 20: 38-59.

Four Seasons of Excavation at Tell el-Hesi A Preliminary Report

D. Glenn Rose

The Graduate Seminary, Phillips University, Enid, OK 73701

Lawrence E. Toombs

Wilfrid Laurier University, Waterloo, Ontario N2M 1C6

with an Appendix by

Kevin G. O'Connell, S.J.

Weston School of Theology, Cambridge, MA 02138

Introduction

The present stage in the history of the Joint Expedition to Tell el-Hesi is an appropriate one at which to attempt a summary of the archeological results of the first four seasons at the site. The first three seasons (July-August 1970, 1971, and 1973) were under the directorship of John Worrell (Holy Cross College). The fourth season (July-August 1975) was directed by D. Glenn Rose (Phillips University). Lawrence E. Toombs (Wilfrid Laurier University) has served as Chief Archeologist in all four seasons.

A major phase of the work of the expedition has been completed and a series of publications covering the Arabic, Hellenistic, and Persian occupations is in preparation under the general editorship of Kevin G. O'Connell. Two preliminary reports have been issued, one by L. E. Toombs (1974) and the other by D. G. Rose and L. E. Toombs (1976).

This report confines itself to the presentation of stratigraphic and artifactual data. Consequently it does not adequately reflect many important and distinctive aspects of the expedition. Notable among these are the volunteer and educational programs conducted in the field; the invaluable on-site work of the specialist staff (including the cultural and physical anthropologists, botanist, geologist, and lithics analyst); and the supporting activity of the camp management personnel, architects, pottery-drawers, conservators, photographers, and recorders. The names of those who participated in these vital functions of the expedition are given in the Appendix to this report.

The expedition gratefully acknowledges the support of the consortium of universities and colleges on which its continued existence depends. The consortium consists of the following eight educational institutions:

Consortium for Higher Education-Religious Studies (Ohio)
Holy Cross College (Worcester, Massachusetts)
Lutheran Theological Seminary (Columbus, Ohio)
Oberlin College (Oberlin, Ohio)
Seabury-Western Theological Seminary (Evanston, Illinois)
Smith College (Northampton, Massachusetts)
Virginia Theological Seminary (Alexandria, Virginia)
Wilfrid Laurier University (Waterloo, Ontario)

Former consortium members are:

Hartford Seminary Foundation (Hartford, Connecticut)
General Theological Seminary (New York, New York)
Ashland Theological Seminary (Ashland, Ohio)

Financial contributions have been made to the Joint Expedition by:

Christian Theological Seminary (Indianapolis, IN)
Golden Gate Baptist Theological Seminary (Mill Valley, California)
Harvard Semitic Museum (Cambridge, Massachusetts)
Phillips University (Enid, Oklahoma)

Valuable assistance has been given in the form of

clerical and other supporting services by Weston School of Theology (Cambridge, Massachusetts).

The generous financial grants provided by The Canada Council (1970), The Smithsonian Institution (1970 and 1971), and The National Endowment for the Humanities (1973 and 1974), the sponsorship of the American Schools of Oriental Research and its officers, as well as the unfailing help of the officials of the Department of Antiquities of the State of Israel are all gratefully acknowledged.

Appreciation must also be recorded for the keen eyes and faithful recording of the many field and area supervisors who worked on the site and whose names are given in the Appendix. Special thanks are due to the hundreds of volunteers who paid hard cash and sacrificed summer incomes to battle the heat, dust, and flies of Tell el-Hesi.

The Site

Tell el-Hesi dominates an undulating plain which runs from west to east about ten km. south of a line from Ashkelon through Kiryat Gat to Beit Jibrin. It is about thirteen km. distant from the Mediterranean coast. The site is founded on a cluster of sand dunes which elevate it above the level of the surrounding plain. It consists of two principal areas of occupation, the Upper City or Acropolis, and the Lower City (fig. 1:A and B). The former occupies a large dune, the original height of which was about 16.70 m. Over the centuries an additional 20.10 m. of the debris of human occupation have accumulated, so that the present summit of the mound is 36.80 m. above the floor of the Wadi Hesi, which forms the eastern boundary of the site. The Upper City is relatively small with the area of its summit being approximately 2,700 sq. m.

The Lower City is more than forty times larger than the Acropolis. It is a roughly rectangular plateau enclosed on the east, north, and west by wadis (fig. 1:C) and bordered on the south by three high dunes with narrow valleys between (fig. 1:D). The Upper City occupies the northeast corner of this plateau. Two ravines cut across the Lower City, one from the east and the other from the west (fig. 1:E). Erosion into these depressions has destroyed the occupational remains on either side, giving the Lower City a curious saucer-shaped appearance. Early Bronze Age structures are, however, preserved on the summit of the southern dune system (fig. 1:D), on a spur of high ground running northwest from the central dune (fig. 1:F), and on a

similar ridge running westward from the Upper City (fig. 1:G).

Although it is too far removed from the sea to exercise direct surveillance or control over the coastal plain, Tell el-Hesi had considerable strategic significance in relation to the ancient road system interior to southern Palestine (fig. 2). A branch of the coastal highway turns eastward and traverses a low ridge about 2.5 km. north of the site. This road follows the line marked by the sites of Um Lakish, Khirbet Aijlan and Abu Suᶜeifan and connects with the old highway from Beer Sheba to Hebron, which followed closely the roadbed of the modern railway. Both of these roads are visible from the site and at closer range from the smaller tells, Quneitira and Sheqef, which were almost certainly satellites of the stronghold at Hesi for at least a part of its history. The location of the ancient roads has been a special interest of the expedition's geologist, Dr. Frank Koucky, and a more detailed report of his investigations will appear in a forthcoming publication.

Hesi thus forms a line of defense north of such larger fortresses as Tell Jemmeh, Tell el-Ajjul, and Tell el-Farah (S). In a more direct way than these sites, it commands the southern approaches to the Shephelah and the Judean highlands. The military importance of the Tell el-Hesi region is underlined by the major battles fought in the area during the Israeli War of Independence in 1948, when for a brief period the site resumed its ancient role as a fortified strong point.

Although Tell el-Hesi lies in a zone of relatively scanty rainfall (about 300 mm. per year), the surrounding plain has considerable agricultural potential, producing at the present time excellent crops of wheat, sorghum, and melons. The productivity of the region not only assured the food supply of the city, but also provided its dependent population with agricultural surpluses for export. Several springs of fresh water are located in the wadi system around the site, but how the water supply within the city walls was guaranteed is as yet unknown.

Previous and Present Excavations

After a monumental struggle to obtain a license to excavate at Tell el-Hesi, Sir Flinders Petrie began work at the site in 1890 on behalf of the Palestine Exploration Fund. Because the top of the tell was under cultivation, Petrie probed the slopes of the mound on all four sides in a series of trenches from

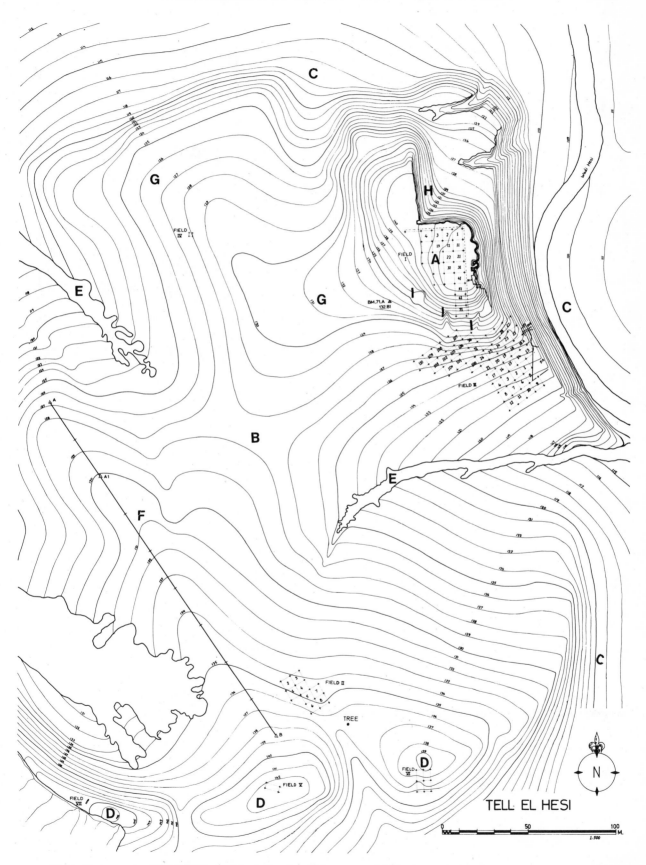

Fig. 1. Contour map of Tell el-Hesi, showing the location of the excavated fields, the numbering of the areas within each, and the principal physical features of the site. Drawing by B. Zoughbi.

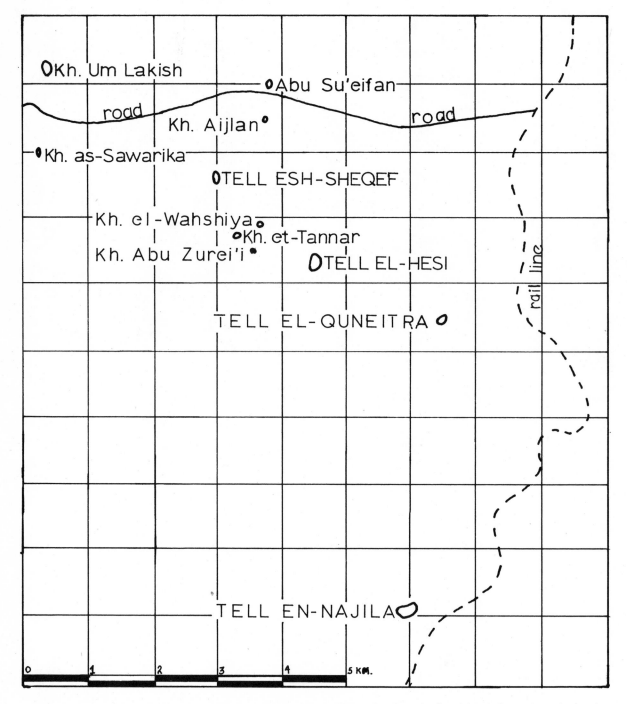

Fig. 2. The environs of Tell el-Hesi. The map shows the tell and its satellites, Quneitra and Sheqef, in relation to the ancient road system. The old road from Beer-sheba probably followed the railway line. Quneitra is about one km. from the N-S road and Sheqef approximately the same distance from the E-W road. Hesi is halfway between in a strategic position to cover the junction. Drawing by L.E. Toombs.

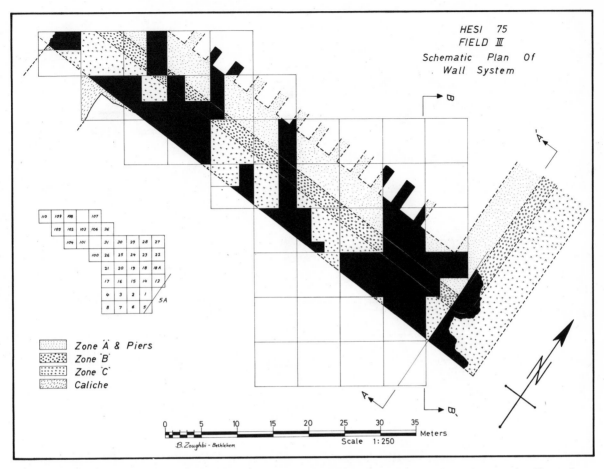

HESI 75
FIELD III
Schematic Plan Of
Wall System

Zone A & Piers
Zone B
Zone C
Caliche

0   5   10   15   20   25   30   35
Meters
B. Zoughbi - Bethlehem   Scale 1:250

Fig. 3. Schematic plan of the walls at the foot of the southern slope (Field III), showing the three zones of construction. The portions of the wall inked solidly were excavated; the remainder is a reconstruction. Drawing by B. Zoughbi.

the summit almost to the base. Petrie's excavations lasted only six weeks and are aptly described by F. J. Bliss as a "rapid reconnaisance." Brief though Petrie's work was, it is a milestone in the history of Palestinian archeology since it represents the first controlled excavation of a Palestinian site and the earliest recognition of the chronological significance of pottery forms (Petrie: 1891).

In 1891 and 1892 during four seasons of approximately three months each, Frederick Jones Bliss continued the project begun by Petrie. His strategy was radically different from that of his predecessor. In a single huge cut at the northeast corner of the tell, he removed nearly a third of the mound from its surface to the natural clay and sand underlying the earliest occupation (fig. 1:H and fig. 4). In its own way Bliss' report (1898) of his work is also a landmark in the archeology of Palestine. It is the first attempt to present the results of a large area-excavation in stratigraphic form. He identified eleven occupation levels which he grouped into

eight strata, or in his own terminology, eight "cities" (see fig. 4).

The work of these pioneers of Palestinian archeology was resumed, after a lapse of more than three-quarters of a century, by the Joint Expedition to Tell el-Hesi. In its first four seasons effort has been concentrated mainly in Fields I and III. Figs. 1 and 3 show the location of these fields and the numbering of the areas within each.

Field I, in the Upper City, was laid out as a grid of 6 x 6 meter squares covering the southeast quadrant of the Acropolis. The two eastern lines of squares (Areas 1, 11, 21, 31, 41, 51, and 2, 12, 22, 32) have been excavated into or below Persian levels. Areas 3, 4, and 13 were opened, but abandoned after one or two seasons. In 1973 Areas 61 and 71 were partially excavated in order to develop a connection between the work on the summit and the fortification system on the southern slope described by Petrie. In connection with this project a section was cut in 1973 along this slope at the wadi face

EASTERN FACE

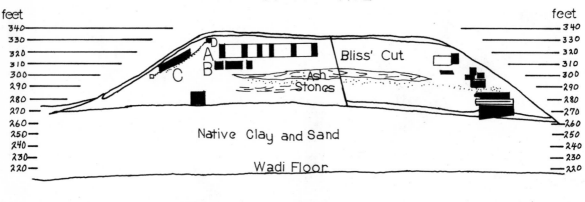

ENLARGEMENT OF BLISS' CUT SHOWING CITY LEVELS

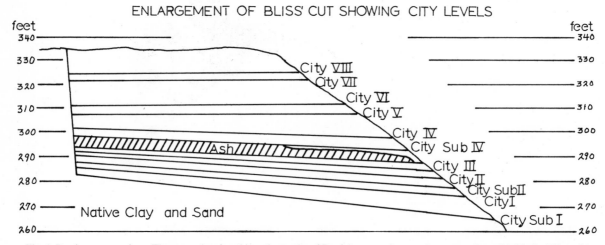

Fig. 4. Previous excavations. The upper drawing shows the results of Petrie's excavations on the eastern slope. A is his "building with long, narrow chambers," B the "Pilaster Building," C the "Manasseh Wall" with the glacis below, and D the supposed termination of the glacis. The lower drawing gives the levels of the eleven occupational strata identified by F. J. Bliss. Adapted from Bliss (1898: pl. 2).

(Area 61A) and in 1975 the section was extended to the north by the opening of Area 51A.

The layout of Field I brings Areas 1 and 2 into relation with the southern face of Bliss' cut and relates the eastern line of squares (Areas 1, 11, 21, 31, 41, 51, and 51A) to the trenches dug by Petrie on the steep eastern face of the tell. The principal structures from these locations as reported by Petrie and Bliss are represented in fig. 4.

In the 1970 season it was decided to investigate a major wall structure, the eastern end of which was visible in the wadi face at the foot of the southern slope of the Acropolis (Field III). Its position at the 119 m. contour line, well below the base of Petrie's trenches into the southern slope, invited the assumption that it was an Early Bronze Age construction, an impression soon dispelled when work began on the wall. In order to determine the

date and nature of the structure, a vertical section was cut across it at the wadi face (fig. 3:A-A'). It soon became apparent that, far from being a single unit, the wall was a composite structure, the end result of at least three phases of building. In order not to prejudice the question of the chronological relationship of these phases, they were designated from north to south Zones A, B, and C.

The excavation strategy now involved a two-fold operation: (1) tracing the wall westward along the base of the southern slope and (2) sectioning the wall in two places near its eastern end in order to determine the method of construction and the date of the three zones (fig. 3:A-A', B-B'). In order to facilitate the tracing of the wall, a grid of 6 x 6 meter squares was laid out with the east and west balks at right angles to the presumed line of the wall. Since squares were opened as dictated by the leap-frog process of pursuing the wall, the numbering system is somewhat erratic. The course of the wall, the lines of demarcation between the three zones, and the numbering system of the grid are shown in fig. 3. The sections through the wall are located in Area 5A, and along the east balks of Areas 1, 14, 18, and 23 (fig. 3).

Both Petrie and Bliss report the discovery of Amorite (i.e., Early Bronze Age) remains in the Lower City. The expedition's first attempt to investigate these proved to be abortive. In Field II (fig. 1) the erosion had removed all Early Bronze Age structures, leaving only the bottoms of two garbage pits belonging to the period. Field II was therefore closed and the investigation of the Lower City moved to a series of probes in areas where the depth of soil seemed greatest. The location of Fields IV, V, VI and VII may be seen in fig. 1. Field IV, a 2 x 2 m. probe on the ridge extending west from the Acropolis revealed two phases of Early Bronze Age housing. Field V, on the central dune on the southern side of the Lower City, began as a 7 x 2 m. probe and narrowed to a 2 x 1 m. excavation. It showed five phases of Early Bronze Age occupation. Whether this is domestic or public in nature is as yet unknown. Field VI, on the easternmost of the southern dunes, showed three phases of construction with walls apparently too large to belong to houses. Field VII, located on the high western dune, was a section only 0.5 m. wide through the occupational debris and the clay and sand below. Here at least three and probably four phases of construction were found, the upper levels of which may be later than Early Bronze Age. The probes just described were exploratory in nature and provide the information on which a full-scale excavation in the Lower City will be based.

The foregoing description will serve to locate the fields excavated by the Joint Expedition and to indicate the strategy by which it approached the excavation of the site. Before presenting the detailed results of the four campaigns so far conducted, mention should be made of the survey project envisaged by the expedition. In order to test its methodology, the survey began in 1973 with an examination of the area enclosed by the wadi system surrounding the tell. The data gathered and the methods employed have been under evaluation since that time, and a wider survey involving a much larger radius around the site is being planned for a subsequent season.

Field I (The Acropolis)

I. The Earliest Remains (Phases Sub-5d:1-4)

In Areas 51, 41, and 31, excavation penetrated to the earliest levels yet reached on the Acropolis. The complex stratigraphic situation existing in these areas is shown in figs. 5 and 6. As fig. 5 indicates, the Phase 5d wall (41.162) was dug down into earlier remains. The stratigraphic chart (fig. 20) shows the position of Phase 5d within the overall stratigraphy of the site. These remains were cleared out north of the wall for the establishment of a large Phase 5d building complex, leaving in place only one fragment of an earlier wall (31.303, fig. 6:B). The excavation for the Phase 5d complex reached the tops of the walls of Petrie's "long range of chambers" which are covered north of Wall 41.162 by the makeup and fill for Phase 5d surfaces (fig. 6:A, B; fig. 4 shows a section of the walls of Petrie's building).

The space south of Wall 41.162 was not cleared out in Phase 5d, but functioned as a waste area in which garbage and ash pits were located. This fact preserved the earlier remains along the southern edge of the tell, providing the only place within the excavated areas where the occupation intermediate between the founding of the "long range of chambers" and the establishment of Phase 5d may be studied. Three levels of occupation can be distinguished beneath the waste area of Phase 5d. The following table, which should be read in conjunction with figs. 5 and 6, summarizes the sequence of occupational levels and shows its relationship to Phase 5d. The excavation of these early occupational levels is not complete and their dating has not been established by a thorough ceramic study. The uppermost level may prove to be Persian in date and in that case should be called Phase 5e, and the lower may have to be further subdivided. Hence, the temporary device of designating them Phase Sub-5d:1, 2, and 3 has been adopted.

Since Phases Sub-5d:2 and 3 are the levels at which excavation ceased, some degree of uncertainty remains as to the details of the phasing. For example, no certainty exists as to what features, if any, in Areas 41 and 51 are to be associated with the "long range of chambers." Therefore, Phases Sub-5d:3 and 4 may prove to be a single phase. Pit 41.178, now assigned to Sub-5d:2, may in fact belong to Phase Sub-5d:3.

PHASE	AREA 51	AREA 41	AREA 31	CONJECTURED DATE
5d	Virtually destroyed by cemetery	Wall 41.162 with waste area to South	Phase 5d walls and surfaces	Persian Period 6th-5th Cent. B.C.
Sub-5d:1	House 51.070 with cobbled outside surface		Removed by Phase 5d walls and surfaces	Babylonian Period 6th Cent. B.C.
	ASH	ASH		Destruction of 587/86 B.C.?
Sub-5d:2	House 51.066 & 51.098	Building 41.163 with pit	Removed by Phase 5d walls and surfaces	End of Israelite Monarchy 7th-6th Cent. B.C.
Sub-5d:3	Early house walls and pit	Largely unexcavated	Fragmentary wall 31.303	? ?
Sub-5d:4	Not excavated	Southernmost wall of "range of chambers" 41.179	"Range of chambers" below 5d fill 31.308, 309, & 310	? ?

The separate elements of the three Sub-5d phases will now be described in further detail.

A. Phase Sub-5d:4 (Petrie's "long range of chambers"). Petrie briefly describes a building almost destroyed by erosion along the eastern wadi face. It consisted of a long north-south wall and six irregularly spaced east-west walls which together formed five rectangular chambers with the eastern wall eroded away (Petrie 1891: 34 and pl. 3). He conjectured (1891: 34) that "Very probably other chambers exist on the other side of the long wall, as a wall was found to run westward at the south end of it."

Excavation in 1975 demonstrated the truth of Petrie's supposition. The tops of three east-west walls and a north-south wall were located beneath Phase 5d walls and fill (fig. 6:A). The southernmost of the east-west walls (41.179) lies immediately beneath a Phase 5d wall and corresponds to the southern wall of Petrie's "long range of chambers." The second and third east-west walls in Petrie's building appeared in Area 31 (31.309 and 31.308) connected by a north-south cross wall (31.310). These walls evidently constitute a second range of chambers west of that described by Petrie. The tops

of similar walls appeared beneath the Phase 5d fill in Area 32 also (32.192, 193, and 194; not illustrated in fig. 6). Whether these constitute a third range of rooms or belong to Phase Sub-5d:3 has not yet been determined. In any event, we are obviously dealing with a very large structure covering almost the whole of the excavated areas.

The walls in question are constituted of large, relatively thin bricks, carefully laid, and of varied composition and color. The fill was removed from part of one of the chambers bounded by Walls 31.309, 31.310, 31.308 and the east balk of Area 31. This fill consisted of a series of layers of compact gray earth containing very little pottery, but with frequent infusions of ash. It filled the chamber to a depth of at least 2.50 m. The fill rested on a level surface of compact reddish earth (31.306), on which no evidence of occupational debris was found. Excavation did not proceed below this surface. No doorways existed in the portion of the chamber excavated. The field reading of the pottery from the fill gave "Iron II/Early Persian" as the date of the latest sherds. This evidence indicates the date of the filling of the chamber, but says nothing about foundation date or the function of the structure. The walls may never have been freestanding, but

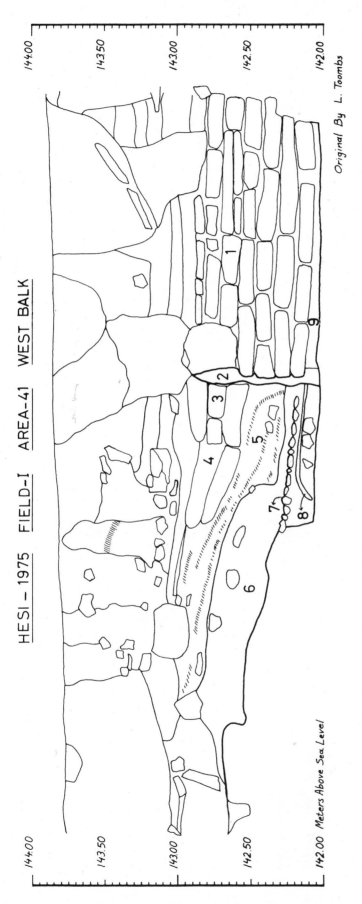

HESI – 1975   FIELD-I   AREA-41   WEST BALK

Original By L. Toombs

Fig. 5. The west balk of Field I, Area 41, showing the relationship of Phase 5d to the Sub-5d levels.
1. 5d wall 41.162.
2. The foundation trench (41.169) for this wall. It cuts 3, 5, 7, and 8 and penetrates into the top of 9.
3. Sub-5d:1 wall 41.158.
4. Brick platform to the south of wall 41.158.
5. Ash layer 41.167/73.
6. Loose gray fill underlying slope 41.163 of Sub-5d:2.
7. Cobbled surface 41.138, belonging to Sub-5d:3.
8. Compact reddish earth layer, running up to 9.
9. The wall of the Sub-5d:4 chamber 41.179 into which the base of the 5d wall (1) is cut.
Drawing by B. Zoughbi.

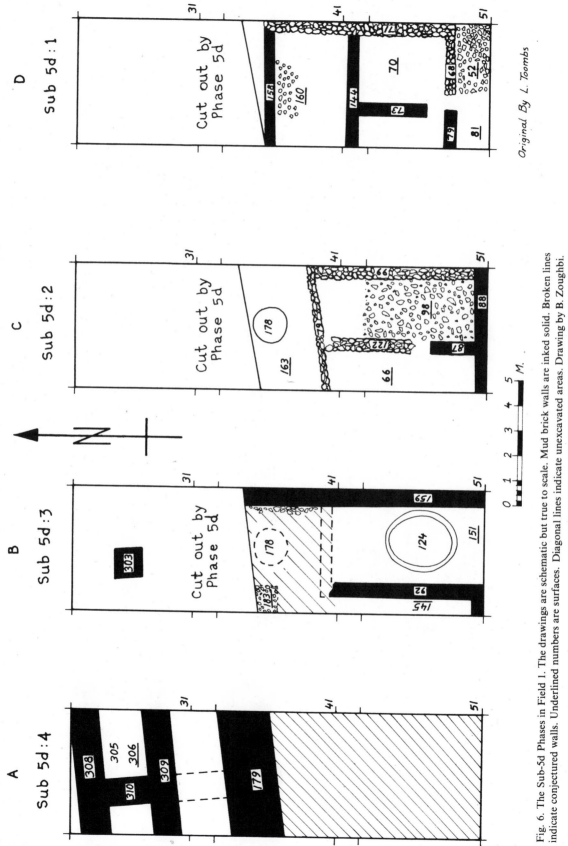

Fig. 6. The Sub-5d Phases in Field 1. The drawings are schematic but true to scale. Mud brick walls are inked solid. Broken lines indicate conjectured walls. Underlined numbers are surfaces. Diagonal lines indicate unexcavated areas. Drawing by B. Zoughbi.

may have served as containers for the fill of a huge platform constructed to raise the level of the mound. In this case surface 31.306 is merely a stage in the filling process. On the other hand, the walls may have formed the chambers of a large building of unknown function, and surface 31.306 may then prove to be flooring for one of the chambers.

An attempt was made to locate the northern extremity of the chambered structure in Areas 2 and 11, but the probes encountered only fill layers. The solution to such problems as the western extent of the structure and what happened at its northern and southern extremities awaits further excavation.

The cut along the wadi face (Area 51A) gives some further information concerning the stratigraphic position of the "Manasseh Wall" (fig. 4:C). This wall, discovered by Petrie, overlies a glacis faced with white plaster. The Area 51A section (fig. 7:1) shows this glacis flattening out and running over a layer of comp·.ct reddish earth which extends southward from tne top of the southern wall of the range of chambers. A similar layer of reddish earth underlies the cobbles of Phase Sub-5d:3 (fig. 5: Layer 8). This evidence suggests that the "Manasseh Wall" and the glacis must be placed after the filling of the chambers and perhaps in conjunction with Phases Sub-5d:2 and 3.

B. Phase Sub-5d:3 (Period of the Monarchy?). Phase Sub-5d:3 is represented only in Areas 41 and 51 (fig. 6:B). It consists of a long narrow room bounded on the east (51.159), west (51.092), and north by walls of hard, gray mud brick. The flooring is of compacted earth and through it a large oval pit with a mud brick rim is cut (51.124). The contents of the pit give no evidence of its function. North of this building, excavation reached the surface levels of this phase only in a probe along the west balk. In this probe a surfacing of small cobbles (41.183) is cut by the extreme bottom of the foundation trench for the Phase 5d wall. The cobbles rest on a layer of compact reddish earth which abuts the top of the southern wall of the range of chambers, immediately below the level of the Phase 5d wall (fig. 5: Layers 7 and 8). The surface, therefore, is probably contemporary with the first structures built on top of the filled-in chambers. The only other evidence of this phase so far recovered north of these cobbles is a fragment of a wall (31.303) accidentally preserved beneath Phase 5d fill in Area 31.

Further excavation is required to determine whether any earlier surfaces are associated with Walls 51.092 and 51.159 and to uncover the remainder of the cobbled surface 41.183. However, enough has already been learned to demonstrate that Phase Sub-5d:3 is better built and implies a more prosperous culture than either of its successors.

C. Phase Sub-5d:2 (The End of the Monarchy?). Phase Sub-5d:2 radically altered the building plan of the previous phase (figs. 5 and 6:C). In this phase a ridge of high ground ran along the southern edge of the summit. On this ridge stood a structure of which two rooms are preserved in the excavated area. The north-south Walls 51.099 and 51.122 are represented only by stone sockets, and the same is true of the east-west Wall 41.079. The southern wall is a mud brick structure (51.088) at the edge of the slope. The interior surfacing of the southeastern room is of cobblestones which had subsided over the fill of Phase Sub-5d:3 Pit 51.124. North of the building an area with a beaten-earth floor (41.163) contains Pit 41.178 and may have been a courtyard associated with the building to the south. To this phase belongs a small black burnished juglet and probably also a finely-made ring-burnished bowl. The relationship of Pit 41.178 to the surfacing has, however, not been clarified. It is tentatively assigned to Phase Sub-5d:2, but may in fact belong to the preceding phase.

The remains of this structure are covered by a layer of ash, in places striated by water-washing and in places lying in pockets as much as 0.25 m. deep. Imbedded in the ash was a total of six juglets of a late Iron II type (Registry nos. 73, 74, 75, 151, and 167 [from 1973] and 369 [from 1975]). The field analysis of the pottery from the ash layers agrees in general with a date around 600 B.C.

D. Phase Sub-5d:1 (The Babylonian Period). The Phase Sub-5d:1 builders had to contend with a heap of rubble. They leveled off some of the debris, filled the worst of the holes with red bricky material, and built a house of fired mud brick. Its ground plan follows the general lines of the Phase Sub-5d:2 structure and parts of three rooms are preserved (fig. 6:D). The floors, mostly destroyed by Muslim graves, were apparently of beaten earth. The construction of the walls is much inferior to that of Phase Sub-5d:3. The eastern wall (51.071) is made of stone, the western (51.073) and northern (51.144) walls of mud brick with some stone used in the construction. The southern cross-wall is brick on stone foundation, and the extreme northern cross-wall (41.158) is brick founded on debris. A well-laid

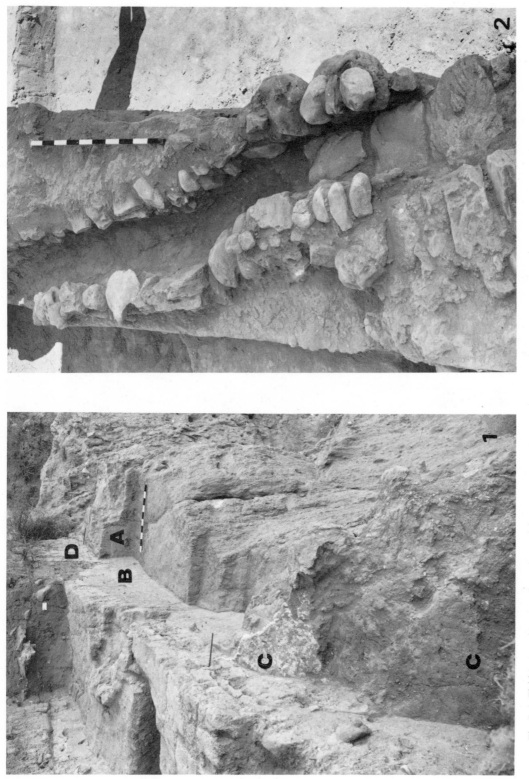

Fig. 7. 1. Field I, Area 51A, cut along the wadi face on the east of the Acropolis, looking north. A is the top of the southern wall of Petrie's "long range of chambers." B is the thin orange layer, originating at the top of the wall and sloping rapidly to a level below that of the hard plaster glacis (C). D is the Phase 5d (Persian) wall built directly on A.

2. The portion of the Phase 4c (Hellenistic) drain found in the Field I, Areas 31/32 balk, looking north. The large stones in the floor of the drain are the northern limit of the catch basin from which the drain was fed.
Photos by J. Whitred.

cobbled surface (51.052) extends from the south wall of the building to the southern edge of the tell.

The type of materials used and haphazard way in which they are put together suggest an impoverished rebuilding of a destroyed town in which the builders were using material salvaged from the earlier city. The red color of the brick may be caused by its exposure to heat during the destruction rather than by kiln firing.

The stratigraphic sequence of Phases Sub-5d:3, 2, and 1 corresponds so closely with the political events in Israel at the end of the 7th and beginning of the 6th centuries B.C. as to suggest a tentative dating of these levels. If the ash layer represents the destruction of Tell el-Hesi by the Babylonian armies in 587/86 B.C., then Phase Sub-5d:1, which overlies the ash, represents a period of depression after the Babylonian conquest. Phases Sub-5d:3 and 2 would then belong to the end of the Israelite Monarchy and would show a decline in the period just before the Babylonian invasions (Phase Sub-5d:2). The revival of the city, represented by Phase 5d itself, could be accounted for by Persian interest in the site as a supply and garrison depot for the Egyptian campaigns. Confirmation or denial of this hypothesis will depend on the results of the laboratory study of the pottery now under way.

II. The Persian Period (Phase 5)

A. *Phase 5d (fig. 8:A).* As already indicated, the Phase 5d builders established the southern line of their construction about 9.0 m. north of the southern edge of the tell. They made no architectural use of these 9.0 m. but used the area for shallow pits in which ash and garbage were deposited. One of these pits yielded a beautiful travertine rhyton with a kneeling horse supporting the drinking horn.

The best preserved remains of the phase are located in Areas 32, 31, and 41. Two north-south and two east-west walls form a casemate-like structure. Its southern limit is a wide mud brick wall (41.162), paralleled 2.5 m. to the north by a somewhat slighter wall (31.225/32.158). These, together with the Cross-walls 32.176 and 31.229, form a rectangular chamber 5.2 x 2.6 m., entered by a doorway through the northern wall. This room is apparently one of a series along the southern edge of the Acropolis, since Wall 41.162 extended eastward to the wadi face where it appears in section in Area 51A (fig. 7:1), and Wall 31.225 runs westward

through Area 32 (as Wall 32.158).

The construction of these walls is distinctive. They are built of mold-made, sun-dried mud bricks of regular size. The faces of the walls are often formed by a row of such bricks set on end, and the walls were given a coat of smooth mud plaster above the surface level (fig. 9:2). The flooring is beaten earth laid over a thin, compact layer of make-up. Little evidence of occupation remains on these surfaces since they were apparently cleared off before the rooms were filled up by the Phase 5c builders.

The pitting operations of Phase 5a have wreaked havoc with the Phase 5d remains north of the "casemate" complex, and fragments of only three additional walls remain. Two of these, located in Area 1, seem to form a T-junction, which may have been the corner of two rooms. The third wall, situated in the balk between areas 22 and 32, is only a tiny fragment of brickwork with the characteristic Phase 5d plaster face. It has been partially demolished by the ditch dug for the Hellenistic drain (see below IIIA), and its eastward extension, if any, has been lost to Phase 5a pits in Area 21.

It seems likely that the casemate-like structure ran along the east side of the summit as well as along the south and that the T-junction in Area 1 is part of the eastern range of rooms. The scrap of wall in Area 22/32 may be part of a chamber built into the southeast angle of the casemate. These suggestions, which are illustrated in broken lines in fig. 8:A, have no higher status than guesses, based in part on a similar building uncovered by Bliss along the north and east edges of his cut and reported by him as belonging to City VII. (Fig. 19 gives a reproduction of Bliss' drawing of City VII.) It is worth noting that in Bliss' excavations as well, no structures were found in the central portions of the site. The impression created is of major construction around the edges of the site, enclosing what amounts to a large open courtyard area.

Attempts to clarify the situation at the northern extremity of Field I during Phase 5d have so far met with little success. The problem is most acute in Area 2. Below the Phase 5c surface the layers slope rapidly downward to the north as if they had fallen over a terrace wall or down a steep incline (Fill 2.141, fig. 8:A). On top of these sloping layers numerous animal bones, some showing evidence of butchering and fire, were found. The slope was evidently used as a refuse dump between Phases 5d and 5c. Since, however, the surfaces on which these layers rest have not been uncovered, it is impossible

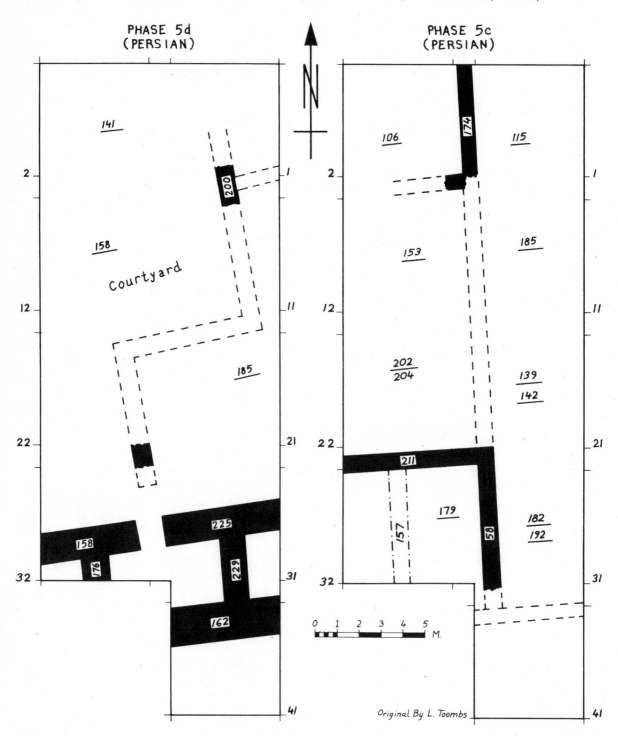

Fig. 8. Phase plans of the two earliest Persian phases (5d and 5c). Broken lines indicate conjectural walls. Wall 32.157 is indicated in Phase 5c, but more probably it belongs to Phase 5b (fig. 10). Drawing by B. Zoughbi.

to say whether the level of the Phase 5d city dropped rapidly at this point because of terracing or some similar operation or whether the sloping layers are the result of a breakdown of Phase 5d structures.

The surfaces and fills of Phase 5d produced trefoil arrowheads (fig. 18:5), fibulae, bone spatulas and needles, spindle whorls and loomweights, projectile points (fig. 18:5), and a large number of Attic ware sherds, including one portraying a snarling dog. A ceramic figurine of the fertility goddess (fig. 18:3) and a finely-cut black steatite scarab with no inscription on the underside (fig. 18:4) also came from these layers.

B. Phase 5c (fig. 8:B). Phase 5c inaugurates a new building plan, the main lines of which persist throughout the rest of the Persian Period. The casemate-like structures of Phase 5d are abandoned and a new alignment of walls appears. These are best preserved in the northern and southern portions of the excavated areas, but unfortunately they are largely destroyed by later pitting activity in the central portion of the field.

The western side of the field was occupied by a building or buildings with walls of gray sun-dried brick, narrow in comparison to those of Phase 5d. In Areas 31/32 the northeast corner of a room appears. It is bounded by Walls 32.211 and 31.058, and is surfaced with a beaten-earth floor (32.179). The southern limit of the chamber could not be established with certainty because of the depredations of the Muslim graves. In the northern part of the field the southeast corner of a second room was found, its surface being laid directly over the Phase 5d fill (1.141). Its eastern wall (1.174) is well-preserved, but its southern wall is only a fragment. The beautiful little green faience figurine shown in fig. 18:8 came from the fill for this building.

Between these two chambers the phase has been pitted out almost completely. To obtain an impression of the extent and destructiveness of this pitting activity the reader should compare figs. 8:B and 11:B. The Hellenistic pits left only narrow strips of undisturbed earth on which surfaces could be traced but on which the identification of brickwork was extremely difficult. The line of Wall 31.058 is connected on fig. 8:B with that of Wall 1.174 on the basis of the change of surfacing along that line and the detection of traces of brickwork in the balk between Areas 21 and 22.

The most striking feature of Phase 5c occurs along the east side of the field. In Areas 31, 21, and

11 a buildup of striated layers of alternate dark ash and light gray earth indicates residues from an agricultural operation such as a threshing floor. The ash has a high content of grain.

C. Phase 5b (fig. 10:A). The fundamental change between Phases 5d and 5c appears to have been a shift from a public and official use of the tell in 5d with a large building complex surrounding an open courtyard to a more settled and domestic type of occupation in 5c in which agricultural operations were conducted near the living quarters. This .endency continued into Phase 5b.

In this Phase the building plan of Phase 5c continued in use with the construction of some new walls. The area in which the striated layers of Phase 5c occurred was no longer used for agricultural purposes and was divided into two rooms by the construction of Walls 21.117 and 11.240. The northern of these had a beaten-earth floor (21.125) while the southern was surfaced with flagstones (31.095). The large Phase 5c room in Area 32 was also subdivided by the construction of Wall 32.157. The smaller eastern chamber, thus created, was clearly employed for domestic purposes since Oven 32.171 with an associated ash pit was set into its floor.

To the north of this building the pits again made the identification of the wall system impossible, and only the surfaces shown in fig. 10:A could be established with certainty. Of these surfaces, 22.199 is especially interesting. It was overlaid by a heavy deposit of broken pottery, including numerous examples of fine Attic ware sherds, of which the best example is the krater rim shown in fig. 18:1.

In Area 1 a deep-founded square structure built of fired brick (1.126) functioned as an underground storage chamber during this phase.

D. Phase 5a (fig. 10:B). The building plan of Phase 5a follows closely that of its predecessor, particularly in the southern part of the field. The continuity between the phases is further emphasized by the continued use of Oven 32.171. One major departure is the elimination of Wall 11.240 and the construction, a little further to the north, of Wall 11.078, which had the effect of enlarging the Phase 5b room. Another innovation was the filling up of the underground chamber and its use as a small room with the installation of Floor 1.054. A splendid ceramic ram's head came from just north of Wall 22.211.

Fig. 9.
  1. Phase 4b (Hellenistic) stone building in Field I, Areas 22 and 32, looking east. A indicates the surviving walls of the structure, cut by Muslim burials (B).
  2. Phase 5d (Persian) casemate-like building in Field I, Area 31, looking west. A indicates the plaster-faced walls of the structure, with the southernmost wall cut away to show the top of the earlier wall on which it rests (B). C is the Phase 4c (Hellenistic) drain and water-catchment, preserved in the west balk.
Photos by W. Nassau and J. Whitred.

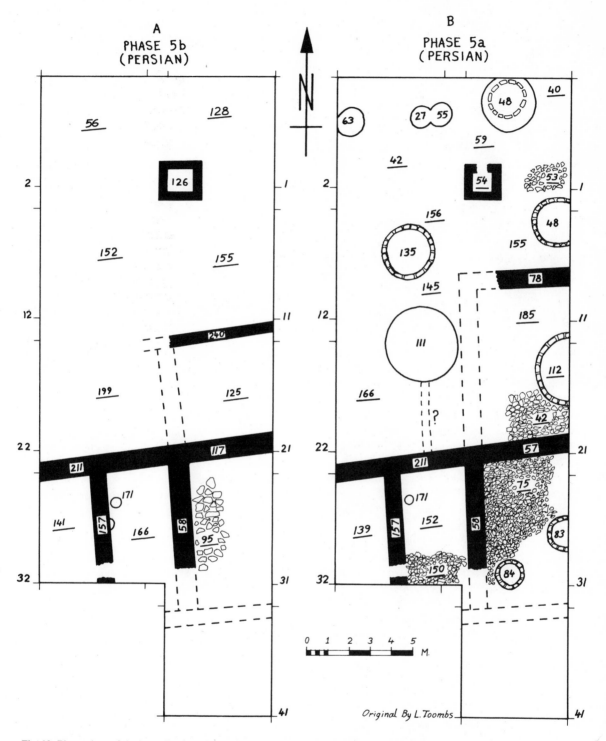

Fig. 10. Phase plans of the latest Persian phases (5b and 5a). Broken lines indicate conjectured walls. The extent of the cobbled and flagstone surfaces is not certain, since they were found in fragmentary condition. Drawing by B. Zoughbi.

Phase 5a was marked by the extensive use of cobblestones as surfacing. As shown in fig. 10:B, four patches of cobbles are preserved (1.053, 21.042, 31.075, 32.150). The reason for the introduction of cobbling may have been to provide a hard, dry surface for the handling of grain gathered for storage. The short length of drain in Area 22 between Wall 22.211 and Pit 22.111 may have been installed in this phase in order to keep the grain-handling area free of water.

The most distinctive feature of Phase 5a is the construction of brick-lined storage pits in two rough north-south lines. These pits range in depth from 2.5 m. to 3.5 m. and are ingeniously made. The initial excavation for the pits was carefully cut to size and the earthen walls were studded with large, angular stones which gave purchase to the brick lining, since the bricks were pressed against them while still soft and allowed to dry in place. The most elaborate of these pits is 1.048, which was relined several times and gives evidence of having had a vaulted brick roof at one stage of its existence. The lower levels of the brick-lined pits contained layers of ash produced, on the evidence of the botanical remains, by the burning of straw and chaff. Lawrence E. Stager (1971) has interpreted this phenomenon as the result of fumigating the pits against rodents and other vermin. Such a procedure was evidently necessary since the sides of the pits are honey-combed with rodent runs. A second type of pit, represented by 2.027, 2.055, and 2.063, is small and unlined. These pits were probably used for auxiliary storage of some kind.

Pit 22.111 is an anomaly. It is large in size, but lacks a brick lining, and it is uncertain whether it originated in the latest Persian or the earliest Hellenistic phase. Most probably it was dug in Phase 5a and was at that time brick lined. It was, however, reused in Phase 4c as a sump for the drainage system. The fill in Pit 22.111 was midden material, rich in botanical remains and artifacts (Stewart: forthcoming).

III. The Hellenistic Period (Phase 4)

The interpretation of Phase 4 is complicated by two factors. All the deep graves of the Muslim cemetery (Phase 2) cut into Phase 4 levels, breaking up the stratigraphy and often destroying surfaces and structural features at crucial points. In addition, the large-scale pit digging which took place toward the end of the Hellenistic Period seriously disrupted the earlier remains. The sub-phasing of the Hellenistic Period is, therefore, less than satisfactory except in Areas 22 and 32, where two phases of construction (fig. 11:A) can be identified with certainty. These are designated Phases 4c and 4b.

A. *Phase 4c in Areas 22 and 32.* Phase 4c is represented by a wall fragment, a number of beaten-earth surfaces, and a stone-built drain. The wall, the northern face of which is supported on a low foundation of field stones, runs along the southern edge of Area 22. A Phase 4b stone building erected directly on top of this wall destroyed the structure of which the wall was a part. A number of fairly well-defined surfaces (12.137, 22.169, and 32.135) may be assigned to Phase 4c, as well as Oven 32.089 and the ash-covered area associated with it. The most prominent feature of Phase 4c is its drainage system. This begins at the south as a wide catch basin, the floor of which consists of large, flat stones, and continues north in a slightly curving course until cut off by Pit 22.111 (fig. 7:2). The drain was lined with irregularly-shaped field stones pressed into the earthen sides of the trench and was covered with flat stones, four of which were basalt slabs cut from old grinders. Where Pit 22.111 intersects the drain, traces of a plastered lip were found. It seems more likely, therefore, that the pit served as a sump for the drainage system than that a redigging of Pit 22.111 accidentally cut off the northern extremity of the drain.

Two artifacts from Phase 4c deserve special mention. The first is a lekythos, complete except for the rim and part of the neck, found in a shallow pit immediately below Phase 4b Wall 32.021. The second is a whole juglet recovered from the fill immediately below the 4c surfacing in Area 32 and therefore possibly of Phase 5 origin.

B. *Phase 4b in Areas 22 and 32.* At the beginning of Phase 4b a layer of hard, bricky earth was laid over the Phase 4c remains, filling and covering the drain. At the same time Pit 22.111 was probably filled and put out of use. On the bricky leveling layer a stone building was erected in the western half of Areas 22 and 32. Three rooms of this building, bounded by Walls 32.050, 32.021, and 22.013, are preserved. The main north-south wall, about 1.0 m. wide, is built of two faces of field stones with rubble fill between. The east-west walls are slighter. All

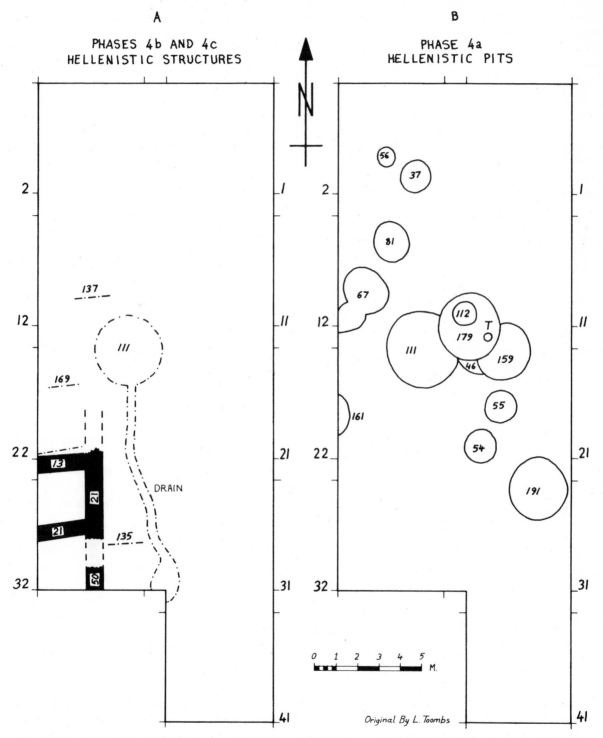

Fig. 11. Phase plans of the Hellenistic phases (4a-4c). Broken lines indicate conjectured walls. Broken lines with dots indicate Phase 4c walls and surfaces. Drawing by B. Zoughbi.

three walls are preserved four to five courses high, but are badly disturbed by Muslim graves (fig. 9:1). Only random patches of surfacing can be assigned to Phase 4b.

C. Phase 4 outside Areas 22 and 32. Outside of Areas 22 and 32 precise phasing of the Hellenistic remains is impossible since they exist only in isolated fragments. In all areas stumps of mud brick walls appear. The best preserved of these is the corner of two walls found in Area 11. Area 2 provides a remnant of a mud brick wall on a stone foundation. Three segments of stone-built walls were also found. Arguing on the basis of architectural similarity, the stone walls may tentatively be assigned to Phase 4b and the brick-on-stone to Phase 4c. The purely brick structures have no analogy in Areas 22 and 32, where the Hellenistic phasing is clearest.

Three patches of well-laid flagstones in Areas 2, 13, and 21 belong to Phase 4, but the surfacing is, in general, composed of compact earth. Water runnels cut through this surfacing, indicating that the area was unroofed. The surfaces merge irregularly into one another, but where extensive patches are preserved in Areas 1, 3, and 12, two distinct phases of surface buildup can be distinguished. These probably correspond to Phases 4c and 4b.

D. The Hellenistic pits. The history of the pits in Field I presents a complicated problem. As we have seen some of the pits were dug at the end of the Persian Period (Phase 5a) and filled at the beginning of the Hellenistic era (Phase 4c). Some, however, such as Pit 22.111, remained in use until the second Hellenistic phase (4b). At the end of the Hellenistic Period (Phase 4a) pit digging activity was renewed. The new pits are unlined and seem to have been kept in use for a short time only, after which they were filled in and other pits dug. In the complicated tangle in the center of the field, for example, five pits intersect one another. The assignment of all the Hellenistic pits to Phase 4a is, therefore, an oversimplification. It is, however, the best that can be done with the evidence available. No structures can with confidence be associated with the pits of Phase 4a, although some of the fragmentary brick walls may belong to buildings contemporary with them.

The fill in all the pits consisted of midden material containing a great deal of pottery of Hellenistic date. It was a valuable source of botanical and osteological specimens, as well as artifacts. The pits

provide evidence of a spinning and weaving industry in the form of numerous spindle whorls, loom-weights, and bone spatulas. They also contained iron, bronze, and chert blades, fibulae, beads, pieces of basalt bowls, and numerous other objects. Notable among the artifacts are two sherds with faint traces of writing, the two amulets pictured in fig. 18:7 and 9, and a "scarab" on which the customary beetle was replaced by the figure of a seated baboon. The evidence of the pit fills indicates that the settlement of the tell in Hellenistic times was more prosperous and more residential than the preserved remains suggest.

E. Summary. The Hellenistic occupation of Tell el-Hesi seems to have developed in three stages. The first, marked by construction in mud brick on stone foundations, was mainly residential in the southern part of Field I, with open air surfaces to the north and east. This stage was followed by a more prosperous settlement in which stone construction was common. The third phase represents a decline in residential occupation and the use of the summit primarily as a storage area.

This sequence may help to explain the plan of Bliss' City VIII (fig. 19). The drawing shows the three types of structure described above: a substantial stone building, several brick walls on stone foundations, and other walls of mud brick alone. Bliss' plan probably represents the whole of the Hellenistic occupation in the northeast quadrant of the site, the three phases being represented on the same drawing. The large number of ovens shown on the plan supports this suggestion. The Joint Expedition discovered the remains of five ovens and three ash pits or fireplaces in the Hellenistic levels.

IV. The Arabic Period (Phase 3)

Sometime after the close of the Hellenistic Period the summit of the tell was roughly leveled, probably to adapt it for agricultural use. Layers of compact soil were laid down, and the tops of the pits, where subsidence of the loose fill had created depressions, were plugged with bricky earth. However, during the long period from the end of Hellenistic occupation to the establishment of the Muslim cemetery (Phase 2), the summit of the tell was used only occasionally and sporadically. The accumulation over the leveling layers is mainly a buildup of loess in successive levels, as if the surface were open to the action of wind and water throughout the period. This impression is supported by the virtual absence from the Acropolis of Roman, Byzantine, and early Arab sherds. None of the characteristic Ummayid cream wares or Abbaysid glazed wares are found and only random sherds of the Roman and Byzantine Periods occur. All three periods are, however, represented in surface finds from the valley south and east of Tell Sheqef. In all probability the Roman, Byzantine, and early Arab settlements abandoned the restricted area of the summit in favor of the more expansive valley floor.

The earliest evidence of post-Hellenistic occupation is an oven built into the fill of Hellenistic Pit 11.179 (fig. 11:B). However, this installation cannot be dated. Most of the surviving evidence of Arab occupation apparently falls into the Turkish period. This consists of fragments of mud brick and adobe walls of slight construction and without stone foundations which may be no more than garden-plot or sheep-fold dividers. The associated surfaces are of compacted mud with occasional fire and ash pits. A few garbage pits are also found.

The only coherent structure belonging to Phase 3 is a semicircle bounded by a low adobe wall. A mud-plastered drain, beside which a water jar was found, runs up to this installation. It has been suggested that the structure is an animal pen and that the summit of the tell may have functioned for a time as an outdoor market, but no convincing evidence for or against this hypothesis is available.

V. The Muslim Cemetery (Phase 2)

Describing his excavations in the northeast quadrant of the tell, F. J. Bliss (1898: 122) wrote, "Immediately under the surface we found many graves." He identified the graveyard as Arab and suggested (1898: 123) that it was "not more than two or three centuries old. I place it as far back as that because, until we covered it [sic!] its existence did not seem to be known, no objection being made to my digging there by the Arabs." The Joint Expedition has found no reason to dispute Bliss' dating.

The cemetery described by Bliss extended also to the areas excavated by the Joint Expedition. Every square produced its quota of graves, thickest along the eastern edge of the summit and thinning out toward the west. Areas 31 and 41 contain the heaviest concentration of burials. In both areas as many as five graves have cut successively into one another. The Muslim cemetery is, however, not confined to the summit of the tell. In Field VI on the easternmost of the southern dunes stands the stone foundation of a small building, the shrine of a minor Muslim saint. Numerous graves are located along the ridge of this dune. Close-packed graves are found on the central dune as well. In the small probe in Field V no less than 14 burials occurred. No Arab burials were found on the slopes of the tell, in the Lower City, or on the western dune. The graves found on the southern slope of the tell were Persian in date (see below, "Field III [The Southern Wall]: Persian Period Burials"). It is probable that the presence of the shrine accounts for the popularity of the site as a burial ground. When the communities which revered the saint moved from the area, his shrine fell into ruin and the cemetery ceased to be used. Its existence was soon forgotten, and the summit of the mound was brought under cultivation by the new inhabitants.

The Muslim cemetery was originally laid out in parallel north-south rows of graves, but repeated use of the cemetery soon destroyed the regular pattern of burials. Interments were made between the rows, and new burials were cut into older graves, sometimes removing part of the skeleton in the earlier burial. When bones were dug up in the excavation for a new grave, they were interred in a shallow pit. This practice accounts for the large number of disarticulated and partial skeletons found near the surface.

The typical burial was at the bottom of an oval shaft of a length adapted to fit the body. The shaft was dug through the loosely compacted loess layers until the harder earth of the ancient occupational levels was encountered. It was then narrowed by about 5-10 cm. on either side and continued downward a further 25-30 cm. The body, clothed in the garments of daily life but not placed in a coffin, was laid in the narrow bottom of the grave. The grave was commonly dug with the long axis roughly east-west and the body was placed with the head to the west in an extended position on the back. The right hand was stretched out at the side and the left placed over the pelvis. The head was turned over the right shoulder so that the eyes looked toward Mecca (the typical position is illustrated in fig. 12:2). After the body had been placed in the grave the cyst was covered with four or five flat capping stones which rested on the ledge where the grave narrowed. Fig. 12:1 shows a grave excavated to the point where the capping stones are exposed. The shaft was then filled with loess material removed during its excavation.

Numerous variations from the typical burial pattern occur. Some graves are stone lined as well as

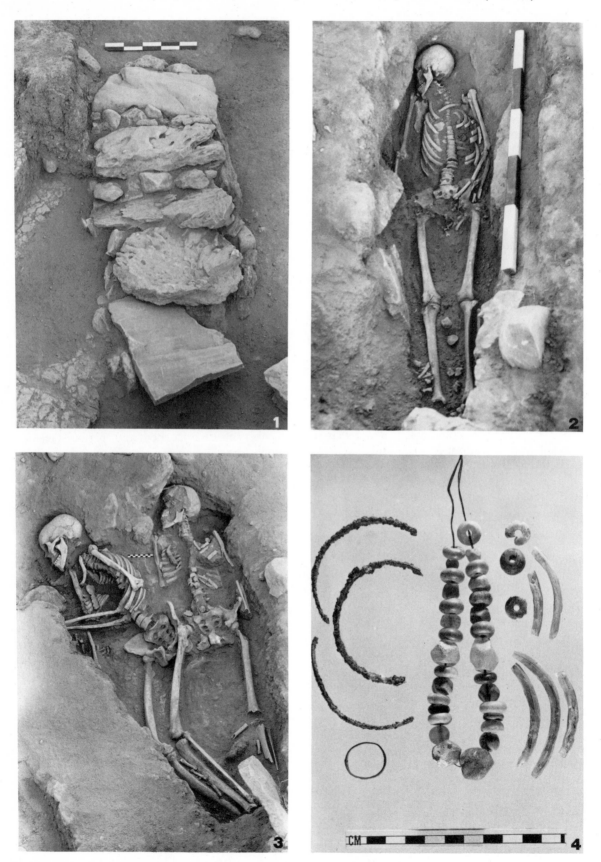

Fig. 12. Muslim burials of Phase 2. Photos by T. Rosen and J. Whitred.
1. Large cap stones covering a burial cyst.   3. A unique double burial in the same cyst.
2. Typical position of the skeleton.   4. Jewelry buried with a young woman.

stone capped. Others have linings of packed mud, while a large number of graves are neither capped nor lined. In some cases the body rests on its right side either extended or loosely or tightly flexed. In four cases the body was placed face down on the stomach with the head turned to the south. In one burial the standard position was reversed. The head was in the east end of the cyst with the eyes looking north. Four skeletons, each of which had elongated skulls, a type rare in the cemetery, had the bones stained a reddish hue. One man over seven feet tall was buried in a grave deeper and better built than those of his neighbors, perhaps as a tribute to his unique size. The skeleton of a young woman was found with her severed skull resting on her abdomen. According to local report beheading was a punishment for adultery among some Bedouin tribes. The bodies of a young woman and a somewhat older man were found in a single grave, the lower part of their bodies in contact and the upper separated from one another by a low wall of earth (fig. 12:3). A second case of multiple burial involved the body of an infant (0-6 months) resting in the lap of an older child (18 months-3 years). Five children who had apparently died at the same time were buried in a single pit in Area 12, each skeleton carefully separated from the others by earthen walls. There is a single case of the burial of an infant in an earthen jar.

The grave furnishings are simple in the extreme. Women were buried with their jewelry: glass and metal bracelets and anklets, bronze and iron finger and toe rings, a variety of beads in glass and semi-precious stones, and one or two pendants. Fig. 12:4 shows a typical collection of jewelry from a single grave, the burial of a young female (22.207). The burials of males were usually without grave furnishings of any kind. The major exception is a grave in which five side-spouted water jars were placed in the shaft immediately over the cyst.

The proportionately large number of infant burials in the cemetery testifies to the high death rate among children in the Arab community to which the cemetery belonged. The infant burials are usually relatively shallow, and this fact gives the impression that they are chronologically later than the deeper burials in the cemetery. It has been suggested that near the end of its residence in the Hesi area the Arab community suffered a plague of severe proportions which took its toll mostly among the children. However, since the Muslim custom is to bury a body approximately chest deep (Granqvist 1965: 36), the depth of the burial depends on the

height of the deceased, and children's graves would naturally be shallower than those of adults. The exceptionally deep grave of the seven-foot "Goliath" mentioned above conforms to this principle. The depth of the graves below the existing surface is, therefore, of little stratigraphic value.

For a number of reasons successive phases of the cemetery cannot be determined. All the shafts were cut from so close to the present surface that their tops are obliterated by cultivation and the depth of the graves is an unreliable stratigraphic index. The cemetery sub-phases, given in the "Phasing Summary" (fig. 20), are therefore not to be interpreted as chronologically distinct periods of use. The cemetery was almost certainly used continuously from its establishment to its abandonment. The sub-phases merely represent physically superimposed layers now found within the cemetery. The children, probably because of their smaller size, were buried in shallower graves than the adults. The first preliminary report (Toombs 1974:21,27) listed three sub-phases in the history of the cemetery, stratigraphically distinguished from one another, and described these in terms of a preparatory phase and two successive phases of use. This reconstruction was based on the erroneous assumption that the graves were dug from the levels at which their stone cappers were found. When in 1973 the shafts of the graves were recognized the original conclusions had to be abandoned. The description given in the preliminary report is misleading and unreliable.

VI. Military Trenching (Phase 1)

When work began on the site in 1970 the summit was scarred by partially filled military trenches. Three large, rectangular depressions, located at the southeast corner of the tell and at the southeast and northwest corners of Bliss' cut, marked the position of major rifle pits or machine gun emplacements. A larger depression below the crest of the mound in Areas 3 and 13 probably represented the location of the command post. These entrenchments were connected by a series of crawl-trenches which zig-zagged through the excavated areas. The trenches showed evidence of multiple use, since in many places two or three trench floors were found. Before excavation took place the trench system was cleared of accumulated debris and yielded a miscellaneous collection of "artifacts," including plastic bags, spent cartridges, and iron nails.

Trenching occurs on the southern dunes also. A line of rifle pits runs along the crests of all three dunes. The combination of trenches on the summit of the tell and along the dunes controls the highest ground in the area and provides a commanding view over the terrain, particularly to the south. According to local report, the summit was fortified by the Turks during World War I and the trenching was renewed during the War of Liberation in 1948 when the Hesi area was the scene of intense fighting.

Field III (The Southern Wall)

The circumstances of the discovery of the southern wall have already been indicated, and a preliminary description of the method of excavation and of the three zones of construction has been given (above, "Previous and Present Excavations"). The interpretation of the date of the wall and of the function of the three zones in relation to one another underwent a series of changes as excavation progressed. The preliminary report of 1970-71 (Toombs 1974: 28-31) represents an early stage in this process and requires correction and revision in the light of the later evidence.

The horizontal extent of Zones A, B, and C is shown in plan on fig. 3, which also indicates the position of the two sections through the wall (A-A' and B-B'). A schematic drawing of section B-B' is presented in fig. 13, and the sequence of photographs in fig. 14 shows crucial stages in the development of section A-A' through the eastern end of the wall.

I. Zone A

A. Foundation. The northernmost of the three zones in the southern wall (Zone A) was founded in a deep trench cut at an angle of 70° into the foot of the southern slope. The trench penetrated three distinct layers of earlier material: gross debris (marked "Fill" in fig. 13), a series of almost horizontal, water-deposited layers ("Wash" in fig. 13), and a poorly-sorted debris layer containing many brick fragments ([2] in fig. 13). This sequence of layers is called "earlier fill" to distinguish it from "later fill" in the foundation trench itself. Only the northern face of the trench is preserved, the southern being obliterated by Zone B construction.

In the bottom of the trench a massive platform of irregularly shaped stones was laid as a foundation for the Zone A brickwork. Many of these stones are freshly quarried chalk, but sandstone, limestone, and conglomerate rock also occur, as well as a few stones robbed from earlier buildings. The stone platform stood 10 to 13 courses (a little under 2.0 m.) high and was about 4.5 m. wide at the top. Its top was carefully leveled in preparation for the brick superstructure. The northern face of the platform rested against the side of the trench, conforming to its slope; the southern was constructed almost vertically. This stone foundation was examined only at the eastern end of Field III (Areas 5A, 18, and 23) and may not, therefore, represent the nature of the foundation along the whole length of Zone A.

In Area 5A, where the eastern end of the wall system was cut away in order to produce section A-A', a stone layer, apparently associated with the Zone A foundation platform, extends eastward under the Zone B construction (fig. 14:4). Moreover, a line of stones, integrally connected with the Zone A foundation, extends northward along the eastern slope of the tell (fig. 14:4). These observations are crucial for the stratigraphic sequence of the three zones. They show that Zone A originally extended eastward to the wadi face, where it turned northward and continued, at least for some distance, along the eastern slope. It follows, therefore, that the Zone B builders by-passed the eastern extremity of Zone A and produced their own rounded corner at the wadi face. Zone B must, consequently, be a later construction than Zone A.

Along the eastern slope of the tell, the whole wall system is eroded away, except for a surviving fragment of the inner face of the Zone A foundation. An exploratory trench into the wadi face above this stone line (Area 22A, fig. 1) tended to confirm the reconstruction suggested above. The cut showed precisely the same stratigraphy as that of the "earlier fill" described above: gross debris above water-deposited layers, above brick-filled debris. The obvious conclusion is that the Area 22A cut is located just inside the line of the Zone A wall, now destroyed by erosion.

The layers of "earlier fill" are interesting, both for their pottery content and for the suggestions they give of earlier construction predating Zone A. The water-laid layers must have been deposited against a major wall structure. This could not have been Zone A, which cut the layers after their deposition, but must have been an earlier wall destroyed in the building of Zone A. The brick-filled debris over which the wash layers ran could only have been deposited at a still earlier period. Zone A, therefore, comes late in a series of structures at the foot of the southern slope. The pottery of the "earlier fill" contains a large quantity of Early and Late Bronze

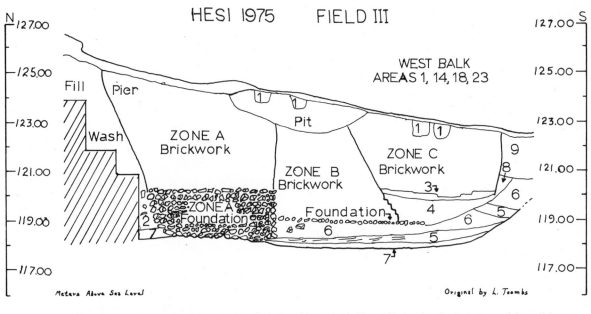

Fig. 13. Simplified section through Field III along the west balks of Areas 1, 14, 18, and 23 showing the three zones of the wall down to foundation level. The numbered layers are identified as follows:

1. Persian Period graves.
2. Bricky fill through which the Zone A foundation was cut.
3. The plaster foundation of Zone C.
4. Zone B fill in foundation trench 8.
5. Chert filled clay/sand layers.

6. Sand fill.
7. Virgin sand.
8. Zone B foundation trench.
9. Brick detritus.

Age sherds and a smaller number of Iron I and Iron II forms. Field analysis indicates that the latest sherds in the "earlier fill" belong to the transition between Iron II and the Persian Period, while the "later fill" in the foundation trench itself contains sherds identified as clearly Persian Period in origin. This evidence, subject to revision when a more detailed study of the pottery is completed, indicates that Zone A was founded early in the Persian Period, perhaps replacing structures in use up to the end of Iron II. The most interesting single piece of pottery came from the "earlier fill" in Area 22A. It was a fragment of a Late Bronze Age deep bowl with a band of red paint on the lip. Below the rim was a molded figure of the fertility goddess in low relief with only the legs and feet missing.

B. Brickwork. The Zone A bricks are approximately 55-60 x 25-30 x 10-15 cm. in size. They vary in color through several shades of brown and possess a very high clay content with numerous limestone flecks. They are laid in regular courses to a preserved height of about 4.0 m. Both the southern and eastern faces of the brickwork are vertical.

C. Westward extent. As fig. 3 shows, Zone A extends westward through the excavated squares for a distance of approximately 60 m. The western

corner has not yet been reached. The entire width, a uniform 4.5 m., has been exposed in five places along its length (Area 5A, a large exposure in Areas 13, 18, and 23, and narrower exposures in Areas 31, 106, and 108).

D. Piers. A curious feature of Zone A is the presence of slighter walls of the same type of brickwork extending northward at right angles to the main wall into the southern slope of the tell. Five piers have been partially or completely exposed. They vary somewhat in width (from 1.25-1.35 m.) and in length (from 2.50-3.75 m.), the shorter piers being at the western end. On the basis of the five examples investigated, the piers appear to have occurred at regular intervals of about 2.5 m. along the northern face of the wall. The piers are bonded into the main wall and are, therefore, contemporary with it.

The piers never appeared above ground level. They were constructed in stages within the foundation trench of the wall and were embedded from top to bottom in the "later fill." Between the piers, and sometimes beneath them, the bottom of the trench was covered with a thick platform of brick as much as ten courses deep. This platform was encountered in both Areas 23 and 107, but was not investigated in depth. It may be the top of an earlier wall shaved off by the Zone A builders or part of the early stages of construction of the wall itself. From this platform the bases of the piers climb step-wise up the steeply sloping sides of the foundation trench. Level layers of mud brick occur at various heights within the fill representing, no doubt, working platforms set in at various stages of the brick-laying and filling process.

The tops of the piers and the filled-in foundation trench were covered by a platform composed of three courses of mud brick. Traces of this capping occurred in Areas 23 and 28, but it was best preserved in Area 107. How far the capping extended up the slope or whether it was general along the length of the wall is not known. The function of the piers and capping can only be conjectured. The piers may have been devices for keying the wall into the slope, and giving it stability, with the cappers functioning as part of the lower stages of a glacis or terracing up the slope, as an erosion control system, or simply as a brick walkway along the inside of the wall.

II. Zone B

A. Foundation. Zone B was apparently built in order to widen the Zone A wall. Its foundation trench (Layer [4] in fig. 13), was dug from the south against the outer face of Zone A. The trench cut through layers of chert-filled soil alternating with layers of sand fill ([5] and [6] in fig. 13) and bottomed out over sand about half way down the stone foundation of Zone A. Over the sand on the leveled floor of the trench, a single close-packed layer of stones provided the foundation on which the Zone B brickwork was erected. The stone foundation extended about 0.60 m. beyond the southern and eastern faces of the wall.

B. Brickwork. The Zone B bricks are mold made and of fairly regular size (50-55 x 25-30 x 10 cm.). They are very pale brown (Munsell 10YR 7/4) in color and have a high sand content with almost no limestone flecks. These distinctive bricks are set flush against the southern face of Zone A and are laid in regular courses, except at the rounded southeast corner where they are laid in radial patterns in order to bring the wall around smoothly in a semicircular arc. In the lower 1.20 m. of the wall the brick courses are progressively set back from one another, giving the wall a batter of about 30°. The batter continues in the upper portion of the wall, which is faced with a layer of smooth plaster.

Ground level was probably between the unplastered and plastered segments of the wall.

C. Extent. The Zone B brickwork, a uniform 2.0 m. in width, runs along the outer face of Zone A for the full 60.0 m. investigated. The whole length of its southern face is plastered, and the plaster line forms a sharp demarcation between Zones B and C.

The most interesting part of the Zone B construction is its curved southeast corner. This semicircular corner was at first identified as a tower, but is now seen to be simply the rounded corner of the Zone B wall. Outside the wall, just west of the corner, a sump filled with large stones was found. It probably functioned to trap the water which drained off along the south face of the wall. Immediately to the north of the corner, Zone B passes around the preserved end of the Zone A wall, stepping up over a stone layer associated with the Zone A foundation platform (see below, "Pre-wall Structures in Field III"; fig. 14:3,4). Unfortunately erosion into the wadi has destroyed the northern extension of Zone B north from the rounded corner (fig. 3).

III. Zone C

A. Foundation. Zone C is founded on a higher level than either of the other construction zones in the southern wall. Its foundation trench, like that of Zone B, is dug from the south. It was a shallow excavation, only slightly below the ancient ground level, meeting Zone B just below the level of its plaster face. In this trench a layer of mud plaster, 0.25-0.35 m. thick, was laid, and the lowest course of the Zone C brickwork was pressed into the plaster while it was still wet. The plaster foundation sloped upward at its southern end in such a way as to throw the weight of the superstructure back against the face of Zone B.

B. Brickwork. The Zone C bricks are mold made and variable in size within narrow limits (50-60 x 30-40 x 10 cm.). They are yellowish brown (Munsell 10YR 5/4) in color and have a high clay content with numerous limestone flecks. The bricks are laid in regular courses. For the most part the Zone C brickwork is pressed directly against the plastered face of Zone B. In Area 103, however, a loose fill containing large pieces of chert was packed between the northern face of Zone C and the southern face of Zone B. In Area 5A a similar phenomenon was observed, only here the patching was between Zones A and B. A plug of mud plaster, visible in fig. 14:4, was pressed in between the faces of the two zones.

The brickwork evidently had a tendency to settle to the south, pulling the zones apart, and the cracks which developed were repaired by plugging with a variety of filling material. The southern face of Zone C was probably nearly vertical, but has been badly worn by erosion.

C. Extent and external features. Zone C is about 4.5-5.0 m. in width and extends through the excavated areas for slightly more than 60.0 m. At its southeast end it runs beyond the rounded corner of Zone B, which it encases completely. The northward course of Zone C along the wadi face has been eroded away, and the reconstruction in fig. 3 is based solely on probability.

Certain external features are preserved along the southern face of Zone C. At several points surfaces of bricky material heavily infused with limestone flecks extend along the wall face. These may have been road surfaces outside the wall. At one point a deep pit filled with the same bricky material was uncovered. This pit was probably used for the manufacture of bricks used in the wall construction.

The most puzzling of the external features of Zone C occurs in Areas 105 and 110. A band of bricky material, harder and darker in color than the brickwork of the wall itself, extends along the wall face for about 3.05 m. The band then turns away from the wall at right angles and runs southward out of Area 105, creating what appears to be a wide platform against the outer face of Zone C (fig. 3). A tiny triangle of what may be the western face of this platform appeared in Area 110, but the exposure is too small to make the reconstruction in fig. 3 absolutely certain. Since the bricky material is exceedingly hard and individual bricks within it are difficult to identify, the bricks of the platform were probably laid wet. Where brick coursing could be determined, the individual bricks appear to be unusually large, averaging 50 x 90 cm. At the present stage of excavation the most likely explanation of this bricky platform is that it is the base of a tower projecting southward from the Zone C wall. The depth of the platform (0.85 m. below the base of Zone C) makes it improbable that the brickwork is the foundation of a roadway.

The topography of the site would suggest that the southern wall should corner and begin to run northward near the western end of the present excavations. No evidence of this turn has been found, although the bricky platform may represent construction at or near such a corner.

D. Earlier structures. Imbedded in Zone C in Area 105 was a patch of brickwork different in color and composition from the rest of Zone C (fig. 15:2.B). The bricks measure 27 x 48 cm. and are composed of a sand/clay mixture. A probe dug against the face of this fragment revealed that the bricky platform, described above, ran *under* Zone C and up against this earlier wall. The wall fragment thus appears to have belonged to a structure predating Zone C, and the bricky platform seems to have had more than one phase prior to its incorporation in the Zone C construction. These points will remain obscure until a section is cut through the western end of Zone C.

IV. Pre-wall Structures in Field III

In the description of the three zones of the southern wall, mention is made of evidence for earlier structures disturbed by, or underlying, or imbedded in it:

1. The stratigraphy of the "earlier fill" through which the Zone A foundation trench was cut (above, "Zone A: Foundation");

2. The brick layers between and beneath the piers of Zone A (above, "Zone A: Piers");

3. The water course sealed beneath the foundation of Zone C (below, "Date and Function of the Southern Wall");

4. The fragment of wall encased in Zone C in Area 105 and the bricky platform associated with this fragment (above, "Zone C: Earlier Structures").

Three additional structures should be added to this list: two walls within the "earlier fill" in Area 107 and a stone-built drain in Area 5A.

In Area 107 the foundation trench for Zone A did not cut through pure fill as it did in Areas 23 and 22A. Instead it intersected two walls situated one above the other (fig. 15:1). The upper of these is oriented northwest to southeast on a line roughly paralleling Zone A. Traces of similar brickwork occur in Area 31, so that the wall in question must have had a considerable east-west extent. At least six courses are preserved, and the bricks show evidence of having been exposed to fire. The lower wall, found only in Area 107, is oriented north-south. Its eight courses of yellow sandy brick rest on a foundation of stones cemented together. On both sides of the wall destruction debris consisting of charred wood and fallen bricks is piled. Neither wall has as yet been investigated, and no estimate of date or function can be given.

Beneath the Zone B sump (above, "Zone B: Extent"), a section of a stone-built drain was

Fig. 14. Progressive stages in the cutting of the Field III, Area 5A section through the defensive wall at the foot of the southern slope. A, B, and C are the successive zones of construction in the wall. A', B', and C', are the foundations of these zones. D is the foundation trench for Zone C. E is the unplastered lower portion of Zone B. F is a pier springing from the Zone A brickwork. G is the beginning of

the long section through the wall in Areas 1, 11, 18, and 23. The increasingly complicated nature of the construction is revealed as the excavation proceeds. See text for fuller description. Photos by T. Rosen, W. Nassau, and J. Whitred.

uncovered. It was traced to the south balk of Area 5A and picked up again 10.0 m. further south in Area 5. The drain has vertical sides, an arched roof, and a flat bottom paved with large stones. It is 1.0 m. high and 0.75 m. wide. It runs roughly parallel to the main wadi, draining southward in the direction of one of the smaller east-west ravines (fig. 1:E). The drain ran up to and under the Zone B rounded corner. When the Zone B construction was removed, the drain, now roofless and plugged with stones, was seen to run beneath the Zone B construction until its rapid slope upward to the north brought it to the level of the stone foundation where it ceased altogether (fig. 14:4). The drain was not, therefore, functional at the time of any of the zones and must predate all three.

More ambiguous is the presence beneath the Zone B foundation of a close-packed layer of stones, south of the Zone A foundation platform (fig. 14:4). This stone layer ends abruptly at the Zone A foundation and seems to have been laid up against it. If this is true, the stone layer must be intermediate in date between Zones A and B. The conclusion is, however, based solely on observation of the surface of the layer, a notoriously unreliable criterion unless supported by vertical evidence. The nature and function of the stonework cannot be elucidated until a portion of it is removed and its foundation studied.

V. Persian Period Burials

After the southern wall system went out of use, a deep pit was scooped out of the decaying brickwork (fig. 13), probably as a mine for bricks to be used in other construction. This pit quickly filled up with water-laid earth, and the fill of the pit, as well as the area around it, became the site of a small cemetery. This burial ground has been studied by Dr. Michael Coogan (1975), and only its general features and stratigraphic significance will be discussed here.

The graves cluster thickest along the wadi edge (Areas 13, 1, and 5) and thin out to the west (Areas 14, 2, 15, 3, and 16). Superficially the burials resemble those of the Muslim cemetery on the summit. The cysts, frequently capped with flat stones, are at the bottom of ovoid or rectangular shafts. The graves, like those of the upper cemetery, are oriented east-west. In the lower cemetery, however, the same attention is not given to the orientation of the body. The head was frequently, though not invariably, placed in the eastern end of the grave. The deeply-flexed position is common, and a wider variety of grave furnishings occurs than

in the upper cemetery. For example, a juglet was associated with Grave 2.004, a dagger with 1.007, and a toggle pin with 1.001. The pottery and artifacts indicate a date late in the Persian Period.

The cemetery provides a *terminus ante quem* for the southern wall. The wall went out of use and successively became a mine for bricks and the site of a cemetery before the end of the Persian Period. The abandonment of the wall as a functional structure and the employment of its top for other uses may reasonably be coordinated with the latest Persian phase (5a) on the summit, when the Acropolis was predominately a grain storage area (above, "Field I [the Acropolis]: Phase 5a," and fig. 20).

VI. Date and Function of the Southern Wall

Excavation of the southern wall began at the eastern extremity of Zone C (figs. 3 and 14:1). The foundation trench was carefully excavated, but its clearance was complicated by a filled-in gulley where heavy runoff had flowed eastward into the wadi. The sub-foundation pottery of Zone C contained a preponderance of 10th-9th century B.C. sherds. Zone C was, therefore, tentatively dated to the beginning of Iron II. Zone B was obviously earlier than Zone C, and Zone A, on the evidence of its foundation trench, had to be dated to the Persian Period. This gave the chronological sequence B/C/A, with Zone A being interpreted as a Persian Period repair and consolidation of the inner or northern face of the wall system.

The evidence of the two major sections (A-A' and B-B') now makes it clear that the true construction sequence is Zone A/Zone B/Zone C, the wall being progressively widened southward as each zone was added. It has also been shown that earlier structures existed along and near the line of the southern wall and that erosion eastward toward the wadi was heavy. In all probability, pottery washed down from the earlier structures skewed the evidence in favor of an early date for Zone C. However, with the establishment of the A/B/C sequence and the firm dating of Zone A to the Persian Period, this conclusion must be abandoned, and the entire history of the southern wall must be placed within the Persian Period.

The original fortification of the southern slope may have been related to Persian plans for the conquest of Egypt. Tell el-Hesi could hardly have been a jumping-off point for a military expedition against Egypt, but it would have been useful as a depot for food supplies and as a station for reserve troops. The heavy runoff from the tell continuously threatened the existence of the southern wall and made constant repair and reconstruction necessary. The three zones of construction represent three major stages in this process. Sometime during the Persian Period, probably at the end of Phase 5b or the beginning of 5a, the wall system was allowed to fall into disuse, and its superstructure underwent rapid decay.

The southern wall evidently fulfilled a double function. It provided a first line of defense for the city and helped check the erosion of the slopes of the mound. Unfortunately we do not know the original height of the brick superstructure or any of the three zones and cannot, therefore, say whether they constituted a free-standing defensive wall or merely provided a steep scarp at the foot of the slope.

VII. Chalcolithic Occupation in Field III

Excavation in Area 5, south of the southern wall, uncovered a circular structure, 2.50 m. in diameter, with adobe walls preserved to a height of 0.40 m. No interior or exterior surfaces were preserved. The pottery associated with the structure dated from the Late Chalcolithic or the very beginning of the Early Bronze Age. The evidence was insufficient to establish whether or not the structure was a dwelling, but the configuration suggests the "hut circles" found at Arad and nearby Tell ⁾Ereini.

Survey and Probes

The survey project (briefly described above) began in 1973 as a surface survey of the Lower City

Fig. 15.
1. Field III, Area 107, looking north and showing the earlier walls through which the trench for the Zone A brickwork cut. A is a wall of dark-colored mud brick running east-west, parallel to Zone A. B is a north-south wall of yellow brick at right angles to Zone A, and with destruction debris piled on either side (C).
2. Complex Zone C construction in Field III, Area 105. Heavy caliche-filled layering (A) runs at right angles to the face of Zone C and may represent a corner in the wall. B is a fragment of lighter-colored brickwork imbedded in Zone C. D is the foundation trench of Zone C.
Photos by J. Whitred.

and its immediate environs. The ground to be surveyed was laid out in 50 x 30 m. areas. Each area was examined by a team of four, working according to an established pattern. Ten minutes were devoted to walking over the area and noting its surface features. An additional twenty minutes was given to the systematic collection and recording of the ceramic, artifactual, and lithic material. This system gives an equal number of person/hours to each area and, if the membership of the team remains the same, insures consistency of observation. Absolute consistency cannot, however, be maintained because of such factors as fatigue, time of day, and development of skill as team members become more practiced in observation.

For recording purposes each area was treated as a unit except where the topography made this undesirable. In these cases the area was subdivided into topographical zones, the number 53.2, for example, referring to Area 53, zone 2. The survey resulted in a series of maps showing the density of distribution over the site of the pottery of the various archeological periods.

Early Bronze Age sherds were most heavily concentrated on the southern dune system (fig. 1:D) and on the ridge running west and north from the base of the tell (fig. 1:G). On the dunes only occasional sherds later than Early Bronze were found, suggesting that this was the only period of occupation represented there. Conclusions based on surface examination remain inconclusive unless checked by excavation. Since, in any event, it was desirable to examine the extent and nature of Early Bronze Age occupation on the site preparatory to more extensive excavation in the Lower City, Fields IV, V, VI, and VII were laid out and exploratory probes were dug in each field (fig. 1).

The probes provided an opportunity for experimentation in excavation techniques. In Field V the initial layout was in 1.0 x 1.0 m. squares, and excavation and recording were controlled by these small units. In Field VI the ash layer was gridded in 1.0 x

Fig. 16. Probes into the Early Bronze Age remains.
1. Two phases of Early Bronze Age housing are seen in the balk of Field IV.
2. The stratification of Field V, drawn in fig. 17B, is shown here photographically.

1.0 m. squares, and the grid was photographed as each 2 cm. layer was removed. The grid, combined with the sequence of photographs, should make possible a complete reconstruction of the destruction layer, showing the position within it of all pottery and artifacts. If the experiment proves successful, it may become the basis of a method of dealing with living surfaces on which substantial deposits of pottery and artifacts are found.

I. Field IV

A 2 x 2 m. probe on the western shoulder of the ridge (fig. 1:G) revealed Early Bronze Age housing immediately beneath a 0.75 m. surface layer disturbed by deep plowing. Two phases of construction occurred, marked by the rebuilding of walls. Each had at least two sub-phases, identified by the relaying of floors. The walls were of mud brick without stone foundations and only two bricks wide. The floors were of beaten earth or thin plaster

(fig. 16:1). Numerous sherds from domestic vessels and two whole pots, one of which is pictured in fig. 18:2, were recovered from these surfaces. All stratified pottery was EB III in date.

II. Field V

The Field V probe was established in relation to two large, cut stones visible on the surface which, it was thought, might be in their original position and indicate the presence on the central dune of a large public building. However, the stones, whose circular shape suggested column bases, proved to have been displaced from their original location in fairly recent times. Fig. 17:B shows the east balk of the probe. In reading the section it should be remembered that at the 140.35 m. level the section steps back 2.0 m., so that the upper and lower portions of the section are not continuous with one another. The lower part of the section is shown in fig. 16:2.

3. Field VI, looking north. The balk drawn in fig. 17A is on the left of the photograph.
4. Field VII showing the stratification drawn in fig. 17C.
Photos by W. Nassau and J. Whitred.

Field V has the greatest depth of occupational remains, and virgin soil had not been reached at a depth of 3.25 m. where excavation ceased. The probe revealed at least five phases of use of the central dune. The latest (Phase 1) consists of debris layers (2, 3, and 4) and the Muslim graves dug through them. The first structure encountered (Phase 2) was a wall (6) with its associated ashy surface (9). The pottery indicated that this was an Early Bronze structure, although a Late Bronze date cannot be absolutely ruled out. Below the foundation of the wall (6) a more substantial mud brick wall (11), with its associated surface (13), ran roughly east-west across the probe (Phase 3). Just beneath the foundation of this wall runs an ash-covered surface (15), overlying a dark, ashy, pottery-filled layer (16). These layers cover a thick deposit of ash mixed with sand (17). Thus Phase 4 represents a period of occupation for which no walls appear in the probe. A debris layer (18) containing many fallen bricks and resting on a heavy ash deposit (19) represents the destruction of Phase 5. Again, no walls are present in the probe. The solid bricky layer (20) below the ash may represent the flooring of Phase 5 or the beginning of the brick-work of a new phase. Excavation stopped at this point.

The function of the walls in Field V has not been established. Since surfaces exist to the south of them, they can have nothing directly to do with a major defense system; whether they are house walls or interior walls within a large building cannot yet be decided. The surfacing and the installations on it indicate domestic use. The two major ash layers (14 and 19) suggest two destructions during the Early Bronze Age, and the field readings of the pottery place the entire stratigraphic sequence within EB III.

III. Field VI

In the Field VI probe cut into the southern slope of the eastern dune (fig. 1), the overburden of debris was less than in Field V, and the Early Bronze Age remains were just below the surface. Fig. 16:3 shows the probe, viewed from the south, and fig. 17:A gives a drawing of its west balk. As in Field V, the latest phase consists of pitting activity (layer 2) and Muslim burials. One especially well-built cyst with its stone capping intact was dug into the northeast corner of the probe. The latest structure (Phase 2) is an imposing mud brick wall (6) which angles across the probe from southwest to northeast. It is composed of bricks of various colors and

composition and is preserved nine courses high. Its width is unknown since it extends beyond the northern limits of the probe. A heavy layer of wood ash (5), filled with flat-lying EB III sherds, lies at the base of the wall. The ash layer covered the top of another wall (7), the orientation of which is uncertain. This wall (Phase 3) is associated with a surface of hard-packed reddish earth (8). Lower brickwork (9) underlies the red earth surface, but whether it is a separate building phase or the foundation for the surface is unknown.

The wall structures of Field VI are too substantial to be house walls. Their size and orientation suggest a defense system along the southern edge of the eastern dune or the outer wall of a public building. Layer 5 gives evidence of the violent destruction by fire of the latest Early Bronze building in the field. All the pottery recovered from Field VI is EB III in date.

IV. Field VII

Almost the entire crest of the western dune (fig. 1:D) has been eroded away into the wadi system to the south. If any Early Bronze Age structures existed here, all that is left of them is the extreme northern portions of the buildings. To test whether any such remains survived, the geologist's probe into the southern slope of the dune was trimmed to a width of 0.50 m. and the section was drawn (fig. 17:C). Layers 3 and 4 consist of bricky material in which no coursing could be distinguished with certainty. They rest on a layer of plaster (5) which may be the remains of a surface. If this dubious structure is designated Phase 1, the second phase is a mud brick wall (6) resting on water-laid earth (7). Beneath this layer is a second mud brick wall (8) which is associated with an ash layer (9), a pebble surface (10), and a second ash layer (11; Phase 3, or possibly Phases 3 and 4). The lowest ash layer overlies caliche-filled earth, in which some possible mortar lines were detected.

The orientation of the two mud brick walls in the section (layers 6 and 8) seems to be east-west, along the ridge line of the dune. The surfaces extend southward from the walls which may, therefore, be the northern boundaries of rooms, the southern portions of which have been destroyed by erosion.

Since there is no common point of reference for the four probes, the sections cannot at this stage be correlated with one another. Field V appears to have the most complete Early Bronze sequence, which is represented only in part in Field VI; consequently which of the two ash layers in Field V

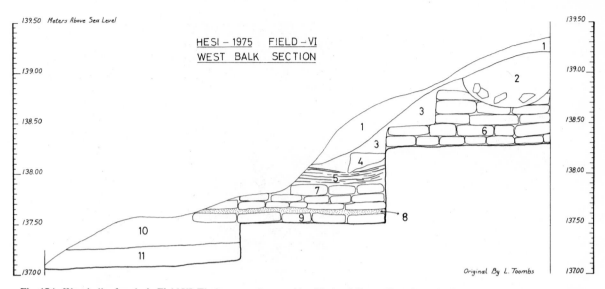

Fig. 17A. West balk of probe in Field VI. The layer numbers are identified as follows: (1) surface, (2) pit containing stones, (3) decayed brick, (4) fallen brick, (5) ash layers, (6) mud brick wall, (7) mud brick wall, (8) hard-packed reddish surface, (9) mud brick, (10) compact gray earth, (11) hard, caliche-filled earth.
Drawing by B. Zoughbi.

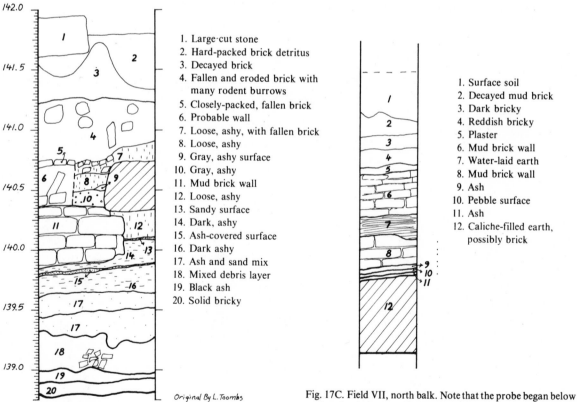

1. Large-cut stone
2. Hard-packed brick detritus
3. Decayed brick
4. Fallen and eroded brick with many rodent burrows
5. Closely-packed, fallen brick
6. Probable wall
7. Loose, ashy, with fallen brick
8. Loose, ashy
9. Gray, ashy surface
10. Gray, ashy
11. Mud brick wall
12. Loose, ashy
13. Sandy surface
14. Dark, ashy
15. Ash-covered surface
16. Dark ashy
17. Ash and sand mix
18. Mixed debris layer
19. Black ash
20. Solid bricky

1. Surface soil
2. Decayed mud brick
3. Dark bricky
4. Reddish bricky
5. Plaster
6. Mud brick wall
7. Water-laid earth
8. Mud brick wall
9. Ash
10. Pebble surface
11. Ash
12. Caliche-filled earth, possibly brick

Fig. 17B. Field V, east balk. Note that the upper part of the section (above 140.35 m.) is set 2.0 m. further east than the lower portion. Drawing by B. Zoughbi.

Fig. 17C. Field VII, north balk. Note that the probe began below surface level. Scale 1:25. Elevation unknown. Drawing by B. Zoughbi.

1

2   3

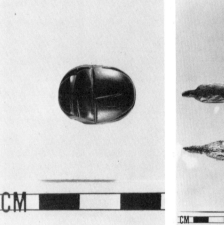

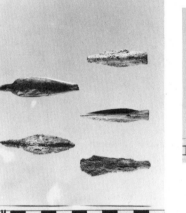

4   5   6

Fig. 18. Selection of artifacts.   7
  1. Attic ware krater rim from Phase 5b
  2. Early Bronze Age vessel from Field IV
  3. Ceramic figurine from Phase 5d
  4. Black steatite scarab from an early Persian context
  5. Projectile points from various Persian contexts
  6. Finger rings from Muslim burials   8   9
  7. Faience amulet from the Hellenistic fill in a Persian pit
  8. Fragment of a green faience figurine from Phase 5c
  9. Carved ivory amulet from the Hellenistic fill in a Persian pit
Photos by T. Rosen, W. Nassau, and J. Whitred.

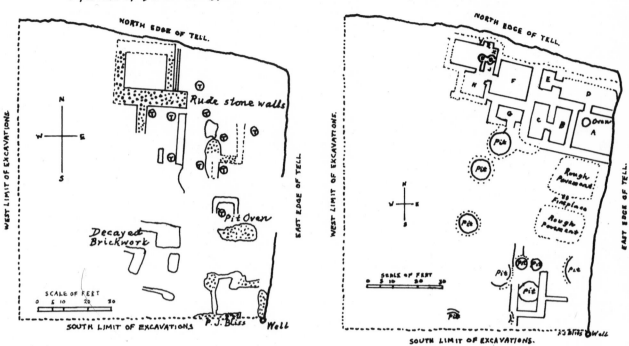

Fig. 19. Reproduction of the plans of Bliss' Cities VIII and VII. These cities appear to correspond to Phases 4 (Hellenistic) and 5 (Persian). Adapted from Bliss (1898: 111 and 115).

corresponds to the destruction level in Field VI remains undetermined.

The probes have, however, fulfilled their main purpose. They demonstrate that the Early Bronze Age occupation (predominantly, if not exclusively, EB III) is extensive and covers virtually the whole of the Lower City, except for the slopes of the central wadis (fig. 1:E), as well as the lowest levels of the tell itself. They also give a good preview of the location of public structures and housing areas. The western ridge and possibly the western dune were occupied by houses. The central dune is probably a housing area, although it may have been occupied by a single large building. A massive structure, possibly a defensive wall, ran along the southern edge of the eastern dune. Further excavation of the Early

Bronze Age levels should give a diversified picture of the culture of the period both in its public and domestic aspects.

Fig. 20 summarizes in tabular form the results of the first four seasons of excavation at Tell el-Hesi. Work on Phases 1 through 5 in the Acropolis area, probably equivalent to Bliss' Cities VIII and VII (fig. 19), has been completed and will be published in final form in the near future. Sufficient data on the southern wall has been gathered to justify a detailed publication of the structure. The major emphases of the next stage of excavation will be a broad exposure of Early Bronze Age structures and the exploration of the Iron Age remains on the summit.

Manuscript completed in January, 1975.

PHASE NO.	SUB-PHASE	PERIOD	DATE	CHARACTERISTICS
1		Modern	After A.D. 1900	Turkish, Egyptian and Israeli military trenching, reaching from the present surface to Phase 4 levels.
2		Late Arabic	Yet to be determined	Muslim cemetery. Fields I, V and VI.
	2a			Infant burials near the surface of the mound.
	2b			Burials of both children and adults in a prepared cemetery area.
3		Late Arabic	Yet to be determined	Pits, hearths, packed earth surfaces and fragmentary walls, probably associated with agriculture and/or stock raising.
4		Hellenistic	3rd-1st cent. B.C.	Three sub-phases, badly damaged by graves and trenching. Field I only.
	4a			Cultural decline marked by much pit digging. Many pits filled at end of period.
	4b			Stone-constructed building and agricultural surfaces. Drain of 4c filled up. Some pit digging.
	4c			Brick building on partial stone foundation. Stone-built drain with water catchment. Many Persian pits filled in at the beginning of the sub-phase.
5		Persian	6th-4th cent. B.C.	Four sub-phases. Fields I and III.
	5a			Square brick Building 1.126. Latest use of brick Structure 31.058. Numerous deep pits, mainly for grain storage. Persian Period burials in decayed tops of Zones A, B and C walls in Field III.
	5b			Building 1.126 used as underground chamber. Structure 31.058 in use. Disappearance of 5c agricultural residues. Multiple resurfacing and use of flagstones and cobbles. Zone C wall in Field III constructed ?
	5c			Founding of Building 31.058. Agricultural residues and outside surfaces. Zone B wall in Field III constructed ?
	5d			Extensive excavation into earlier remains south of Wall 41.162. Casemate-like building in south-east quadrant. Open air surfaces to the north-west. Zone A wall in Field III constructed ?
Sub 5d				Not a true phase, but a sequence of levels as yet only partially studied. The assignment of the defensive walls to the sub-phases is conjectural.
	1	Persian/ Iron II	6th cent. B.C.	Relatively poor house construction on a brick platform over the ash layer. Northern portions removed by 5d construction.
				ASH
	2	Iron II	7th-6th cent. B.C.	House 51.098. Manasseh wall on southern slope ? Northern portions removed by 5d construction.
	3	Iron II		Brick-built house with Pit 51.124. Glacis on southern slope ? Northern portions removed by 5d construction.
	4			Large building with narrow chambers under 5d walls and fill to the north of 5d Wall 41.162. Date and function unknown.
EB		EB III	27th-24th cent. B.C.	Four or five phases of Early Bronze Age occupation in Fields IV, V, VI and VII probes. Domestic occupation in Fields IV and V. Major walls in Field VI. Type of occupation in Field VII unknown. Heavy destruction layer within the EB period.

Fig. 20. Phasing summary. The phasing does not represent all periods of occupation on the site, but only those investigated by the expedition. The conclusions presented, particularly in respect to all phases earlier than 5d, are tentative and subject to revision. The phasing of the wall structures on the southern slope is merely plausible and will, of course, be altered and refined when the slope is excavated.

APPENDIX

Staff of the Hesi Expedition (1970-1975)

Project Director
John E. Worrell (1970-74, on leave 1974-75), Hartford Seminary Foundation, Holy Cross College
D. Glenn Rose (*Acting Director*, 1974-75), Phillips University

Senior Archeologist (title changed to *Archeological Director* for 1974-75 season)
Lawrence E. Toombs (1970-75), Wilfrid Laurier University

Administrative Director
Philip J. King (1970-73), St. John's Seminary, Boston College
Kevin G. O'Connell, S.J. (1973-75), Weston School of Theology

Volunteer and Educational Program Director
Harry Thomas Frank (1970-75), Oberlin College
Louis Gough (*Assistant*, 1973), Ashland Theological Seminary
Jack B. van Hooser (*Associate Director*, 1975), Seabury-Western Theological Seminary

Camp Managers
Susan Simmons (1970-71)
Lawrence and Dorothy Ingalls (1973-75)

Consortium Director
Charles U. Harris (1971-75), Seabury-Western Theological Seminary

Overseers and Consultants
G. Ernest Wright (1970-74), Harvard Divinity School
Reuben Bullard (1970-73), University of Cincinnati
Edward F. Campbell, Jr. (1970-75), McCormick Theological Seminary
Michael Hammond (1973-75), Columbia University, Duke University
Garmon Harbottle (1971-75), Brookhaven National Laboratory
Philip J. King (1973-75), St. John's Seminary, Boston College
Frank Koucky (1973-75), College of Wooster

Edward Sayre (1971-75), Brookhaven National Laboratory
Jeffrey Schwartz (1970-75), Columbia University, University of Pittsburgh
Lawrence E. Stager (1973-75), The Oriental Institute, University of Chicago
Robert Stewart (1970-75), Sam Houston State University
John E. Worrell (1975), Holy Cross College

Medical Director
Melvin K. Lyons, M. D. (1970-75)

Camp Doctor
Melvin K. Lyons, M. D. (1971-73)
Al Donovan, M. D. (1971)

Camp Nurse
Dorothy Ingalls (1973-75)

Field Supervisors
Linda Ammons (1973), Harvard University
W. Jack Bennett (1970-75), University of Southern California
Michael D. Coogan (1973-75), St. Jerome's College, The Albright Institute of Archeological Research
Ralph Doermann (1973-75), Lutheran Theological Seminary
John Matthers (1973-75), The Institute of Archeology
D. Glenn Rose (1973), Phillips University
Karen Seger (1975), Hebrew Union College
Lawrence E. Stager (1970-71), Harvard University, The Oriental Institute

Survey Director
John L. Peterson (1973-75), Seabury-Western Theological Seminary

Surveyor
Bishara Zoughbi (1970-75), The Albright Institute of Archaeological Research

Architects
David Voelter (1970)
Bishara Zoughbi (1970-75), The Albright Institute of Archaeological Research

Photographers

Theodore Rosen (1970-71), Hebrew University

Wilhelm Nassau (1973-74), Wilfrid Laurier University

James Whitred (1975), Wilfrid Laurier University

Eugenia Nitowski (1975), Andrews University

Geologists

Abdulhossein (Alan) Baharlou (1970), Phillips University

Reuben Bullard (1971), University of Cincinnati

Frank Koucky (1973-75), College of Wooster

Botanists

William Robertson (1970), Sam Houston State University

Robert Stewart (1971-74), Sam Houston State University

Elizabeth Porter (1975), Texas A & M University

Cultural Anthropologists

Robert Rhoades (1970), Phillips University

Michael Hammond (1973-74), Columbia University

Stuart Peters (1975), State University of New York

Physical Anthropologists

Jeffrey Schwartz (1970-74), Columbia University, University of Pittsburgh

Janet Sawyer (1970), Harvard University

Lynn Fisher/Emmanuel (1971-73), New York City University

Susan Ford (1975), University of Pittsburgh

Ceramists

Joel Plum (1971)

Richard Finman (1973-74), Northwest Connecticut Community College

Neutron Activationist

Dorothea Brooks (1971-75), Brookhaven National Laboratory, Hartford Seminary Foundation

Artists

Anne Carter/Pritchard (1970), Wilfrid Laurier University

Judy Hammond (1971-73), Columbia University

Dorothy Ingalls (1975)

Peter Jenkins (1971), Wilfrid Laurier University

Patricia Koeber (1970), Wilfrid Laurier University

Katharine Korrell (1974), Northwest Connecticut Community College

Tom Stone (1970), Wilfrid Laurier University

Shelly Wilcox (1971), University of Southern California

Coders (1971)

Erika von Conta, Patricia Koeber, Patricia MacLaughlin, and Joel Nordenstrom, all of Wilfrid Laurier University

Registrars

Mary Bennett (1971-75)

Anne Carter/Pritchard (1971-73), Wilfrid Laurier University

Carolyn Rose (1975)

Mary Schmieder (1970), Wilfrid Laurier University

Martha Smith (1973-75), Seabury-Western Theological Seminary

Muff Thomsen (1970)

F. Carolyn Toombs (1973-75), Wilfrid Laurier University

Area Supervisors

Linda Ammons (1970-71), Harvard University

W. Boyce Bennett (1973), General Theological Seminary

Jeff Blakely (2 weeks in 1973, 1975), Oberlin College, University of Wisconsin

Dorothea Blow (4 weeks in 1975), Wilfrid Laurier University

Dorothea Brooks (1970), Hartford Seminary Foundation

Kevin Clark (1973), Claremont Graduate School

Michael D. Coogan (1970-71), St. Jerome's College, The Albright Institute

Barbara Dart (1975), Wilfrid Laurier University

Ralph Doermann (1970-1971), Lutheran Theological Seminary

J. Kenneth Eakins (1975), Golden Gate Baptist Theological Seminary

Carol Epley (1971, 4 weeks in 1973), Phillips University

Valery Fargo (1975), The Oriental Institute

David Freedman (1970), Occidental College

Larry Herr (1973), Harvard University

Peter Jenkins (1973), Wilfrid Laurier University

Richard Kuns (1970-73), Hartford Seminary Foundation

Hank Lay (1973), Claremont Graduate School

Yechiel Lehavy (1971), University of Pennsylvania

Cherie Howard Lenzen (1975), Johns Hopkins University

Lucia Lerner (1971)

Maurice Luker (1973), Emory and Henry College

Burton MacDonald (1971, 1975), St. Francis Xavier University

Marjorie Ward Mahler (1975), Oberlin College, Duke University

R. Edward Maitland (1975), Oberlin College

Ellen Messer (1970), University of Michigan

Lydia Newcombe (1973-75), Wilfrid Laurier University

Mark Papworth (2 weeks in 1970), Oberlin College

S. Thomas Parker (1973-75), University of California in Los Angeles

Cymbrie Pratt (1970), Wayne State University

Carol A. Redmount (1973-75), Oberlin College, Harvard Divinity School

Robert Rhoades (4 weeks in 1970), Phillips University

D. Glenn Rose (1970-71), Phillips University

Diane Saltz (1971-73), Harvard University

Carola Schulte (2 weeks in 1975), Brandeis University

Peter Schweitzer (1973), Oberlin College

Supervisor-in-Training

Eugene Roop (1975), Earlham School of Religion

Volunteers

There were 45 to 85 volunteers, many of them students at consortium schools or other institutions, each season.

Other Personnel

Technical men each season were Nasser Diab Mansur (Abu ⁽Issa) and Jabber Muhammad Hasan (Abu ⁽Abid) from the village of Balata, assisted as necessary by other technical men and workmen from Balata and Taanach. Important support services were provided each year by Doris and Farid Salman of the Jordan House Hotel in Jerusalem and by Samir Khayo of Jerusalem, food supplier for 1973 and 1975. In 1970 the expedition lived in the nearby city of Kiryat Gat, thereafter in a tent city on the site. The cooks for 1973 and 1975, Muhammad Ali Sourki (Abuᵓl ⁽Ez) and Harbi Marzouk Tanbour (Abu Najjar), were particularly important to the success of the expedition in those two seasons.

BIBLIOGRAPHY

Bliss, F. J.
    1898   *A Mound of Many Cities.* London: Palestine Exploration Fund.
Coogan, M.
    1975   A Cemetery from the Persian Period at Tell el-Hesi. *Bulletin of the American Schools of Oriental Research* 220: 37-46.
Granqvist, H.
    1965   *Moslem Death and Burial.* Helsinki: Söderström.
Petrie, W. M. F.
    1891   *Tell el-Hesy (Lachish).* London: Watt.
Rose, D. G., and Toombs, L. E.
    1976   Tell el-Hesi, 1973 and 1975. *Palestine Exploration Quarterly* 108: 41-54, pls. 1-5.

Stager, L. E.
    1971   Climatic Conditions and Grain Storage in the Persian Period. *Biblical Archaeologist* 34: 86-88.
Stewart, R. B.
    Forth-   Archeobotanic Studies at Tell el-Hesi 1973. In
    coming   *Economic Botany.*
Toombs, L. E.
    1974   Tell el-Hesi, 1970-1971. *Palestine Exploration Quarterly* 106: 19-31, pls. 1-6.

Excavations at Carthage 1975
The Punic Project: First Interim Report

Lawrence E. Stager

The Oriental Institute, University of Chicago, Chicago, Illinois 60637

The present flurry of building activity, particularly in the eastern suburbs of Tunis, is ineluctably reducing and eroding the anepigraphic sources for reconstructing Carthage's past. The Campagne Internationale de Sauvegarde de Carthage was organized partly in response to these growing problems in order to recover, through archeological research, more of the history of ancient Carthage and to preserve this monumental heritage. In response to the formal invitation issued by Dr. A. Beschaouch, the Director of the Institut National d'Archéologie et d'Art, to the American Schools of Oriental Research to participate in the international campaign, we launched the "Punic Project," sponsored by the Harvard Semitic Museum, in conjunction with the "Roman Project," sponsored by the Kelsey Museum of the University of Michigan.

The American excavations were supported in 1975 by a major grant from the Smithsonian Institution, supplemented by contributions from the Harvard Semitic Museum, the Oriental Institute (University of Chicago), and the University of Missouri—St. Louis.

We are extremely grateful to Dr. Beschaouch, who has helped us immeasurably in realizing many of our objectives for the first season. We are indebted to Dr. M. A. Ennabli, the Conservateur du Site de Carthage, for his able assistance in implementing the necessary strategies for meeting those objectives. Without the tireless efforts and preparations of the Reverend Thomas D. Newman, Administrative Director of the American Schools of Oriental Research, and Mrs. Newman, the Punic Project could not have begun.

The 1975 campaign started April 19 and continued through June 4. The staff totaled 17 in the field.

The primary objective for the first season was to determine the northern extent of the Tophet ("Precinct of Tanit") and its relationship to the Rectangular Harbor (probably Appian's *emporion;* see figs. 2, 3). The latter led into the Circular Harbor to the north. Recent archeological discoveries by the British team tend to support the identification of the Circular Harbor with the Punic military port mentioned in Appian (Hurst 1975: 17-22). One of our long-range goals is to develop a stratigraphically controlled sequence of Punic remains at Carthage. We made a series of deep soundings at points along the line of the main trench with the hope of finding Punic material. Not too surprisingly, most of the discoveries of the first season were Roman; but Punic levels were reached in deep probes, ca. 3.00 m. below ground level. In those stratigraphic sections we observed a range of human occupation from the early 4th century B.C. to the 7th century A.D. Groundwater, but not bedrock, was reached in the deeper probes.

Vaulted Building

The Vaulted Building appeared less than half a meter below ground level. It was completely covered by ancient debris, often mixed with modern refuse. In the east portion of the structure we exposed nearly 100 m.² of floors and wall foundations (figs. 5, 6).

The Vaulted Building was built ca. 400 A.D. and later remodeled. All that was preserved of the original structure is a rugged plaster floor (e.g., A1.007, fig. 7) that had been laid over leveling fills of varying thickness. Beneath the fill material were three parallel vaults, oriented northwest-southeast, which provided foundations for the building. The west end of the Vaulted Building lies under what is now the Rue des Suffètes (figs. 3, 5, 19). Wall B1.015, about 1.50 m. wide, once sealed the east end of the vaults. Running slightly northeast-southwest, this formed the main east wall of the Vaulted

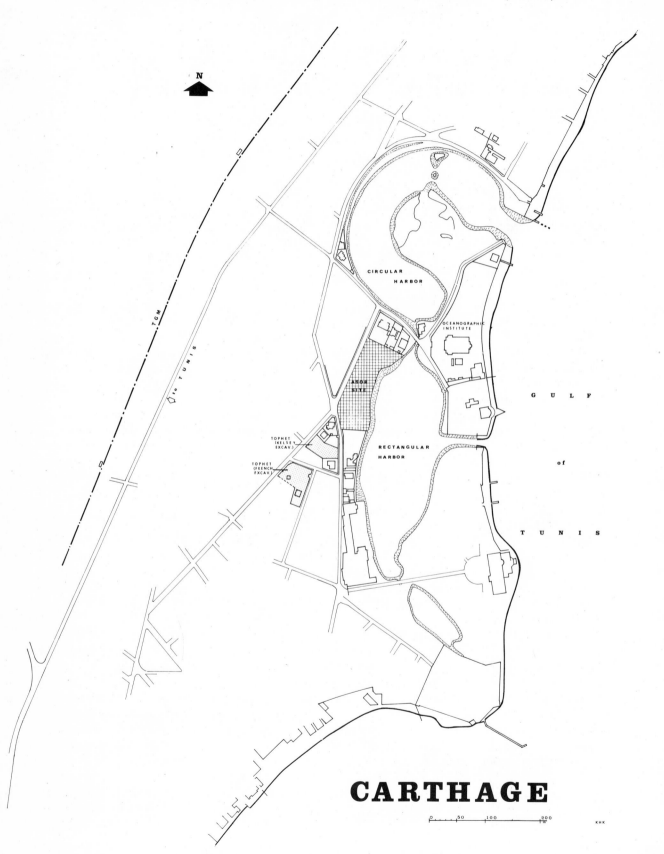

Fig. 1. Map of Carthage.

Building which was aligned with harborside installations 15 m. farther east (fig. 5).

Floor A1.007, 1-4 cm. thick, was composed of slaked lime. The best preserved patches occurred in the west half of A1, but even there the floor was disrupted by later intrusions (figs. 7, 9). Floor 007 sealed an uneven layer of yellow sand and sandstone (fig. 8, A1.011), which contained pottery dating to the second half of the 4th century A.D. (pl. 4:1). Below this was a rich layer of garbage loaded with pottery, charcoal, humus, and bones (A1.013, fig. 8 and pl. 4:2-8). Possibly an earlier floor lay just above the vaults. These deposits were much more homogeneous than the rubble fill thrown in between the vaults (A1.015, fig. 8). The latter contained seven stelae fragments (Appendix A) and a weathered cippus originally from the Tophet, chunks of mosaics, and seven fresco fragments.

None of the fill material sealed beneath Floor A1.007 dates much later than ca. 400 A.D., the *terminus post quem* for the construction phase of the Vaulted Building. The function of the Vaulted Building is difficult to determine. Distributional analyses of artifacts within the various units of the building were of little use in determining function

because of later disturbances. Nevertheless the rustic flooring and the position of the Vaulted Building in relation to other installations farther east suggest this was a storage facility of some kind built near the lagoon or harbor.

Ghost Wall A1.016 (fig. 9) cut through Floor 007 and could be traced intermittently to the northeast corner of A2. Between this robbed-out wall and Wall 015 were patches of a later plaster floor (A1.020), which sealed a garbage pit (A1.022) that had been dug into Vault 1, ca. 500 A.D. (For discussion and illustration of pottery from A1.022, see Hayes 1976: chapter 3. There one can also find a more generous selection of pottery from A1.013 and A1.026 than we have included in this report.)

Probably during this same period of renovation, Well A2.027, just west of Ghost Wall A1.016, was cut through Vault 3. The well was at least 2.00 m. deep and 1.90 m. in diameter. The shaft was lined with sixteen or more courses of well-cut Hamilcar sandstone. Well A2.027 continued to supply water for the inhabitants until late in the 6th century A.D., when it was filled up with various kinds of debris, including a large column of Chemtou marble (fig. 10). By the 7th century A.D. the northeast corner of

Fig. 2. Site of ASOR excavatons looking east toward Lagoon or Rectangular Harbor.

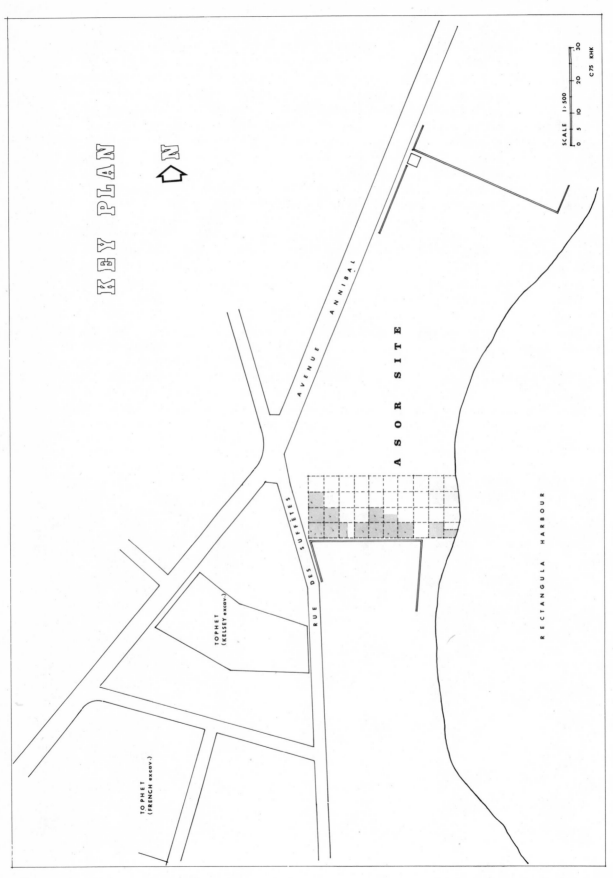

Fig. 3. Site of excavations.

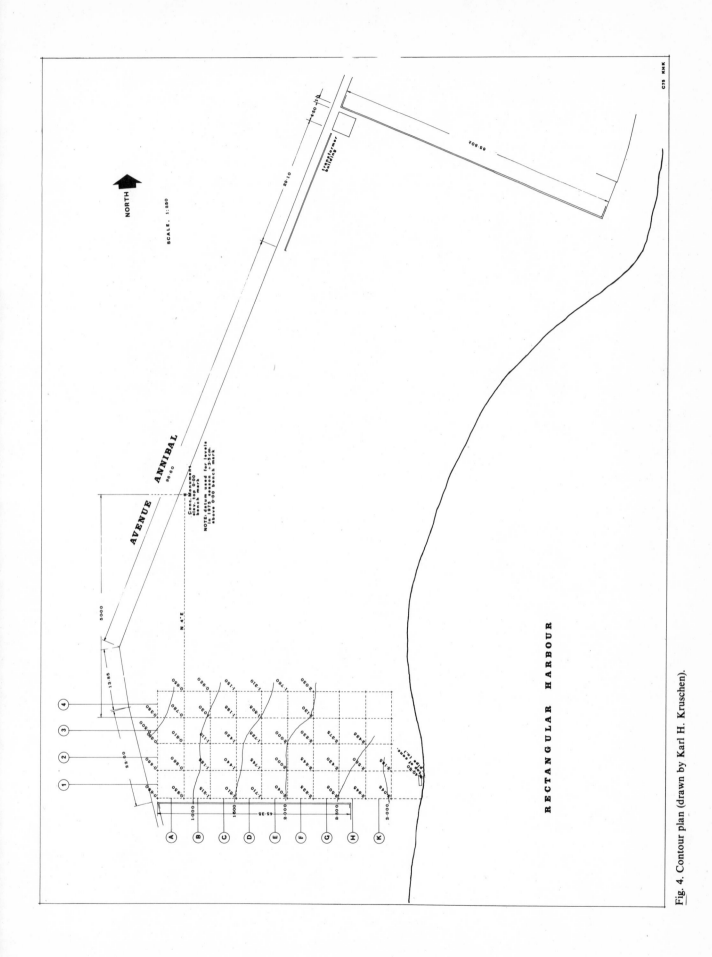

Fig. 4. Contour plan (drawn by Karl H. Kruschen).

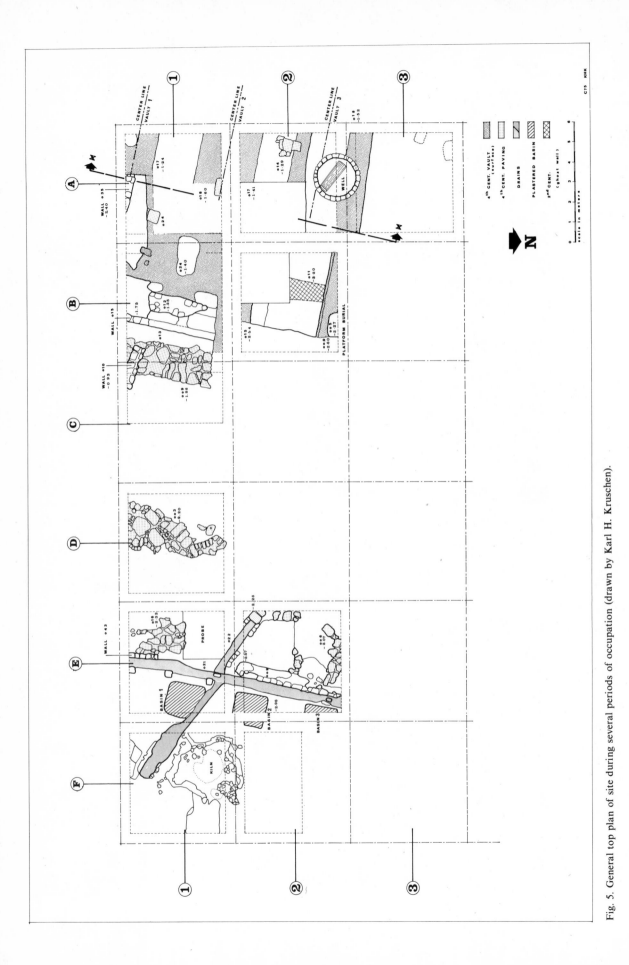

Fig. 5. General top plan of site during several periods of occupation (drawn by Karl H. Kruschen).

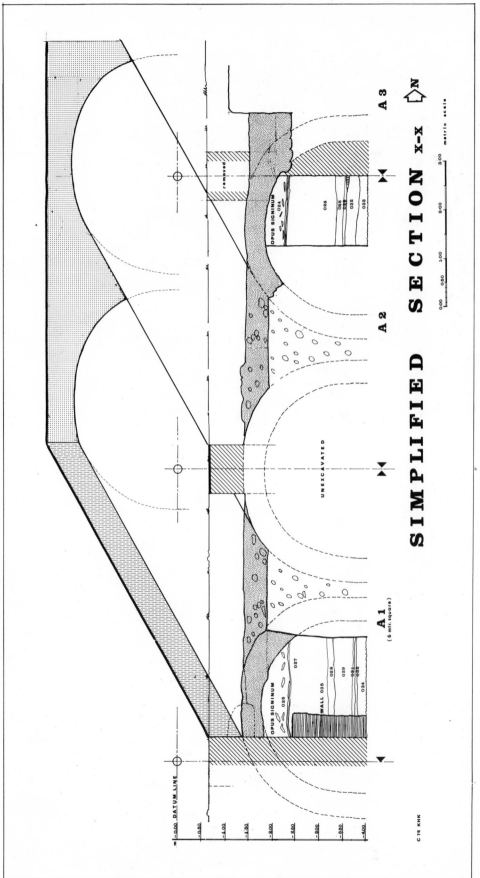

Fig. 6. Schematic section X-X through Vaulted Building (drawn by Karl H. Kruschen and L. E. Stager).

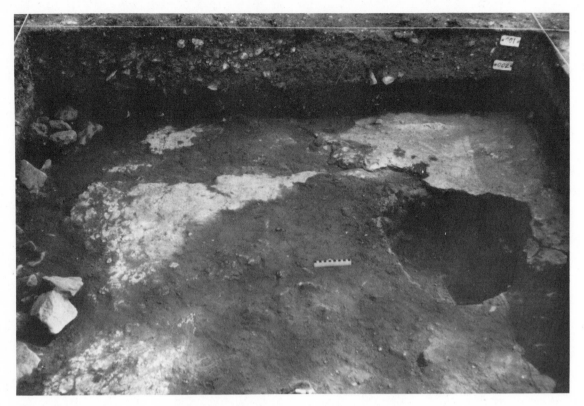

Fig. 7. Patches of plaster. Floor A1.007, looking south.

Fig. 8. West balk of A1 (Photo by Vida Ward).

Fig. 9. A1, looking south, at Ghost Wall 016 to the left and Floor 007 to the right (Photo by Vida Ward).

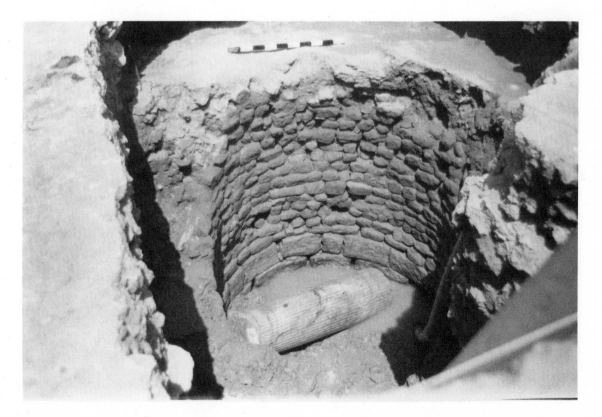

Fig. 10. Well A2.027, looking west (Photo by Vida Ward).

Fig. 11. Burial B2.005, looking north (Photo by Vida Ward).

Fig. 12. E1 probe in northwest quadrant, looking south (Photo by Vida Ward).

the Vaulted Building (Area B2) had been demolished and converted into a burial ground (figs. 5, 11, 23).

Harbor Installations

Aligned with the east end of the Vaulted Building was a low curbing of flagstones (C1.009). The entire area between the vaults and the plastered basins (fig. 5) was paved with slabs of limestone in the late 4th century A.D. (D1.003, E1.016, E2.006) to form an open-air courtyard or quayside.

In the northwest quadrant of E1, 30 m. west of the lagoon, we made a sounding 2.50 m. x 2.50 m. x 2.00 m. The sequence is summarized in the sequence diagram to the right (cf. figs. 12 and 14):

The latest construction phase (E1 probe) consisted of 0.50 m. of leveling fill composed of harbor sand mixed with occupational debris (022, 024). The fill was laid over a thin destruction layer (026) and a band of decomposed sandstone (027). Large flagstones (016) embedded in a very compact matrix of pebbles and potsherds (021) capped the fill.

From this section it appears that the paved area was laid in the late 4th century A.D. (when the vaulted Building was constructed) and continued to be used into the 7th century A.D. (see pls. 2:20-25; 3:1-11).

The flagstones and fill were fronted on the east by Terrace Wall E1.043 (= E2.009), which once stood 0.50 m. high (figs. 5, 14, 15). A shallow, plaster-lined drain (E1.021) ran between the foot of the terrace wall and the plastered basins. The basins had been dug into the fill sediments to a depth of 1.00 m. or slightly more (groundwater hampered further excavation in the basins).

Initially we thought that the basins were later installations cut into a Roman quay. However, in E2, where the plaster connections had not been broken, it appeared that the lining of Drain 021 lipped up and over the rim of Basin 2. This same plaster lining also adhered to the face of Terrace Wall E2.009. Thus there are some stratigraphic reasons for concluding that the flagstones, the terrace wall, and the basins were contemporary. The basins were filled to the brim with refuse in the 7th century A.D. A kiln, possibly for pottery, was dug into the last two phases of the plastered quays. The kiln was in use ca. 650-700 A.D.

The parallel alignment of the Vaulted Building, the paved area with terrace wall, the drain and

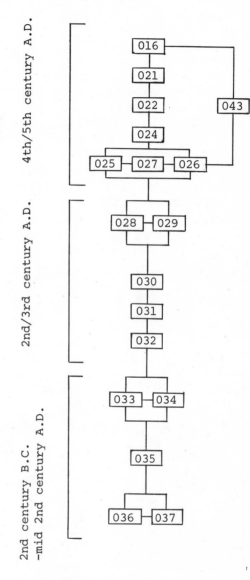

Fig. 13. Sequence diagram of E1.

the three plastered basins indicate that most of the site was occupied by a single, large complex from ca. 400-650 A.D.

As a tentavie hypothesis, we suggested that a *garum* (or "fish-sauce") factory was operating next to the "Commercial Harbor."

But during the second season at Carthage (April-May, 1976), it took only two weeks to put the "*garum*-hypothesis" to rest.

The plaster-lined "basins" proved to be column, or pier, footings that ran in a straight line parallel to the terrace wall and drain. The footings had once contained round boulders mortared in place. When the boulders were later robbed out, a lining of mortar (with occasional stone impressions) was left

Fig. 14. E1 and E2, looking south along Terrace Wall E1.043 = E2.009, with plastered basins on the left (Photo by Vida Ward).

adhering to the sides of the rectangular "basins." Additional proof of this interpretation came from a nearby wall of similar construction. The footing for the wall was only partially robbed out, with many of the mortared boulders still intact. Therefore, during the last phase of the harbor (6th century A.D. and later), we should reconstruct a colonnade, or an arcade, along the harbor front to the west of the quay wall (discovered in Area G1 in 1976).

The earlier plastered quays were replaced by one made of flagstones that paved the way between the colonnade and the warehouse (Vaulted Building). Thus throughout the Roman and most of the Byzantine periods, the western dockside of the Rectangular Basin seems to have been a place of commerce rather than industry.

The probe in E1 revealed two earlier phases of harbor platforms (the ancient quays). A layer of plaster (028, 029) covered bands of yellow sand interspersed with marble chips (030-032). This material, ca. 0.60 m. thick, was imported from a lithic industrial site and deposited as a leveling fill for the harborside (fig. 12). The latest pottery from these sediments provides a date in the 2nd century A.D. for the construction (pl. 3:12-20).

Below the second phase of harbor installations and under a thin layer of occupational debris (033-034) was a hard plaster pavement (035), which had been spread over building rubble (036-037), consisting of sandstone blocks and wall plaster, charred and calcined by fire (figs. 16, 17). The few pottery indicators from this phase date to the 2nd century B.C. (pl. 3:22-27). At present, we are speculating that the building rubble represents the destruction of Punic Carthage, reused as fill for the first Roman harborside.

Vault Construction

We caught glimpses of the vault interiors in B1, where Wall 015, which had sealed the east end of Vault 1, had been robbed out; in A1, where a pit had been dug through the roof of the same vault; in A2, where a late (modern?) intrusion destroyed part of the well shaft that had been sunk deep into Vault 3; and in B2, where the top of the vault had been sheared down 1.25 m. to prepare a flat area for the 7th century A.D. burials.

Usually the vaults were filled almost to ceiling level with occupational debris. One exception to this occurred west of the well in A2. Perhaps those who destroyed part of the well casing also removed much of the debris from inside the vault. There we

Fig. 15. East face of Terrace Wall E2.009, with Drain 021 and Basins 2 and 3 in foreground (Photo by Vida Ward).

Fig. 16. E1.036 destruction debris behind meter stick, E1.037 beach sand fill to the right (Photo by Reuben Bullard).

Fig. 17. E1 probe in northwest quadrant, looking south (Photo by Vida Ward).

Fig. 18. Vaults 1 and 2, looking west. Note keystones at east end of Vault 1, Area B1, left foreground (Photo by Vida Ward).

were able to crawl into the vault and walk through it for 11.00 m. to the west, passing under the modern Rue des Suffètes, to a point at which a vertical wall completely blocked the vault. If this transverse wall marked the western limits of the Vaulted Building, the east-west dimensions of the structure must have exceeded 22.00 m.

The maximum interior width of the vaults was ca. 4.00 m. The foundation levels have not been reached. Contiguous parallel vaults probably shared common side walls from which the arches sprang in opposite directions. The vault roofs, 0.40-0.50 m. thick, were made of cobble- to boulder-sized sandstone held together with mud plaster. The interior was roughly finished, with no traces of smooth plaster lining usually found in vaulted cisterns. Only at the east end of Vault 1 was there an attempt to key in the stones of the roof (fig. 18, cf. the construction farther west in A1). The apex of the vault interior appeared to be the weakest part of the structure. A fairly regular "seam," ca. 0.40 m. wide, marked the line along which the two sides of the vault roof were joined and sealed from the outside

with a layer of plaster (fig. 19).

Inside Vaults 1 (Area A1) and 3 (Areas A2 and B2), where the debris had not been disturbed or removed, the occupational sequence was almost identical. These sediments bore no resemblance to the fill found outside between the vaults and beneath the earliest floor levels of the Vaulted Building (fig. 6). Pre-4th century A.D. layers, including occupational floors and surfaces, were encountered only in the vaults. The vaults were never open for use as cisterns or storerooms; rather, they were subterranean supports for the building above. The builders must have dug a series of parallel foundation trenches into which they laid the side walls of the vaults. After widening the trenches at the top, they laid the roof over earlier strata, thereby preserving them.

Just 50 m. southwest of our excavations, in the northern part of the Tophet ("Precinct of Tanit"), similar vaults were built in the Roman period. Kelsey excavated one of them in 1925. He correctly recognized that the vault had been built over earlier Punic levels. Inside the vault his crew uncovered

Fig. 19. Inside Vault 3 under Rue des Suffètes, looking west. Note ceiling construction (Photo by Robert H. Johnston).

Fig. 20. Foundation vault in Tophet (Kelsey Trench). Note burial urns hanging from ceiling in upper lefthand corner (Photo by Daniella Saltz).

cippi and stelae still standing in place (Kelsey 1926: 35-36 and figs. 14-15). This level corresponded to the "stele surface" found outside the vaults. Today cinerary urns still hang vertically from the vault roof, the necks of the Punic jars embedded in debris adhering to the lower parts of the ceiling (fig. 20).

This type of vault was apparently unique to Carthage. As foundation vaults, they could have been constructed quickly and economically. If swampiness were a problem, this type of construction would have provided more stability than free-standing walls.

Intra-Vault Sequence

The stratigraphic profile established by probes within Vaults 1 and 3 is summarized in the following diagram:

Fig. 21. Sequence diagram for various loci in Areas A1, A2, B2, earlier than the Vaulted Building.

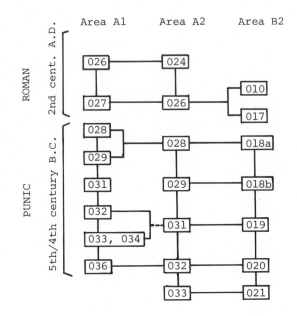

Roman Period— 2nd Century A.D.

Remnants of an *opus signinum* floor, 5 cm. thick, appeared just below the vault roofs in A1.026 and A2.024 (fig. 6). Some of the floor plaster still lay in its original position, but many fragments were dislodged when the vaults were built. The white plaster consisted of a calcium oxide matrix which held an aggregate of marble chips, marine shell fragments, bone chips, and worn tesserae. Flat-lying potsherds were pressed into the surface.

To level up the site in preparation for the floor, the builders imported yellow beach sand containing pockets of gray harbor clay (A1.027 = A2.026). The harbor clay became more concentrated near the base of the deposit (cf. B2.010 and 017, fig. 24). In places this fill was more than 1.25 m. deep. In contrast to the floor and occupational debris above, this sediment yielded very few potsherds and other artifacts.

In B2, where the vault had been truncated in the 7th century A.D., the *opus signinum* floor was completely removed, but the lower levels of the yellow fill remained (B2.010, 017). The straight-sided trench filled with dark brown soil, Ghost Wall 011, appears to be the eastern limits of the *opus signinum* floor. The latest pottery in the trench dates to the 2nd century A.D. When projected south into B1, Ghost Wall B2.011 strikes a line at least a meter inside the east end of Vault 1 (figs. 6, 22, 23). No traces of *opus signinum* were found in the B1 section of the vault (fig. 18).

This stratigraphic evidence suggests that Ghost Wall 011 marked the east side of a 2nd century A.D. building (an earlier "warehouse"?). Sherds from the occupational debris mixed with fragments of *opus signinum*, as well as the latest pottery from the man-made fill, indicate that this structure was built during the reign of Hadrian (pl. 1:1-4). Perhaps the building continued to be used into the 3rd-4th century A.D. before it was replaced by the Vaulted Building.

Punic Period—4th Century B.C.

The side walls of the vaults penetrated all of the Punic deposits excavated and interrupted the horizontal stratigraphic connections. However, in Vaults 1 and 3 the vertical sequence was similar

Fig. 22. Ghost Wall B2.011, looking south (Photo by Vida Ward).

enough to conclude that the same kind of occupation (whatever its exact nature was) characterized this part of the site.

> All of the Punic layers excavated were submerged. To drain the groundwater from these deep probes, we used small pumps driven by gasoline engines. Usually this method required digging a meter-square sump one meter below the level at which we were excavating. The pumps were too inefficient for large-scale clearance. In the probes, however, even under these conditions the supervisors maintained a high degree of stratigraphic control. Striking contrasts of color and texture distinguished the succession of layers.

In both vaults the fill of the Hadrianic structure rested on a layer of gray clay, 0.15 - 0.25 m. thick (A2.028 = B2.018a = A1.031). This layer contained no organic material or laminae, so common to use-surfaces. If this layer was a leveling fill for a floor of some kind, that floor or surface had been removed by later construction. It seems that there was a sizeable gap in occupation between the Punic and Roman remains preserved inside the vaults (see below).

In Vault 1 the occupational debris was 0.25 m. deep. A thin layer of gray clay mixed with charcoal (A1.032) covered yellowish-red sand and a blackened lense of harbor muck (A1.033, 034). Pottery and murex shells were abundant. When wet-sieved, A1.033 yielded a few carbonized seeds: two olive pits, one grain of barley, and three fragments of wheat. All of the occupational debris had accumulated on a surface/fill of yellow beach sand (A1.036), not yet excavated. In Vault 3 a corresponding Punic phase occurred beneath the decomposed sandstone (A2.029 = B2.018b). Dark yellowish-brown soil (A2.031 = B2.019), 0.20 m. thick but thinning out in the southeast corner of A2 (fig. 6), contained much pottery and bits of charcoal. This layer lacked harbor muck but had other hallmarks of occupational debris. Like its counterpart in A1, this locus lay on a bed of imported yellow beach sand (A2.032, 033; B2.020, 021).

The most common local Punic wares in these two phases were holemouth jars with simple (pls. 1:8, 2:6) and flattened (pls. 1:7, 2:7) rims, store jars with

Fig. 23. Ghost Wall B2.011, brown layer in foreground looking west. Note truncated Vault 3 to the right with Burial 005 in lower righthand corner (Photo by Vida Ward).

Fig. 24. West balk of B2 (Photo by Vida Ward).

simple, everted (pls. 1:12-13, 2:1) and rolled (pls. 1:30, 2:19) rims, and cooking pots with an inner ledge (pls. 1:27, 29, 2:14) for a lid.

Unfortunately no stratigraphically derived and carefully dated corpus of Mid-to-Late Punic pottery has been published. For comparative dating purposes we have been forced to rely on over 50 sherds of black-glazed ware, probably manufactured in Greece.

This corpus of imports, all sherds, is small but suggestive. Their fabric is light red to pink in color. There are few inclusions in the well-levigated clay. The pottery was well-fired. Most of the sherds have a thick, lustrous black "glaze," with little or no scaling.

The closest parallels to these imports date ca. 400 B.C. and come from the Athenian agora. Stamped motifs of "linked palmettes round a circle of ovules, sometimes repeated in a second band" appear in the late 5th century and continue into the mid-4th century B.C. in Athens (Sparkes and Talcott 1970: 29). The best parallels to our pl. 2:2 are Sparkes and Talcott 1970: pl. 59:826 and 1025. The

dates range from 425-380 B.C. Rouletting, an attribute usually not much earlier than 390 B.C., decorated other black-glazed vessels imported to Carthage. The bolsal base is a known Athenian form (cf. our pl. 1:24 and Sparkes and Talcott 1970: fig. 6:541).

From macroscopic inspection there seems to be little reason for not regarding the black-glazed ware as imports from Greece rather than from Italy, however indirect the trade route. Because of political hostilities between Athens and Carthage during the 5th-4th centuries B.C., archeologists, following the lead of historians, generally see a sharp decline in Attic imports to Carthage at that time, and often consider the black-glazed ware to be manufactured in Italy. In the light of the above evidence, this view should be reconsidered. A systematic study of black-glazed ware subjected to neutron activation should prove more conclusive for establishing provenances.

Unless the date derived from Attic imports for the two Punic phases found inside the vaults is misleadingly early (and not all of the sediments were fill material), the occupational hiatus in this area lasted more than 400 years. Why was some evidence of a 2nd century B.C. occupation extending into the 1st century A.D. found in Phase 3 (E1) nearer the lagoon, but not beneath the Vaulted Building? Could the Late Punic structures have been hauled down to the harbor front to level up the earliest Roman quay? If so, there were still no remains found in the vaults contemporary with Phase 3, when the Roman harbor was apparently first used. For the present the gap remains an enigma.

From the nature of the sediments and artifacts found in the 4th century B.C. levels, we can conclude, with some confidence, that the Tophet did not extend as far north and northeast as our field of excavation. Inside Vault 1, the north face of a sturdy wall (A1.035) more than five courses high was exposed. Its founding level, somewhere beneath the water table, has not yet been reached, and the south face (partially robbed out) was obscured by the balk in A1 (fig. 6). This wall was in use as late as the 4th century B.C. sediments that abutted it. Perhaps this Punic wall demarcated the northeast limits of the sacred "Precinct of Tanit."

Gary Pratico, Harvard University, drew and inked the following pottery illustrations. During the digging season at Carthage he sawed the sherds in half and traced them at a scale of 1:1. They were reduced photographically to 1:5.

Dean Robert H. Johnston (Rochester Institute of Technology) analyzed most of the illustrated sherds and provided the descriptions opposite the plates.

Abbreviations used in the descriptions:

+	= oxidation
—	= reduction
inc.	= inclusions
w.t.	= wheel thrown
int	= interior
ext	= exterior
BT	= Black-Top ware
BG	= Black-Glazed ware
ARS	= African Red Slip ware
color	= Munsell Soil Color Charts
temperature	= Centigrade
Hayes 11	= Type series after J. W. Hayes, *Late Roman Pottery*

Plate 1.

	Area & Locus	Regis. No.	Type	Surface Treatment	Manufacture	Composition	Firing	Color
1.	A1.026	5325	ARS; Hayes 11	thumb-pressed band below rim	w.t.	very fine water lev. clay; micro-quartz inc.	+; 900°; little lime spalling	ext: 10R 5/8 (red-lustrous) int: same
2.	A1.026	5337	ARS	incised bands and rouletting	w.t.	very fine water lev. clay; micro- quartz inc.	+; 800°	ext: 2.5YR 5/8 (red-lustrous) int: 10R 6/8 light red-matte)
3.	A1.026	5328	BT; Hayes 197	blackened ext. and rim (iron oxide slip?)	w.t.	well lev. clay; quartz inc.	+; ca. 800°; some lime spalling	ext: 2.5YR 3/1 (very dark gray) int: 2.5YR 5.5/6 (reddish brown) core: same
4.	A1.026	5321	BT; Hayes 196	blackened around rim	w.t.; throwing grooves retained on int.; tooled down on ext.	medium fine clay; some quartz inc.	+; ca. 900- 1000°; minimal lime spalling	ext: 2.5YR 5.5/8 (red) int: same; core: 2.5YR 6/6 (light red) slip: 5YR 4/2 (dark reddish gray)
5.	A1.028	8030		incised on rim int.	w.t.	sandy clay; quartz inc.	+; ca. 800°; slightly oxidized core remaining; some lime spalling	10YR 7.5/3 (very pale brown) core: 2.5YR 6/4.5 (light reddish brown)
6.	A1.028	8031	BG	black slip on ext. and int.	w.t.	fine, water lev. clay; micro-quartz and limestone inc.	+ then -; ca. 800-900°	ext: 2.5YR 2.5/0 (black- lustrous) int: same; core: 2.5YR 6/4 (light reddish brown)
7.	A1.028	8044	hole-mouth jar		w.t.; rim finger-formed; outer edge delineated with wooden potter's tool	medium fine clay	+; ca. 800°	2.5YR 5.6/5 (reddish brown)
8.	A1.028	8028	jar		w.t. and wet smoothed	medium coarse clay	+; 750-800°; reduced core	ext: 7.5YR 8/2 (pinkish white) int: 2.5YR 5.5/6 (reddish brown) core: 2.5YR 5.5/0 (gray)
9.	A1.028	8029			w.t.; wet slurry finish on ext.	medium fine clay; quartz inc.	+; ca. 800°; reduced core	ext: 7.5YR 8/2 (pinkish white) int: 2.5YR 6/6 core center: 2.5YR 6/1 (pale red-gray)
10.	A1.028	8045			w.t.	medium fine clay	+; ca. 800°; some lime spalling	2.5YR 6/6 (light red)
11.	A1.028	8057	cooking pot	blackened ext.	w.t.	medium coarse clay; many quartz inc.	+; ca. 800°; some lime spalling	ext: 10YR 7.5/2 (light grayish white--mottled) int: 7.5YR 7.5/4 (pink) core: 2.5YR 6/5 (light reddish brown)

Plate 1.

	Area & Locus	Regis. No.	Type	Surface Treatment	Manufacture	Composition	Firing	Color
12.	Al.028	8027	jar	traces of dark slip below rim ext: red slip band on rim	w.t.	medium fine clay; quartz inc.	+; ca. 800°; some lime spalling	2.5YR 6/6 (light red) slip: 10YR 4.5/8 (red)
13.	Al.028	8032	jar		w.t.	medium fine clay; quartz inc.	+; ca. 800°	2.5YR 6/6 (light red)
14.	Al.029	8276	cooking pot (inner ledge)		w.t.; tooled ext.	medium fine water lev. clay; dark and light quartz inc.	+; ca. 800°; some lime spalling	ext: 2.5YR 5/5 (reddish brown) int: 2.5YR 5/4 (reddish brown) core: 2.5YR 4.5/4 (reddish brown)
15.	Al.029	8283	BG	black slip on ext. and int.	w.t.	fine, water lev. clay; micro-quartz inc.	+ then-; ca. 900°	ext: 2.5YR 2.5/0 (black-lustrous) int: same; core: 2.5YR 6/4 (light reddish brown)
16.	Al.029	8278	bowl	traces of reddish gray slip bands on ext.	w.t.	medium coarse clay; quartz inc.	+; 750-800°	ext: 10YR 8/3 (very pale brown) slip: 5YR 5/2 (reddish gray) int: 10YR 8/3 (very pale brown) core: 5YR 7/2 (pinkish gray)
17.	Al.029	8281	cooking pot		w.t.; wet smoothed finish	medium coarse clay; many quartz inc.	+; ca. 800°	ext: 10YR 8/4 (very pale brown) int: same; core: 7.5YR 7/4 (pink)
18.	Al.029	8047	BG	black slip flaking away from clay body	w.t.	medium fine, lev. clay	+ then -; ca. 900°; some lime spalling	ext: 2.5YR 2.5/0 (black-lustrous) int: same; core: 5YR 5/1 (gray)
19.	Al.029	8046	cooking pot?		w.t.; out-folded rim	fine clay; quartz inc.	+; ca. 800°; some lime spalling	2.5Y 7/2 (light gray)
20.	Al.029	9327	cooking pot		w.t.	medium fine clay; quartz inc.	+ with traces of - around rim ext.; ca. 800°	ext: 7.5YR 7/1 (light gray) int: 7.5YR 8/2 (pinkish white) core: 7.5YR 7.5/2 (pinkish gray)
21.	Al.029	8275	amphora		w.t.; tool-finished rim	dense fine clay; lev. body; small quartz inc.	+; 800-900°; well fired throughout; lime spalling	2.5YR 6/4 (light reddish brown)
22.	Al.029	3614	(no description)					
23.	Al.029	8282	BG askos	black slip on ext.; weak red slip on int.	w.t.; neck added to vessel as separate piece	very fine water lev. clay; some micro-quartz inc.	+ then -; ca. 900°	ext: 2.5YR 2.5/0 (black) int: 10R 4/4 (weak red) core: 2.5YR 6/4 (light reddish brown)
24.	Al.029	8280	BG bolsal	black slip on ext. and int.	w.t.	water lev. clay; micro-quartz inc.	+ then -; ca. 900°	ext: 2.5YR 2.5/0 (black-lustrous) int: same; core: 2.5YR 6/6 (light red)
25.	Al.029	8277			w.t.; tool-finished when leatherhard to give sharply defined base	well lev. clay; small quartz inc.	+; ca 900-1000°; oxidized core; some lime spalling	ext: 7.5YR 8/3 (pink pinkish white) int: 7.5YR 7/4 (pink) core: 2.5YR 5.5/6 (red light red)

Plate 1.

	Area & Locus	Regis. No.	Type	Surface Treatment	Manufacture	Composition	Firing	Color
26.	A1.032	9344	bowl		w.t. and tooled	medium coarse clay; quartz inc.; very thin ware	+; 750-800°	2.5YR 4.5/4 (reddish brown)
27.	A1.032	9332	cooking pot (inner ledge)	partially blackened ext.	w.t. and tooled	medium coarse clay; quartz inc.	+; 800-900°	ext: 2.5YR 3.5/4 (dark reddish brown) int: 2.5YR 5/7 (red)
28.	A1.032	9343	(no description)					
29.	A1.032	9309	cooking pot (inner ledge)		w.t. and tooled	medium fine clay; dark and light quartz inc.	+; 750-800°	ext: 2.5YR 4.5/8 (red) int: same; core: 10R 5/8 (red)
30.	A1.032	9335	jar	w.t.; wet smoothed ext.		medium fine water lev. clay; quartz inc.	+ slight -; ca. 800°	ext: 10R 7.5/3 (very pale brown) int: 10R 6/3 (pale brown) core: same
31.	A1.032	9342	jar/ amphora	micro-layer of clay brought to surface by wet smoothing at end of finishing process	w.t. and wet smoothed	medium coarse clay; many quartz inc.; burned out organic voids	+; 750-800°	ext: 10YR 8/2 (light grayish white) int: same; core: 10YR 6.5/2 (light brownish gray)
32.	A1.033	9347	BG	black slip on ext. and over rim	w.t.	very fine water lev. clay; micro-quartz inc.	+ then -; 800-900°	ext: 2.5YR 2.5/0 (black) int: 2.5YR 6/6 (light red) core: same
33.	A1.033	9350	BG	black slip on ext. and int.; more lustrous on int.	w.t.	fine, water lev. clay	+ then -; ca. 900°	ext: 2.5YR 2.5/0 (black-lustrous) int: same; core: 2.5YR 6/6 (light red)
34.	A1.033	9356	BG	black slip on ext. and int.	w.t.	fine, water lev. clay	+ then -; ca. 900° some lime spalling	ext: 2.5YR 2.5/0 (black-lustrous) int: same; core: 2.5YR 6/4 (light reddish brown)
35.	A1.033	9348	BG	black slip on ext. and int. slip flaking from clay body	w.t.	fine, water lev. clay	+ then -; 850-900°	ext: 2.5YR 2.5/0 (black-lustrous) int: same; core: 2.5YR 6/6 (light red)

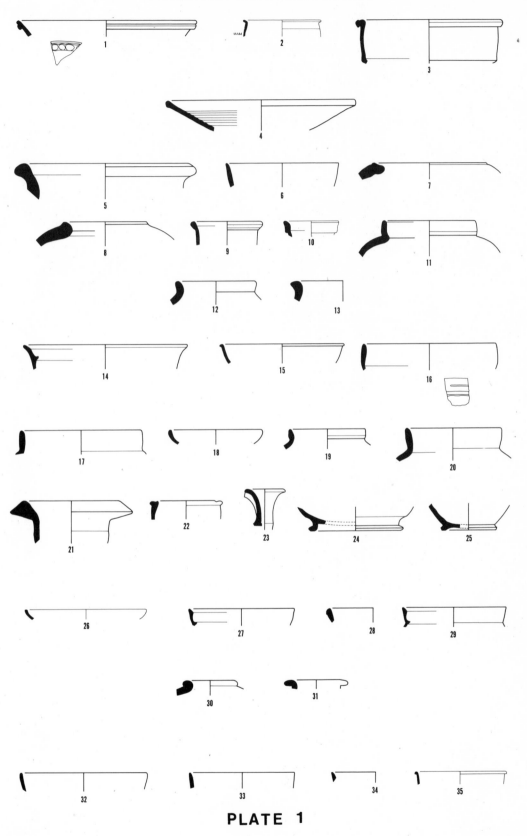

PLATE 1

Scale 1:5

Plate 2.

	Area & Locus	Regis. No.	Type	Surface Treatment	Manufacture	Composition	Firing	Color
1.	A1.034	8833	jar/ amphora		w.t.	medium fine clay; small quartz inc.	+; ca. 800°	10YR 7.5/3 (very pale brown)
2.	A1.034	9330	BG	black slip on ext. and int.; linked palmettes and ovules stamped on int.; reserved circles on ext.	w.t.	very fine water lev. clay; some micro-quartz inc.	+ then -	ext: 2.5YR 2.5/0 (black--lustrous) int: same core: 2.5YR 6/6 (light red)
3.	A1.034	8834	(no description)					
4.	A1.034	9329	deep bowl		w.t.; clay drawn up and laid over to form thick rim; seam is evident; tooled in finishing process	medium coarse clay; dark and light quartz inc.	+; 750-800° some lime spalling	2.5YR 6/6 (light red)
5.	A2.031	8056	bowl	4 bands of iron oxide slip	w.t.	medium coarse clay; quartz inc.	slight -; ca. 800° some lime spalling	ext: 7.5YR 6.5/4 (light pinkish gray) brown slip: 7.5YR 5/0 (gray) int: 10YR 6.5/2.5 (light gray brown)
6.	A2.031	8055	hole-mouth jar		w.t. and wet smoothed	medium coarse clay; quartz inc.	+; 750-800° quickly fired; core with dense organic matter; some lime spalling	ext: 10R 5.5/6 (red light red) int: same; core: 10R 3.5/1 (dark reddish gray)
7.	A2.033	9359	hole-mouth jar		w.t.; reverse rim (anti-splash?); wet smoothed ext. and int.	medium fine clay; voids from burned out organic matter; quartz inc.	+; 800-900°	ext: 10YR 8/3 (very pale brown) int: same; core: 10YR 5/7 (red)
8.	B2.017	8784		blackened ext.	w.t. and tooled	fine, water lev. clay; micro-quartz inc.	+; 750-800°	ext: 10R 5/6 (red) slip: 10R 3/1 (dark reddish gray) int: 10R 5.5/8 (red light red) core: 10R 5/6 (red)
9.	B2.017	8783			w.t.; sharply tooled and wet smoothed	medium coarse clay; quartz inc.	+; ca. 800°	ext: 10YR 8/2.5 (very pale whitish brown) int: same; core: 10R 5/6 (red)
10.	B2.017	8782	jar		w.t.	medium fine clay; quartz inc.	+; ca. 800°; some lime spalling	2.5YR 6/6 (light red)
11.	B2.017	8780	hole-mouth jar		w.t.	medium fine clay; quartz inc.	+; ca. 800°; lime spalling	2.5YR 5.5/6 (light red)
12.	B2.018	9326	deep bowl		w.t. and wet smoothed in finishing process	medium fine clay; small quartz inc.; some voids from burned out organic matter	+; 800-900°	ext: 10YR 7.5/4 (very pale brown) int: same; core: 10YR 6.5/1 (gray)
13.	B2.018	9318	BG	black slip on ext. and int.	w.t.	very fine water lev. clay; micro-quartz inc.	+ then -; 800-900°	ext: 7.5YR 2.5/0 (black-lustrous) int: same; core: 2.5YR 6/4 (light reddish (brown)

Plate 2.

	Area & Locus	Regis. No.	Type	Surface Treatment	Manufacture	Composition	Firing	Color
14.	B2.018	9320	cooking pot (inner ledge)	carbon smudges on ext.	w.t.; tool marks (trimming) on ext.; wet smoothed	medium fine clay; quartz inc.	+; ca. 800°; some lime spalling	2.5YR 6/4 (light reddish brown)
15.	B2.018	8805	bowl	(no description)				
16.	B2.018	9319	jar		w.t.	medium fine clay; quartz inc.; some voids from burned out organic matter	+; 900-1000°; some lime spalling	10YR 7.5/2 (shite)
17.	B2.018	9317	amphora		w.t.	medium coarse clay; quartz and limestone inc.; flecks of iron	+; ca. 750°	ext: 2.5YR 6/6 (light red) int: same; core: 2.5YR 5.5/1 (gray)
18.	B2.020	9923	BG	black slip on ext. and int.; flaking from clay body	w.t. and tooled in finishing process	very fine water lev. clay; some micro-quartz inc.	+ then - ca. 900°	ext: 2.5YR 2.5/0 (black-lustrous) int: same; core: 5YR 7/4 (pink)
19.	B2.020	9322	jar		w.t.; tooled wet smoothed	medium coarse clay; quartz inc.		ext: 5YR 7/4 (pink) int: 10YR 8/3 (very pale brown)
20.	E1.021	135	ARS; Hayes 67A	(no description)				
21.	E1.021	140	amphora	(no description)				
22.	E1.021	137	ARS; Hayes 59	poor quality red slip on ext. and int.	w.t.; design on ext. cut with potter's knife when leather-hard	fine lev. clay	+; 800-900°	ext: 10R 5/6 (red-matte) int: 10R 5/4 (weak red) core: 10R 5/6 (red)
23.	E1.021	142	BT	(no description)				
24.	E1.021	141	BT: Hayes 195	smoke smudged with carbon black	w.t. and tooled	medium coarse clay; quartz inc.	+; ca. 800°; some lime spalling	ext: 2.5YR 4.5/1 (weak red gray) int: 2.5YR 6/4 (light reddish brown) core: 2.5YR 5/7 (reddish brown)
25.	E1.021	136	ARS; cf. Hayes 60		w.t. and tooled	very fine, water lev. clay; micro-quartz inc.	+; 800-900°; some lime spalling	10R 5/8 (red)

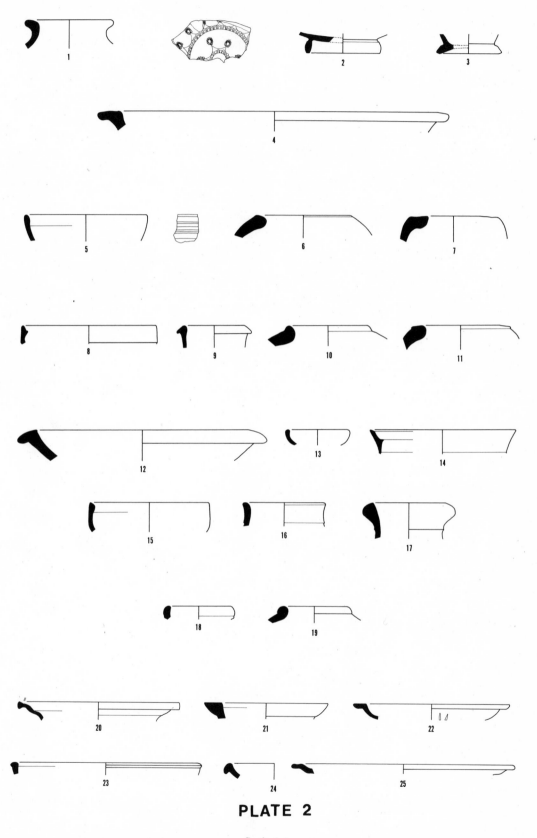

PLATE 2

Scale 1:5

Plate 3.

	Area & Locus	Regis. No.	Type	Surface Treatment	Manufacture	Composition	Firing	Color
1.	E1.021	134	cf. Hayes 92		w.t. and tooled		+; ca. 750-800°	10YR 7.5/3 (very pale brown)
2.	E1.021	139	ARS; cf. Hayes Style A(ii)	red slip and stamped motif	w.t.	very fine lev. clay	+; ca. 800°; some lime spalling	2.5YR 5/6 (red)
3.	E1.021	138	cooking pot (inner ledge) Punic survival sherd		w.t.	fine, water lev. clay; micro-quartz and limestone inc.	+, some - at end of firing; ca. 800°	ext: 5YR 5/1 (gray) int: 5YR 5/2 (reddish gray) core: 10R 5/6 (red)
4.	E1.024	351	BT; Hayes 197	gray slip; wash on ext.	w.t. and well-tooled		+ then -; ca. 850°	ext: 2.5YR 4.5/2 (weak red) int: 2.5YR 6/6 (light red) core: same
5.	E1.024	352	bowl/lid		w.t.	medium coarse clay; light and dark quartz inc.	-; ca. 750°	ext: 2.5YR 5/2 (weak red) int: same; core: 2.5YR 5/6 (red)
6.	E1.024	353	BT crater; survival sherd	smudged ext.	w.t. and tooled	quartz inc.	+; ca. 800°; some lime spalling	ext: 5YR 7/6 (reddish yellow) int: same
7.	E1.024	349	amphora		w.t.	medium coarse clay; dark and light quartz inc.	+; ca. 800°; long and well fired; some lime spalling	2.5YR 6/5 (light reddish brown)
8.	E1.024	1217	Punic "bean pot;" survival sherd		w.t.	medium coarse clay; light and dark quartz inc.	+; 950-1000°	ext: 10YR 8/2 (white) int: same; core: 10YR 7/3 (very pale brown)
9.	E1.024	348	bottle neck	gray wash on ext. and int.	w.t.	fine, water lev. clay	+ then -; ca. 900°	ext: 2.5YR 5/2 (weak red) int: same; core: 2.5YR 6/4 (light reddish brown)
10.	E1.024	1218	Punic bottle; survival piece		w.t.	medium coarse clay; quartz inc.	+; ca. 900-950°; much lime spalling	ext: 10YR 7.5/3 (very pale brown) int: same; core: 10YR 4.5/2 (dark grayish brown)
11.	E1.024	350		traces of gray-black slip on int.	w.t.; tooled; wet-smoothed	medium coarse clay; quartz inc.	+; ca. 800°; some lime spalling	ext: 2.5YR 6/7 (light red) int: 2.5YR 5/4 (reddish brown) core: 2.5YR 6/7 (light red)
12.	E1.029	1260	BT	smudge blackened ext.	w.t. and tooled	medium fine clay	+ then -; ca. 800-900°	ext: 2.5YR 4.5/1 (gray) int: 10R 5.5/8; core: same
13.	E1.030	2263	ARS; Hayes 8	red slip int. and ext.; rouletting on ext. band	w.t. and tooled	micro-quartz inc.	+; ca. 800°; rapid firing	ext: 10R 5/8 (red) int: same; core: 10R 4/1 (dark reddish gray)
14.	E1.030	1269	BT; Hayes 196	smudge blackened rim	w.t.	medium fine clay; quartz inc.	+; ca. 800°; some lime spalling	ext: 30R 5.5/6 (weak red) int: 10R 6/4 (pale red)
15.	E1.030	1288	Tripolitanian Amphora		w.t.	coarse clay; quartz and limestone	+ then -; ca. 900°; some lime spalling	ext: 7.5YR 7.5/4 (pink) int: 2.5YR 6/4 (light reddish brown) core: 10R 5/1 (reddish gray)
16.	E1.030	1294	BT; cf. Hayes 197		w.t.	fine, water lev. clay; micro-quartz inc.	+; ca. 800-900°; some lime spalling	ext: 7.5R 4/1 (dark gray) int: 7.5R 6/8 (light red)

Plate 3.

	Area & Locus	Regis. No.	Type	Surface Treatment	Manufacture	Composition	Firing	Color
17.	E1.031	2325	ARS; Hayes 8	red slip on int. and ext.; rouletting on ext. band	w.t. and tooled ext.	fine, water lev. clay; tiny quartz inc.	+; ca. 900°; some lime spalling	ext: 7.5R 5/7 (red-light red) int: 2.5YR 5/8 (red) core: 10R 5/8 (red)
18.	E1.031	2343	ARS; Hayes 9	red slip on ext. and int.; incised bands and rouletting on ext.	w.t. and tooled	fine, water lev. clay; micro-quartz inc.	+; ca. 900°; some lime spalling	2.5YR 5/8 (red)
19.	E1.032	2239	ARS; Hayes 7	red slip on ext. and int.; incised band and rouletting under rim ext.	w.t.	water lev. clay; quartz inc.	+; ca. 800°; some lime spalling	10R 5/8 (red)
20.	E1.032	2220	BT; Hayes 197	blackened ext.; red slip on int.	w.t. and tooled	some micro-quartz inc.	+; ca. 800°	int: 2.5YR 6/7 (light red)
21.	E1.034 (see 3:13, 17 above)	2342	ARS; Hayes 8					
22.	E1.035	3441	cooking pot (inner ledge)	blackened ext.	w.t. and tool finished; coil handle	medium coarse clay; quartz inc.	+, some -; ca. 850°	ext: 10R 4/1 (dark reddish gray) int: 10R 5.5/6 (weak red) core: 10R 4/7 (red)
23.	E1.035	3443	deep jar	incised band decoration	w.t. and tooled	medium coarse clay; slightly water lev.; heavy dark and light quartz inc.	+; ca. 750°; well fired; some lime spalling	2.5YR 6/6 (light red)
24.	E1.035	3442	amphora		w.t. and wet-smoothed	fine, lev. clay; light and dark quartz inc.	+; ca. 800°	7.5YR 7.5/4 (pink)
25.	E1.036	8002	deep jar		w.t. and tool finished	coarse clay; light and dark quartz inc.	+; ca. 750-800°; some lime spalling	ext: 5YR 7/3 (pink) int: same; core: 10R 4.5/6 (red)
26.	E1.037	1292	jug		w.t. and wet-smoothed	quartz inc.	+; ca. 800°; some lime spalling	ext: 10YR 8/3 (very pale brown) int: same; core: 2.5YR 5/6 (red)
27.	E1.037	1291	bowl		w.t. and wet-smoothed; throwing marks evident	medium coarse clay; dense quartz inc.	+; ca. 800°	10YR 8/3 (very pale brown)

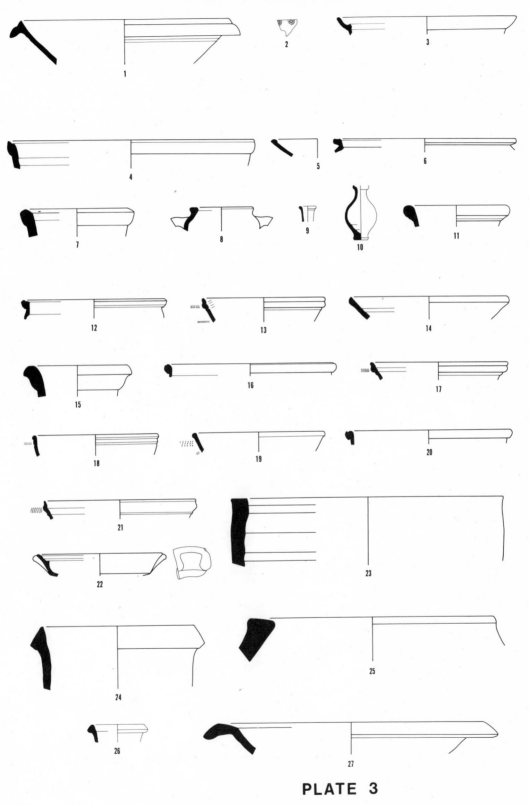

PLATE 3

Scale 1:5

Plate 4.

	Area & Locus	Regis. No.	Type	Surface Treatment	Manufacture	Composition	Firing	Color
1.	A1.011 (see 4:3)	1495	BT; Hayes 195					
2.	A1.013	3299	ARS; Hayes 26	thin red slip on int.; blackened ext.	w.t.	fine, water lev. clay	+; ca. 800°; some lime spalling	ext: 10R 5/6 (red) int: 7.5R 5.5/8 (red-semi-lustrous) slip: 10R 4/1 (dark reddish gray)
3.	A1.013	3331	BT; Hayes 195	blackened rim	w.t. and tooled	medium fine, lev. clay; some light and dark quartz inc.	+ then -; 750-800°	ext: 2.5YR 5/2 (weak red) int: 5YR 6/3 (light reddish brown) core: 2.5YR 6/5 (light reddish brown) brown)
4.	A1.013	3302	ARS; Hayes 61A	red slip with moderate lustre on ext. and int.	w.t.; stick-smoothed and shaped	very fine, lev. clay	+; ca. 850°; micro-lime spalling	ext: 2.5YR 5/8 (red) int: same; core: 2.5YR 6/8 (light red)
5.	A1.013	3313	cf. Hayes 92		w.t.; tooled; wet-smoothed	lev. clay; quartz inc.	+; ca. 800°; some lime spalling	ext: 7.5YR 6.5/4 (light pinkish brown) int: 2.5YR 6/4 (light reddish brown) core: 2.5YR 6/4 (light reddish brown)
6.	A1.013	3303	ARS; Hayes 60	red slip on int. and ext.	w.t. and tooled	fine, water lev. clay; micro-quartz inc.	+; ca. 900°	ext: 10R 5.5/8 (red light red) int: same; core: 10R 6/6 (light red)
7.	A1.013	3329	BT; Hayes 197	gray slip on ext., or exposure to atmosphere	w.t. and tooled; 5 int. grooves made by combing		+; 800-850°	ext: 10R 4.5/1.5 (dark reddish gray) int: 2.5YR 6/5 (light reddish brown) core: 2.5YR 5/5 (reddish brown)
8.	A1.013	3309	jar/ basin		w.t. and tooled	medium coarse clay; quartz inc.; voids from burned out organic matter	-; ca. 900°; some lime spalling	ext: 5Y 8/1 (white) int: same; core: 5Y 6/1 (light gray)
9.	A1.006	4985	ARS; Hayes Style E(ii)	red slip on ext. and int.; incised int.	w.t.	medium fine clay; dark and light quartz inc.	+; 750-800°; some lime spalling	ext: 10R 5/6 (red) int: 2.5YR 5/6 (red-dull) core: 10R 5.5/6 (red light red)

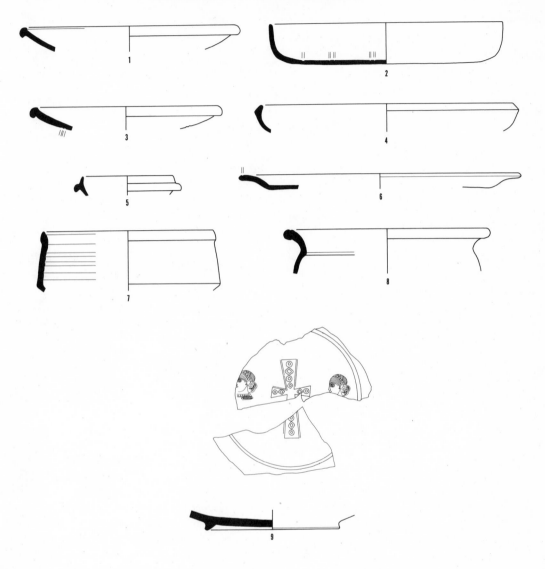

PLATE 4

Scale 1:5

APPENDIX
The Punic Inscriptions

Paul G. Mosca
University of British Columbia, Vancouver, B.C.

Of the stelae and stelae fragments discovered in the 1975 season, only two merit attention in this preliminary report. Both were found in the 4th century A.D. fill deposited between Vaults 1 and 2 (A1.015, fig. 8), but there can be no doubt that they once stood in the Tophet.

Stela 1 (C75.V1.771; fig. 25)

Stela with triangular pediment flanked by acroteria. Micritic limestone. The top of the pediment (including the upper part of the "Sign of Tanit") is broken off but the inscription is complete.

Height (preserved), 42 cm. Width, 17 cm. Thickness, 8.6 cm.
Date: 3rd century B.C.
Transcription: 1. *lrbt ltnt pn b^cl wl^ɔ*
        2. *dn lb^cl ḥmn ɔš ndr bd*
        3. *mlqrt bn ḥn^ɔ bn ɔdy*
        4. *bn mlqrt^cms.*

Translation: 1. To the Lady, to Tinnit "face of Baal," and to
        2. the Lord, to Baal Ḥamon, which vowed *bd-*
        3. *mlqrt*, the son of *ḥn^ɔ*, the son of *ɔdy,*
        4. the son of *mlqrt^cms.*

Stela 2 (C75.V2.772; fig. 26)

Stela with triangular pediment flanked by acroteria. Micritic limestone. The inscription is complete.

Height, 48.8 cm. Width, 14.7/17.6 cm. Thickness, 8.5 cm.
Date: First half of 2nd century B.C.

Transcription: 1. *lrbt ltnt pn b^cl wl^ɔdn lb^c*
        2. *l ḥmn ɔš ndr bd^cštrt*
        3. *bn ḥn^ɔ*
Translation: 1. To the Lady, to Tinnit "face of Baal," and to the Lord, to Ba-
        2. al Hamon, which vowed *bd^cštrt*
        3. the son of *ḥn^ɔ*.

The banal nature of the two inscriptions requires only the briefest comment. The order of both follows the stereotypical votive pattern so familiar from the thousands of late Carthaginian exemplars: (1) supernatural recipients (divine name preceded by the appropriate title); (2) relative *ɔš* + verb *ndr*; (3) dedicant's name followed by genealogy (of varying length). The concluding formula of benediction *k šm^c ql (ɔ) ybrk (ɔ)*, is absent in both inscriptions, nor is there any mention made of the occupation or social standing of either dedicant. Such reticence is not unusual.

The personal names of the dedicants and of their ancestors again occasion no surprise (Halff 1963-64: 61-146, and Benz 1972). The phrase-names *bdmlqrt* (*Bōdmilqart*, "by the hand/power of Melqart") and *bd^cštrt* (*Bōd^caštart*, "by the hand/power of Astarte"), as well as the hypocoristic *ḥn^ɔ* (*Ḥannō*, "favor") recur in hundreds of Carthaginian stelae. The remaining names, *ɔdy* (pronunciation unknown; hypocoristic probably meaning "Father") and *mlqrt^cms* (*Milqart ^camōs*, "Melqart has carried"; cf. Hebrew ^c*āmos*, Amos, and ^c*ămasyāh*, Amasiah), while far less common, are not unknown at Carthage. *ɔdy* is attested in seven other inscriptions, *mlqrt^cms* in thirteen (Benz 1972: 55 and 141).

Lastly, the iconography of our stelae is as

Fig. 25. Stela 1 (Photo by Robert H. Johnston).

Fig. 26. Stela 2 (Photo by Robert H. Johnston).

unexceptional as the inscriptions themselves. Stela 1 preserves only the bottom section of a "sign of Tanit" resting on a base ("autel à gorge"). On the origin and significance of this symbol (with references to the earlier literature), cf. the interesting article of Sabatino Moscati (1972: 371-74). The symbol is also attested in the eastern Mediterranean; cf. E. Linder (1973: 182-87), G. Benigni (1975: 17), and M. Dothan (1974). Stela 2, while inferior in workmanship, is more elaborate in design, containing both typical sacred symbols (crescent and disk, "sign of Tanit," and hand of benediction) and geometric decoration (friezes of wavy horizontal and straight vertical lines framing the inscription proper). Such a combination is again hardly unique; in fact, a stela of almost identical design has recently been published by Mh. Fantar and C. Gilbert Ch. Picard (1975: 51, 57, pl. 15b, stele 6). It is quite possible that the two stelae, although clearly the products of different stonecutters, came from the same workshop.

ACKNOWLEDGMENTS

Staff of the expedition were:

Frank M. Cross (Harvard), *principal investigator and epigraphist*
Lawrence E. Stager (Oriental Institute, University of Chicago), *field director and Punic pottery specialist*

Area Supervisors:

Diane Lynn (Daniella) Saltz (Harvard), also *Punic pottery specialist*
Christopher Carr (University of Chicago)
Stephen Urice (Harvard)
Vida Ward (Phoenix, Arizona), also *photographer*
Giovanni Vitelli (Radcliffe)
Prince Chitwood (Wilfrid Laurier University)

Assistant Supervisors:

P. C. Finney (University of Missouri—St. Louis), *early Christian art and archeology specialist*
Samuel Wolff (University of Chicago)
James Armstrong (University of Chicago)

Sandra Woolfrey (Wilfrid Laurier University), *registrar*
Karl Kruschen (Wilfrid Laurier University), *architect and surveyor*
Gary Pratico (Harvard), *pottery draftsman*
Robert Johnston (Rochester Institute of Technology), *ceramist*

Paul Mosca (University of British Columbia), *Punic epigraphist*
Reuben Bullard (University of Cincinnati), *geologist*

Ambassador and Mrs. Talcott W. Seelye as well as other members of the U. S. Embassy in Tunis provided encouragement and support for our project. Nicole Logan, Monique De Martin, and Donald Cleveland deserve special credit for their assistance in and out of the field.

We are very grateful to the University of Michigan team for sharing with us such expert specialists in Roman pottery as John Hayes (Royal Ontario Museum) and John Riley (University of Manchester); their typological considerations of the ceramics from stratified deposits have provided the chronological framework of this report.

Professor Robert Stewart (Sam Houston State University, Texas) identified the few botanical remains recovered this season by water flotation. We are grateful to Samuel Wolff, graduate student in Near Eastern archeology at the University of Chicago, who made a study of the imported black-glazed ware.

Finally, we gratefully acknowledge the help of Daniella Saltz and Diana Buitron, whose suggestions and criticisms improved this manuscript.

BIBLIOGRAPHY

Benigni, G.

    1975   Il «segno di Tanit» in Oriente. *Rivista di studi fenici* 3: 17-18.

Benz, F. L.

    1972   *Personal Names in the Phoenician and Punic Inscriptions.* Studia Pohl 8. Rome: Pontifical Biblical Institute.

Dothan, M.

    1974   A Sign of Tanit from Tel ᶜAkko. *Israel Exploration Journal* 24: 44-49.

Fantar, M., and Picard, C. G. C.

    1975   Stèles puniques de Carthage. *Rivista di studi fenici* 3: 43-60.

Halff, G.

  1963-64 L'onomastique punique de Carthage, répertoire et commentaire. *Karthago* 12: 61-146.

Hayes, J. W.

    1972   *Late Roman Pottery.* London: British School at Rome.

    1976   Chapter 3 in Vol. 1 of *Excavations at Carthage 1975 Conducted by the University of Michigan,* ed. John H. Humphrey. Tunis: Ceres.

Hurst, H.

    1975   Excavations at Carthage 1974: First Interim Report. *The Antiquaries Journal* 55: 11-40.

Kelsey, F. W.

    1926   *Excavations at Carthage 1925: A Preliminary Report.* New York: MacMillan.

Linder, E.

    1973   A Cargo of Phoenico-Punic Figurines. *Archaeology* 26: 182-87.

Moscati, S.

    1972   L'origine del «segno di Tanit». *Accademia Nazionale dei Lincei: Rendiconti,* ser. 8, 27: 371-74.

Ponsich, M., and Tarradell, M.

    1965   *Garum et Industries Antiques de Salaison dans la Méditerranée Occidentale.* Université de Bordeaux et Casa de Velazquez. Bibliothèque de l'École des Hautes Études Hispaniques, Fascicle 36. Paris: Presses Universitaires de France.

Sparkes, B. A., and Talcott, L.

    1970   *The Athenian Agora XII. Black and Plain Pottery, Parts I and II.* Princeton: American Schools of Classical Studies at Athens.

939
P 92